# PAGANISM PERSISTING

# Exeter New Approaches to Legend, Folklore and Popular Belief

*Series Editors:*
**Simon Young**, University of Virginia (CET, Siena) and
**Davide Ermacora**, University of Turin

Exeter New Approaches to Legend, Folklore and Popular Belief provides a venue for growing scholarly interest in folklore narratives, supernatural belief systems and the communities that sustain them. Global in scope, the series encompasses milieus ranging from ancient to contemporary times and encourages empirically grounded, source-rich studies. The editors favour the broad multidisciplinary approach that has characterized the study of folklore and the supernatural, and which brings together insights from historians, folklorists, anthropologists and many other branches of the humanities and social sciences.

# PAGANISM PERSISTING

## A HISTORY OF EUROPEAN PAGANISMS SINCE ANTIQUITY

**ROBIN DOUGLAS**
and **FRANCIS YOUNG**

UNIVERSITY
*of*
EXETER
PRESS

First published in 2024 by
**University of Exeter Press**
Reed Hall, Streatham Drive
Exeter EX4 4QR
UK

www.exeterpress.co.uk

*Exeter New Approaches to Legend, Folklore and Popular Belief*

ISSN 3049-7329 Print
ISSN 3049-7337 Digital

**British Library Cataloguing in Publication Data**
A catalogue record for this book is available from the British Library

ISBN 978-1-80413-123-7 Hardback
ISBN 978-1-80413-124-4 ePub
ISBN 978-1-80413-125-1 PDF

https://doi.org/10.47788/FWPK6118

Typeset in the UK by BBR Design, Sheffield

Cover image: A pagan sacrifice. Engraving after L. Lombard (1506–1566).
Wellcome Collection. Public Domain Mark.

# Contents

# Acknowledgements

The authors are grateful to Anna Henderson and Nigel Massen of Exeter University Press for shepherding this book towards publication, as well as to the anonymous reviewers of the manuscript for their constructive suggestions. We thank the staff of the British Library, Cambridge University Library and the Bodleian Library, Oxford for their assistance, and Robin Douglas thanks his wife Kelly for her forbearance during the course of this project.

# Abbreviations

| | |
|---|---|
| Ammianus, *Res gest.* | Ammianus Marcellinus, *Res gestae* |
| Apuleius, *Metamorph.* | Apuleius, *The Golden Ass* |
| Augustine, *De civ. Dei* | Augustine of Hippo, *On the City of God Against the Pagans* |
| Bede, *Hist eccles.* | Bede, *The Ecclesiastical History of the English People* |
| *Cod. Justin.* | *Codex Justinianus* |
| *Cod. Theod.* | *Codex Theodosianus* |
| Constantine VII, *De admin. imp.* | Constantine VII Porphyrogenitus, *De administrando imperio* |
| *Corp. Herm.* | *Corpus Hermeticum* |
| *Derveni Papyrus* | Janko, Richard (ed.), 'The Derveni Papyrus ("Diagoras of Melos, *Apopyrgizontes Logoi?*"): A New Translation', *Classical Philology* 96.1 (2001): 1–32 |
| George of Trebizond, *Comp.* | George of Trebizond, *Comparatio* |
| Gregory, *Ep.* | Pope Gregory I, *Letters* |
| Gregory Nazianzen, *Orat.* | Gregory Nazianzen, *Orations* |
| Isidore, *Etym.* | Isidore of Seville, *Etymologies* |
| Isocrates, *Antid.* | Isocrates, *Antidosis* |
| Julian, *Contra Gal.* | Julian, *Against the Galileans* |
| Julian, *Ep.* | Julian, *Letters* |
| Julian, *Ep. ad sac.* | Julian, *Letter to a Priest* |
| Julian, *Orat. 5* | Julian, *Oration 5* (*Hymn to the Mother of the Gods*) |

Libanius, *Orat.*     Libanius, *Orations*

Lucifer, *De reg. apostat.*     Lucifer of Cagliari, *De regibus apostaticis*

Macrobius, *Sat.*     Macrobius, *Saturnalia*

Marullus, *Hymns*     Michael Marullus, *Hymns to Nature*

*PGM*     *Papyri Graecae Magicae*

Plato, *Phaedo*     Plato, *Phaedo*

Plato, *Phaedrus*     Plato, *Phaedrus*

Plato, *Rep.*     Plato, *Republic*

Plato, *Symp.*     Plato, *Symposium*

Plato, *Theaet.*     Plato, *Theaetetus*

Plethon, *Laws*     Gemistios Plethon, *Laws*

Pontius, *Acta*     Pontius Diaconus, *Acta Proconsularia*

Porphyry, *Contra Christ.*     Porphyry, *Against the Christians*

Psellus, *Orat. For.*     Michael Psellus, *Orationes Forenses*

Sozomen, *Hist. eccles.*     Sozomen, *Historia ecclesiastica*

Tertullian, *Apol.*     Tertullian, *Apologeticus*

# Introduction

In the treasury of the Basilica di San Marco in Venice, which is filled with plunder taken from Constantinople during the Fourth Crusade in 1204, is a small glass bowl of Byzantine workmanship which was made in the tenth or eleventh century. This bowl, fashioned in a city that then regarded itself as the centre of the Christian world, is adorned with a series of roundels depicting an unexpected cast of characters. Among them are Zeus, Apollo, Hermes and Ares, along with Odysseus and an augur, while pseudo-Arabic script (nonsense mimicking Kufic Arabic) adorns the bowl's inner lip. It is probable that the original purpose of the San Marco Cup, which was later given handles and repurposed as a chalice for use in the Christian eucharist, was lecanomancy: divination by the use of a bowl. It was thus a transgressive, occult object which drew both on imagery of the old pagan gods and the script of the Muslims who represented the greatest adversaries of the Byzantine Empire.[1] The San Marco Cup is a magical object. But can it be described as a *pagan* object? And if it can, what does that tell us about the persistence of the idea of paganism after antiquity?

One possible answer to these questions is that, by definition, an object produced within a medieval Christian culture—a culture, indeed, that in the case of Byzantium defined itself as the paragon of Christianity—cannot be pagan: because classical paganism was well and truly dead by the eleventh century. In one sense, this is true; no temples were still operating in medieval Constantinople, no sacrifices or libations were being offered. No statues of the gods were venerated, and the citizens of the Eastern Roman Empire were officially Christians. And yet the figures of apparently obsolete pagan gods on the San Marco Cup are disturbingly alive; they are not just turgid, decorative copies of pre-Christian art or stereotyped, schematic representations of allegorical figures. Was the maker (or patron) of the San Marco Cup a pagan—some sort of cultural outlier, or remarkable survivor, in the Christian city of Constantinople who was keeping their true religious convictions concealed?

This is vanishingly unlikely. But it is still not enough to write off an anomalous artefact like the San Marco Cup as a melange of transgressive imagery designed to enhance its magical power. Why was that specific imagery chosen? Why was so much care given to the portrayal of long-dead gods? Is there any sense in which the religious power of paganism can be said to have persisted into the Middle Ages?

The San Marco Cup raises deep questions about the nature of magic, religion and culture. One of those questions is how religions—and indeed modes of religiosity—that are apparently extinct can not only linger as cultural and intellectual forces, but also undergo processes of revival and reanimation over time. This book argues that 'pagan revival' is not a modern phenomenon, confined to the stereotype of twentieth-century suburbanites trying to shake off their post-Christian anomie by dressing as Viking priests or dancing under the moon. The notion that ancient, pre-Christian religious traditions persist in European culture and can be reanimated is, rather, an enduring cultural reality from the fourth century CE to the present day. Revival need not imply survival. Indeed, rather the opposite is true: wholesale revival only becomes necessary when nothing of the original religious outlook remains. 'Paganism', as a self-conscious identity (or series of identities),[2] could arguably come into existence only once the 'old' paganism—of the inherited, unthinking kind—had been completely destroyed. Paganism, moreover, could persist in European societies under non-religious forms for long periods—the vast reservoir of symbols and ideas that made up the legacy of classical culture—between bursts of reanimation in which people chose to reactivate it as fully fledged religious belief or practice.

It is the argument of this book that a hermeneutic of persistence—which holds that elements of paganism continued to exist in post-classical European society, constantly ready to be revived and reanimated—better accounts for the sporadic re-emergence of various kinds of self-declared 'pagans' in different ages than the two established alternatives. These are the 'hermeneutic of survival' which was popular for much of the twentieth century; and the 'hermeneutic of concoction' which has become popular since then. The hermeneutic of survival was the idea that some essence of pagan religion endured beneath the Christian hegemony of the fourth century onwards, at least in most of the former and continuing Roman Empire. This idea is false. Paganism persisted; whether paganism 'survived' is a far more contentious matter. The hermeneutic of concoction is the idea that revived paganism is an unmoored creation of the modern age with at best a superficial connection to the historical pagan heritage. It has been said of the modern pagan movement that, 'like such movements as Scientology, ISKCON, and the Unification Church, it is simply a new religion, one without a long continuity or fully developed history'.[3] Such assessments are undoubtedly true in part—but only in part. They do not account for the very real continuity of paganism in post-classical European culture; and, as we will see in Chapter 5, they ultimately originated in the context of Victorian Christian polemic.

This book's 'persistence' model can be described using a series of metaphors, none of which quite captures it precisely. Paganism might be imagined as a set of ancient desiccated seeds which can be watered periodically so as to bloom afresh. Paganism is an organism preserved in ice which exists in deep metabolic sleep until someone thaws it out. Paganism is a temperamental artist who produces nothing for years but is capable of periodic bursts of astonishing work. Paganism is a volcano which lies dormant between occasional eruptions. Paganism is an unquiet spirit which lingers in the byways of the culture, waiting to be summoned. ('A spectre is haunting Europe, the spectre of paganism.') Europe's polytheistic religious traditions have always been subject to continual reinvention and reimagining. But in the same way that folklorists now reject the stereotyping of folklore as the old, the lingering and the recondite, so we ought to set aside the idea that 'pagan' traditions can be detected only in the form of 'survivals' from the ancient past. Nor should we interpret modern engagement with these complex and persisting traditions as inauthentic or superficial, a leisure activity akin to *Star Trek* cosplay.

Europe's pre-Christian traditions have persisted and re-emerged under many different forms: as intellectual speculations, as artistic conventions, as cultural *topoi*, as esoteric traditions, and—most fascinatingly—as outright revivals or attempted revivals of pagan religion. Whereas the word 'survival' implies something left over, a relic of a former worldview that is somehow preserved beneath the accreted weight of subsequent religious and cultural developments, 'persistence' implies no such claims. The persistence of paganism is the continued significance of themes from the pre-Christian religious traditions of Europe—seeds ready for the watering can, organisms in ice ready to be thawed—which can periodically be fashioned into revived pagan religions without the need to invoke dubious claims about the concealment of identities, covert religious practices, or underground beliefs. The pagan theme can persist without continuing to live as a coherent and unbroken mode of religiosity.

Chris Gosden, writing about the history of magic (an endeavour very much adjacent to the historiography of paganism, as we shall see), has made a similar argument in favour of an 'invented and reinvented' tradition as people and cultures 'played with a series of long-lasting themes'. There is no need to imagine a line of transmission of secret knowledge to explain the persistence of magic and magical practices; the past is not so much a river flowing from past to present between defined banks, as 'a lake from which we draw resources, which come to exist as part of our present'.[4] This book is an attempt to draw some of the boundaries of the lake in which European culture deposited the detritus of paganism, and an attempt to tell the story of those who have, from time to time, ventured into its depths to retrieve and reassemble the components of pagan belief and practice.

## Speaking of pagans

Any book about 'paganism' must tackle the knotty question of whether 'paganism' really exists. This is in reality two questions: were (or are) there such people as 'pagans' in Europe? And can the collective identity of these people be meaningfully labelled with the term 'paganism'? On the face of it, these questions might seem to be absurd: of course we know that polytheistic worshippers of pre-Christian gods and followers of pre-Christian traditions of cult existed in Europe. But the question is one of onomastics rather than ontology, at least in the first instance: should we use the term 'pagan', coined by Christians in late antiquity, to refer to the followers of pre-Christian cults, and should we reify all such cults as 'paganism'? There are powerful arguments against the use of either 'pagans' or 'paganism'; if they are convincing, and there is no such thing as 'paganism' and it is not a meaningful term, then a book about 'paganism persisting' is by definition stillborn, and a fruitless enterprise.

Exactly what early Christians meant by the word 'pagan' is itself a contested question. In the beginning, there were no pagans. The word 'pagan'—or rather, the Latin word *paganus*—was not used in ancient Europe to describe anyone's religious beliefs or practices. This changed only at the very end of antiquity, in the fourth century CE, when Christians adopted the term as a way of referring to people who continued to follow pre-Christian polytheistic traditions. No-one really knows why they did this. Scholars have tried to extrapolate from the known non-religious meanings of *paganus* in Latin to work out what the term meant to the Christians who started applying it to their unconverted neighbours. The word was often used to refer to inhabitants of the countryside, and it may be that it was employed by Christians in the sense of 'country bumpkins', in reference to polytheism supposedly surviving for longer in rural areas than in cities. *Paganus* could also mean 'civilian', and a rival theory holds that it was meant to draw a contrast with the Christian 'soldiers of Christ'. A third theory is that it denoted a person who was attached to their *pagus*, or native district, with its traditional religious cults. A final proposal maintains that it simply meant 'outsider'. This is not the place to settle this etymological disagreement: none of the theories proposed to date is entirely satisfactory, and nothing turns for our purposes on which of them (if any) is correct. We need only note that the term seems to have had somewhat pejorative overtones.[5]

Christian authors did not use the term 'pagan' with much consistency, sometimes labelling any religious practice or belief they disapproved of as 'pagan'—a habit that would accelerate with the advent of colonialism, and later with the Reformation.[6] When employing the term, Christian authors generally meant 'anyone, at any period, who is not a Christian, a Jew or a Muslim'.[7] 'Pagan' has thus served primarily to describe what someone is *not*. It is an othering term. Its basic purpose is to label outsiders: 'We are Christians; you are pagans.'[8] Furthermore, in a modern context 'pagan' is generally a word with geographical limitations; it refers to the pre-monotheistic religions of the Old World, while other terms such as 'indigenous religion' or 'traditional religion' are conventionally applied to the pre-Christian religions of those peoples with whom Christian missionaries came into contact from the early modern period onwards. This book adheres to that—admittedly rather arbitrary—geographical use of 'pagan', and focuses on the traditions of the Old World.

It might seem to follow from the use of 'pagan' as an othering term that to use the very terms 'pagan' and 'paganism' is to yield to a 'Christianization of the mind' that scholars ought to be avoiding in non-confessional and post-confessional discourse in the historiography of religion. The classicist Harriet Flower emphasises the need to understand 'the world BC' ('before Christianity') on its own terms—to the extent that such a thing is even possible—'independent of pervasive comparisons and contrasts with various monotheisms'.[9] There were no such people as 'pagans' and no such thing as 'paganism', merely the immense variety of pre-Christian cults and cultic practices that filled Europe before the advent of the monotheistic religions. To label these as 'pagan' is to begin any historical enquiry already burdened with a set of othering assumptions that prevent us from seeing the true diversity, distinctiveness and value of the world of pre-Christian religion. This is the view taken by (for example) Gian Luca Grassigli, who advocates abandoning the Christian–pagan dichotomy, and the term 'pagan' itself, as reflecting 'a modernistic and ultimately colonialist attitude'.[10] Likewise, David Petts rejects an 'essentialist' model of Christianity and paganism that envisages the two approaches to the sacred as mutually exclusive opposites, or rivals for people's allegiance.[11]

One difficulty with this onomastically iconoclastic approach is that it leaves us with the problem of what words to use instead of 'pagan'. We have already used the term 'pre-Christian' as a potential alternative, yet if we are concerned with avoiding a 'Christianization of the mind', then 'pre-Christian' is a deeply problematic choice—suggesting that paganism can only be defined in relation to Christianity, and in a position of chronological priority to it—which seems to carry the even more controversial implication that Christianity always replaces and supersedes paganism, with a sort of historical inevitability (which, as we shall see in Chapter 2, is historically untrue). Other options are available, such as 'polytheistic' for example. Yet the adoption of such a term leads us deep into the thickets of religious studies: were/are all European paganisms polytheistic? Where does this leave animists, or henotheists, or syncretists, or Shamans?[12] Defining paganism in terms of belief seems to be on a hiding to nothing, given that paganism—as we shall see in Chapter 1—is an approach to religion that is emphatically not defined by *belief*. Similarly 'ancestral religions', another potential alternative term, is not without its problems, laden as it with potentially problematic assumptions about heredity, communal identity and even race that do not seem to do justice to the fluidity of pagan religions—and potentially play into the hands of contemporary far-right movements that seek to lay claim to 'native faiths'.

A further difficulty with abandoning the terms 'pagan' and 'paganism' is that they are used today by followers of contemporary religions inspired by the cult traditions of pre-Christian Europe. While by no means all contemporary paganisms are 'reconstructionist', seeking specifically to replicate in close detail what ancient pagans may have done (indeed, reconstructionist polytheists are in a minority among contemporary pagans in the English-speaking world), and few contemporary pagans claim seriously to be in literal historical continuity with ancient pagans, contemporary paganisms are nevertheless well-established minority religious traditions in many European countries, as well as in the wider world. Contemporary pagans sometimes suffer marginalization and discrimination. If historians of religion were to refuse to use a term by which followers of contemporary religions link their own practices with those of their perceived predecessors, this could have an adverse impact on contemporary pagans, and certainly on relations between contemporary pagan communities of practitioners and academia. Paradoxically, contemporary pagans have embraced the idea that their religious paths are defined in relation to the monotheisms from which they differ. Thus Michael York defines paganism in terms of 'sacred relationships and experiences that reach beyond monotheism'; according to York, paganism is 'outside conventional institutionalized religious practises' and de-emphasises reliance on revelation or scriptures.[13]

The historian of religion is faced with a paradox when it comes to 'paganism': on the one hand, it might seem that a more respectful, less 'Christianocentric' approach to ancient paganism is to reify it as a faith tradition equally worthy of consideration, alongside the great monotheistic faiths. But to do so is itself to impose a Christian conceptual framework on paganism; indeed, even calling it 'paganism', as if to reify it as a single coherent ideology, is arguably a Christianizing act. On the other hand, if historians refuse entirely to label or reify pre-Christian cults and rites as having no meaningful coherence, this seems a denigration of pre-Christian religious traditions, denying them the opportunity to be considered the cultural or intellectual equals of the 'great' monotheisms. It risks adopting an implicit hermeneutic of monotheistic supremacy, simply because monotheism has become the conceptual baseline of what we imagine religion to be.

The use of the terms 'pagan' and 'paganism' will always be controversial. But the authors of this book take the view that there is a middle course to be steered between the ahistorical reification of a monolithic '-ism' that never was on the one hand, and abandoning language and concepts readily recognizable to most readers on the other. Rather like 'magic' and 'religion', 'paganism' is an unavoidably contested term in intellectual and religious history, yet one that continues to be used both inside and outside the academy. An excessively prescriptive approach to language, here and elsewhere, risks alienating the academy from wider culture, and it is often preferable to continue using widely recognized terms hedged with appropriate qualifications, rather than jettisoning them altogether. The idea of paganism undeniably originated as an 'other' (imagined or otherwise) against which Christianity defined itself; but such intellectually and culturally constructed 'others' are nonetheless realities, not least because people will sometimes come to identify with, and internalise, an othered identity. Just as some people in the contemporary world identify proudly as pagans in the area of religion, and do not hesitate to appropriate an originally pejorative term, so the term 'queer' (likewise originally pejorative) has become a positive identity in the area of sexuality and gender.

What, then, are the caveats which should attend the terms 'pagans' and 'paganism'? Already the subtitle of this book hints at the most important caveat of all: that it is more accurate to speak of multiple 'paganisms' than of a single monolithic 'paganism'. Not only were the cults of pre-Christian Europe bewildering in their variety, differing from one another in drastic and fundamental ways, but they differed also from subsequent revivals of paganism and from contemporary paganisms. The temptation to treat all 'paganism' as essentially the same, as mere religious window-dressing to an underlying basic 'pagan' idea, is not so much buying into a Christianocentric perspective—*interpretatio Christiana*, as it were—but into an older *interpretatio Romana* that held together the Roman Empire. When Julius Caesar tried to make sense of the religion of the Gauls and Tacitus interpreted the religion of the Germanic tribes, they sought to assimilate other paganisms to the Graeco-Roman cults and deities familiar to them. It is not only the 'Christianization of the mind' that the historian of religion must strive to escape, but also a 'Romanization of the mind' that is itself part of the pagan past, in which Graeco-Roman religion becomes a standard by which all other paganisms are to be measured.

While most scholars have long since abandoned *interpretatio Romana* as an approach to Europe's pre-Christian religions (consciously, at least), a herme-neutic that may be equally unhelpful has sometimes come to replace it: namely, Indo-Europeanism. While there can be no doubt that most of Europe's languages (along with languages of Central Asia and the Indian Subcontinent) have a common ancestor that linguists have reconstructed as Proto-Indo-European, the notion that reconstructed Proto-Indo-European can also be used to reconstruct the 'original' religion of the steppe peoples who brought Indo-European languages is much more contentious. It does not follow from the fact that people spoke a single language that they also followed a single religion, yet some comparative mythologists have proposed with all the certainty of Caesar or Tacitus that an Indo-European pantheon can be reliably constructed from whom the various attested pantheons of pre-Christian Europe descended.

Comparative mythology may have its merits, but for historians of religion it represents a problematic and potentially ahistorical approach to the history of religion which shades into cultural anthropology. The distinctive features of individual cults, and their distinctive histories, are of secondary importance if what matters is the 'ur-mythos' from which all paganisms can be assumed to descend. Such assumptions make historicist approaches to European paganisms redundant; they are all simply expressions of an original Indo-European pantheon and mythology, and it is as valid to search for this 'ur-mythos' in recent folklore as in older historical records. What results is a 'headlong rush to catch glimpses of a lost mythical world' without much critical analysis of the sources, with scholars of mythology adopting a 'holistic' approach to inter-preting a very diverse range of evidence.[14] Yet *interpretatio Indo-Europeana* seems worryingly like the *interpretatio Romana* that preceded it, projecting a Hesiodic conception of a divine pantheon back into the distant prehistoric past that was, in all likelihood, a literary creation of the seventh century BCE. Europe's paganisms deserve their own histories, their distinctiveness deserves recognition, and they deserve to be studied on their own terms.

An issue related to the use of the terms 'pagan' and 'paganism' to identify Europe's pre-Christian religious traditions is the question of whether we should use the terms 'neopagan' and 'neopaganism' for modern pagan revivals. For the authors of this book, the answer is a resounding 'no'. The term 'neopagan' is rarely if ever used by contemporary pagans to describe themselves,[15] and often carries pejorative connotations—not least the implication that contemporary paganism is in some sense unreal, inauthentic or undeserving of respect as a religious tradition. The vitality and growth of contemporary paganism make it impossible to sustain in good faith an argument that revived paganism is not a 'real' religious tradition (although it is important to be clear that according basic respect to a religious tradition does not require the historian or the scholar of religious studies to accept the historical account that a religion gives of itself). It is part of the argument of this book that once the religio-cultural dominance of a traditional pagan outlook is disrupted, every subsequent iteration of 'paganism' will take the form of a revival. 'Neopaganism' is a problematic term because it presumes a single process of pagan revival, occurring in the nineteenth and twentieth centuries, which has led to the existence of contemporary pagan religions. It is precisely that historiography of pagan revival that this book sets out to challenge: there has not been one pagan revival, but many throughout history. To call someone a 'neopagan', therefore, is essentially meaningless. All paganism after antiquity is 'neopaganism', and it makes no sense to confine the term to pagans living in the last couple of centuries.[16] The authors of this book prefer the terms 'pagan revival' or 'revived paganism', which can refer to any revival movement from the Emperor Julian's Neoplatonic paganism to Gerald Gardner's Wicca.

## Defining paganism

If, for the sake of argument, we are willing to accept that it is possible (and desirable) to use terms such as 'pagans' and 'paganism'—even if only as conceptual placeholders, and with appropriate caveats—then how is paganism to be defined? There are two broad approaches to this problem: defining paganism negatively, and defining it positively. The word 'pagan' itself can be produced as a witness in favour of negative definition, if we accept that 'pagan' was a pejorative term developed by the early Christians. A pagan is someone as yet untouched by (or actively rejecting) the Abrahamic monotheisms, following instead their ancestral cults.

This vague negative definition underlies the Christian usage of the term 'pagan' since antiquity. Christians have deployed the word in a range of different contexts with a meaning which reduces to little more than 'not us', plus perhaps a vague link to polytheism. Indigenous peoples colonized by European empires; Catholics after the Reformation; freethinking atheists; taboo-breaking artists; followers of totalitarian political movements—all of these have been called 'pagans' at one time or another. Each of these uses of the word has had *some* connection with its original semantic field of the pre-Christian peoples of the Roman Empire; but the connection is sometimes tenuous. The status of the term 'pagan' in historical Christian discourse might be compared with the status of the term 'fascist' in modern political rhetoric. Calling someone a fascist is essentially a way of banishing them from the moral community. Some kind of comparison with the politics of Mussolini and Hitler is usually intended, but the connection may be rather remote.

It follows that a downside of the negative approach is that, like denying any meaningful coherence to the concept of 'paganism' itself, it risks denigrating the pagan from an implicitly Christian or post-Christian hermeneutical perspective, where the pagan is an absence of confessional monotheism— a mere void waiting, perhaps, to be filled either by proselytism or materialist disenchantment. Should we adopt the alternative approach of defining paganism positively, we are faced with the task of identifying characteristics shared by all pagans. This is not straightforward. One definition which has emerged from religious studies scholarship is this: 'Paganism is an affirmation of interactive and polymorphic sacred relationship by individual or community with the tangible, sentient, and nonempirical.'[17] This formulation is useful as an academic tool for exploring different styles of religiosity; but it is based on an understanding of paganism which is so broad that it loses touch with historical and common understandings of the concept. Notably, it would include various expressions of Christianity.

If an academic definition does not fit, we might try a practitioner one. The UK's Pagan Federation, with contemporary pagans in mind, defines a pagan as 'A follower of a polytheistic or pantheistic nature-worshipping religion', and paganism as 'A polytheistic or pantheistic nature-worshipping religion',[18] but these are definitions that raise as many questions as they offer answers for the scholar of religious studies. The very term 'follower' derives from Christianity, which conceptualized religion as a 'way'; the idea that pagans worship nature is dependent on an abstract concept of nature with its origins in the Romantic movement; and the distinction between polytheism and pantheism is likewise a sophisticated philosophical one that few pagans of the past are likely to have recognized. Indeed, some scholars would take issue with the idea that paganism is a religion at all. Nevertheless, while not all pagans have been or are polytheistic, it is not unreasonable to suggest that the worship of the divine diffused between divine personalities or natural forces has generally been characteristic of paganism: generally speaking, paganism has lacked a tendency towards emphasizing a unified personal conception of the divine (although some pagan philosophical traditions, such as Neoplatonism, are comfortable with a belief in a single ultimate divine reality which transcends even the gods themselves).

The most sophisticated attempt to define 'paganism' in its modern sense(s) is that of Ronald Hutton, who has written of four 'languages' or discourses which have characterized talk of paganism since the nineteenth century. The first two languages are associated with conservative circles and the latter two with radical thought. The first language is the traditional Christian conception of pagans as the despised other: 'pagans are people who bow down to idols, offer up blood sacrifices, and represent the religious aspect of human savagery and ignorance'. The second language is the language of classicism, in which the pagan Greeks and Romans are admired for their high culture even though they were deficient insofar as they lacked knowledge of the Gospel of Christ. The third language reflects the syncretic idea that paganism and Christianity are different expressions of the same fundamental religious truth; and the fourth language actively and specifically celebrates pagan varieties of religion as 'joyous, liberationist, and life-affirming traditions'.[19] If we are looking for a conceptual framework to understand modern perceptions of paganism, Hutton's scheme is the best available. But it does not really give us a clear diagnostic to use for determining whether someone's beliefs do or do not make them a pagan (save that Hutton argues that it was the fourth of the languages that was embraced by the founders of modern paganism).

Trying to define paganism positively as a belief system may be barking up the wrong tree. It is almost a cliché to observe that paganism is primarily a matter of ritual practice rather than belief. Even here, however, it is problematic to define paganism as 'non-Christian (or pre-Christian) religious practices'. Ancestral ritual practices in ancient Europe did not, by all accounts, admit a clear distinction between 'religious' and 'secular' rituals, which begs the question of what counts as religious practice to begin with. For instance, medieval Christian writers often dwelt on the funeral, burial and marriage rites of still pagan peoples, but there is no reason to take such rites as diagnostic of pagan religiosity. They were, rather, part of a religiously neutral festive culture which was only 'pagan' if critics chose to interpret it that way—such as drawing attention to the equipping of the dead for the afterlife, which suggested a lack of Christian understanding.[20] One of the authors of this book has advanced a case for the possibility of pagans adopting Christian ideas and imagery in fourth-century Britain in the context of the strange mixture of Christian and pagan themes in the Thetford Treasure.[21]

Early approaches to paganism in newly converted societies reveal a more complex attitude than what popular culture leads us to believe about the imposition of Christianity. In medieval Iceland, for example, a prohibition on pagan sacrifice was accompanied by acceptance that people might continue pagan practices in private (see Chapter 2 below), and Adam of Bremen noted that Norse Christians continued to engage in rites honouring pagan gods. During the eighth-century conversion of Germany, the popes expressed concern about the validity of baptisms performed by priests who were also officiants in pagan cults.[22] Late antique and early medieval Christian mission engaged, in practice, in a process of negotiation with pre-Christian beliefs and practices—openly suppressing some, overtly Christianizing others, and tacitly tolerating others still. Iconoclasts who defaced and destroyed major pagan sites may not have bothered with the cults of lesser deities such as nymphs and fauns, and the nymphs endured, even in Greece itself (something that will be discussed in Chapter 3 below).[23] Writing in the 1930s about the Christianization of Greece, Campbell Bonner observed: 'The last battles were not merely against the worship of the great Olympians, but also against Isis, Sarapis, Mithra, Asklepios, against stubborn village cults of godlings and heroes, against astrology and black magic.'[24] This approach assumes, however, that Christian missionaries always considered these elements of pagan culture worth fighting. In the early stages of its conversion, a society is often only as Christianized as it needs to be.

The language of 'pagan survival' is problematic because it carries with it the assumption that Christianity *replaces*, as a matter of course, every aspect of pre-Christian belief and practice. Yet Christianity did not immediately replace pre-Christian rites of betrothal, marriage, burial or commemoration of the dead in most European societies, only later stepping in to take control of these aspects of life as pagan traditions withered or were forgotten.[25] What constituted acceptable Christian behaviour changed over time, thereby allowing those who failed to meet the required standards at any time to be labelled as 'pagan'.[26] However, the Christian church itself had its own internal ways of distinguishing pagans from non-pagans—it had to, since its purpose was to evangelise the pagans and therefore to know who they were. From a canonical point of view, a pagan was someone unbaptised, since the baptised fell under the jurisdiction of the church's law; and in addition, from a theological and moral point of view a pagan was a violator of the First Commandment—an idolater who worshipped images as deities and offered sacrifice to them. The act of sacrifice to a named deity—which might take the form of a mere libation of drink or grain, or animal (and even human) sacrifice—arguably set someone apart as definitively pagan in a way less ambiguous than inhumation practices, for instance.

Even sacrifice is not without its difficulties. Libations and sacrifices were offered not just to idols or deities, and their intent was not always worship, but rather a kind of placation. Offerings to fairies remained common in the modern Balkans and other parts of southeastern Europe into the twentieth century,[27] but we would be unlikely to classify the making of offerings to fairies (such as the Irish practice of putting out saucers of milk or cream on May Eve) as full-blown pagan cult, any more than the placatory offerings made by ritual magicians to spirits are really 'sacrifices' in the old, pagan sense. Here we run up against a difficulty even larger than the definition of paganism, which is beyond the scope of this introduction: namely the definition of religion itself, and what makes something a religious rather than merely a ritual, mystical, placatory, magical or 'superstitious' act. A further problem is pagan self-definition: many people have called themselves pagans (or 'heathens', which serves as the Germanic equivalent of the Romance term), or at least acquiesced in receiving the appellation from others, yet their beliefs might otherwise be described as mystical, pantheistic, deistic, agnostic or atheistic. Should we accept people as pagans simply because they choose to describe themselves as such, even if such self-identification is undertaken as a deliberate act of cultural or religious transgression, or an attempt at blasphemy?

Related to the idea of pagan survival is the idea of a 'pagan tradition', which can be understood in both a strong and a weak sense. In its strong sense, the pagan tradition is the idea that paganism must be passed on from generation to generation to remain alive, and to remain real. Thus Pierre Chuvin, writing of the reappearance of paganism in the writings of Gemistos Plethon in the fifteenth century, mused that 'By whatever means, the torch [of paganism] was passed during the three centuries that separated the closing of the school of Harran and Plethon's apprenticeship with Elissaios.'[28] This is the historiography of paganism as a mystery religion, somehow covertly passed down from generation to generation even when there is apparently no evidence of its existence—because how else could it re-emerge into view at a later date? Yet a weaker interpretation of the pagan tradition is also possible: a tradition can be passed down both as living practice and as a much more general cultural memory. In the case of paganism, the latter is a great deal more likely than the former; and it is the argument of this book that paganism re-emerges periodically through revivals. But there is no reason to conclude from this that paganism has always remained a living practice between those revivals, as though human beings are incapable of drawing something obsolete from the past and bringing it to life again: watering the seeds, defrosting the ice, and so on.

For all the difficulties of attempting to define what paganism is, and who pagans are, the fact remains that the category of paganism remains one that people seem to find useful; some name must be given to that other way of thinking about religion that preceded the dominance of the monotheistic faiths in Europe, even if it is a way of thinking we now find it difficult to reconceptualise or imagine. A pragmatic definition of paganism, which allows discussion of the subject to proceed—since discussion will happen anyway—is preferable to unending anxiety about the precise demarcation of who or what was pagan. It is such a pragmatic and 'minimalist' approach to the category of paganism that is adopted by Hutton, who tentatively defines paganism as 'the pre-Christian religions of Europe and the Near East', understood as 'active worship of the deities associated with those old religious traditions'.[29] Once again, various elements of this definition are open to question and to problematization; but it is necessary to start somewhere.

## Histories of paganism

Chris Gosden has observed that there exist two broad tendencies in the historiography of European paganism: one tendency emphasises 'a radical break brought about initially by the coming of Rome and then the Christian world that emerged fully after the fall of the Roman Empire'. A second approach emphasises 'deep but hidden continuities between so-called pagan Europe and the present'.[30] Taken to its extreme, the first approach is merely the history of Europe's conversion to Christianity (or Islam), with the Continent's pre-monotheistic cults mere foils to the advancing tide of Abrahamic confessions. Given that Europe's pagans beyond the Greeks and Romans left few written records of their own, the temptation to tell the religious history of Europe as one of monotheistic triumph over the indistinguishable mass of essentially irrelevant traditional cults has proved a strong one, especially for historians who are not especially focused on the niceties of religion and belief. History is not so much written by the victors as by the victors' archivists, and the character of the archive is decidedly Christian in authorship. On the other hand, the second strand of historiography Gosden identifies can easily become the kind of wishful thinking about 'survival' we have already critiqued in this introduction, privileging ideas of an underground pagan religious tradition for which there is precious little historical evidence.

In one sense, any book avowedly focused on the history of paganism after antiquity is already taking the second of Gosden's paths; if we consider paganism important enough to deserve a history, then we are starting with a conviction that pagan religions are something more than a curiosity of the vanished ancient past. Having said this, there is a fine and important literature on the conversion of Europe which takes pre-Christian religion seriously, even if its primary focus is not the nature of pagan religion itself but the transition from one mode of religiosity to another. Examples include the collection edited by Martin Carver, *The Cross Goes North* (2006) and David Petts's helpful book *Pagan and Christian*.[31]

The most longstanding scholarly discourse focused specifically on the persistence of pagan themes beyond antiquity in European culture is perhaps to be found in art history. Here there is a long tradition of scholarly engagement with the significance of the pagan gods in medieval and Renaissance art—and with the question of whether Renaissance interest in pagan deities should be considered an aesthetic choice, an elaborate form of symbolism or personification of abstract ideas, or a genuine temptation to revert to pagan cults.[32] Another direction taken by the historiography of European paganism has been to consider the question of the 'last pagans': what was the last recorded moment at which a region could be said to have been pagan? The last pagans of Rome and its empire were the subject of an influential study by Pierre Chuvin and, more recently, studies by Alan Cameron and Edward Watts.[33] Other 'last pagans', namely the pagans of the Baltic, were the subject of a recent book by Sylvain Gouguenheim.[34]

However, as Chuvin observed, 'it is much easier to point out the first time an event occurred than the last',[35] and this is as much true of the historiography of paganism as that of Christianity. Despised cults sink into obscurity within societies energised by new modes of belief, becoming the preserve of the elderly, the poor, the rural and the culturally irrelevant. By definition, the last embers of a dying faith are obscure to the historian, and the final stages of a declining religion (and, in paganism's case, a declining mode of religiosity) raise questions about what is 'authentically pagan' and what counts as syncretism, mere nostalgia, or revival. As Hutton has observed, the danger here is that we fall into 'endless, and irreconcilable, arguments over the extent of the survival of the essence of a religion when the people who professed it have been formally converted to another'.[36] The trope of 'the last pagans' is not altogether historically useful—not because such people did not exist, but because they are often historically untraceable, and there will always be some uncertainty as to their identity.

One way to avoid the difficulties attendant on a history of religious decline is to concentrate on the vitality of the pagan idea in the post-classical world. Serious research on this subject began to appear in the last decade of the twentieth century, although the earlier work of Margot Adler in the 1970s also deserves honourable mention here.[37] This period saw the publication of Graham Harvey's *Listening People, Speaking Earth* and Philip Davis's semi-scholarly polemic *Goddess Unmasked*, as well as an edited volume entitled *Paganism Today*.[38] But the principal product of the 1990s was Ronald Hutton's magisterial work on the prehistory and history of modern pagan witchcraft, *The Triumph of the Moon*, which virtually inaugurated an entire field of study dedicated to modern paganism.[39] Hutton's *Triumph* implicitly established chronological parameters for the historiography of modern paganism, which generally begins in the decades around 1800 at the earliest. The present study transgresses that periodization by covering a much longer period; and indeed it is not primarily concerned with modern paganism, even if the development of the modern pagan revival provides the latter part of the story. While Hutton adopted a teleological approach, taking the religion of Wicca as the endpoint of his study and tracing its earliest origins, this book is not about the development of any particular pagan path or practice; stillborn revivals and religious dead ends are of equal interest in this history of the persistence of the pagan idea. The present book is thus complementary to the literature on modern revived paganisms rather than an avowed contribution to that increasingly crowded field.

While the pagan revival of the mid-twentieth century has produced flour-ishing religions—indeed, arguably a new 'world religion'—with more or less coherent conventions of membership, worship, and even sacred texts, this was not the case with earlier pagan revivals. But the purpose of this book is not to search history for movements that resembled the pagan revival of the twentieth century, but rather to interrogate what the revival of paganism has looked like at different times—even when it has enjoyed very limited success. The 'pagan revival' of the Renaissance was very different from those of the eighteenth century, and different again from Gerald Gardner's revival. A question that naturally arises, therefore, is how a *genuine* 'pagan revival' should be distin-guished from a cultural or aesthetic revival of pagan themes? A related question is the extent to which a *philo-pagan*—someone who is a lover of pagan ideas and themes, of whom there were many throughout medieval and early modern history—can be considered a pagan. These are difficult questions to answer, but the approach of this book is to focus on individuals and groups whose enthusiasm for paganism seems to have exceeded mere cultural interest, tipping them into assertions of the theological truth of pagan beliefs and the revival of pagan religious practices. While it is important to exercise caution in identifying 'revivals', therefore, the argument of this book is that there were clearly individuals and groups who celebrated a specifically pagan *religiosity* between the fourth and twentieth centuries.

Studies of paganism and the pagan idea in the period between the end of antiquity and the Romantic period that is Hutton's *terminus post quem* for the pagan revival are perhaps scarcer now than the scholarship on contemporary pagans. Ludo Milis's collection *The Pagan Middle Ages* (1991) remained firmly under the spell of 'survivalism';[40] Prudence Jones and Nigel Pennick's *History of Pagan Europe* (1995) was another early effort in this direction,[41] but it appeared at a time when it inevitably relied on antiquated secondary sources, and it similarly rested on the problematic survivalist conceptual framework. Ken Dowden's *European Paganism* followed in 2000, offering a thematic and anthropological rather than chronological and historical approach to the phenomenon of pagan religions, and stretching from prehistory to the Middle Ages. For Dowden, pagan*ism* understood as a confession or ideology was 'an impossible contradiction': paganism is non-credal religion, and consists entirely of the observance of ritual.[42]

One difficulty with this rather prescriptivist approach to paganism as non-credal is that it makes it difficult to deal with the phenomena of pagan revivals in post-conversion societies, and to explain the relationship between the original paganism and such attempted revivals. Chas Clifton and Graham Harvey's *Paganism Reader* (2004) seeks to trace pagan ideas in a continuous train from antiquity to modern times, albeit in the form of an anthology of texts rather than a narrative history.[43] Hutton's grand historical synthesis *Pagan Britain* (2013) is chronological and historical, but while he seeks to illuminate the nature of pagan religiosity, Hutton is not primarily concerned with the question of the continuity of paganism in the post-conversion world—an idea he had largely rejected in an earlier book.[44] Niketas Siniossoglou's *Radical Platonism in Byzantium* (2016) is an impressive account of post-classical tendencies which were bound up with persisting paganism, but its focus (like that of Hutton's book) is specific, being localized in this case to the Byzantine Empire.[45] A final, recent book, Liz Williams's *Miracles of Our Own Making* (2021) seeks to tell the entire story of paganism up to modern times. It is informative and well written, but since it is aimed at a popular audience it is not able to deal fully with the theoretical and evidential depth of the subject.[46]

In the 2010s, the fields of intellectual and literary history gave rise to a scholarly literature whose focus is not so much paganism as a historical phenomenon but the reception and perception of 'imagined pagans'. Examples include Marion Gibson's *Imagining the Pagan Past* (2013), John Marenbon's *Pagans and Philosophers* (2015), Sarah Salih's *Imagining the Pagan in Late Medieval England* (2019) and Paroma Chatterjee's *Between the Pagan Past and Christian Present in Byzantine Culture* (2021).[47] Salih argues that in medieval England the largely imagined pagan became a sort of cultural focal point 'for thinking about human relations with the past, with human culture, with the material world, with the supernatural'. Salih's approach of 'thinking with pagans' is perhaps comparable to Stuart Clark's idea of 'thinking with demons' or Simon Ditchfield's 'thinking with saints';[48] pagans, whether real or imagined, were 'good to think with'. While it is of great scholarly importance, however—including to this present book—such literature avowedly restricts itself to the pagan *idea*; the reality or otherwise of pagan religiosity, and the question of revivals of actual paganism, lie beyond its scope.

In his most recent work Hutton has emphasized the possibility of pagan-seeming figures and beliefs arising in the post-conversion world, focusing in his book *Queens of the Wild* (2022) on the characters of Mother Earth, the Fairy Queen, the Lady of the Night, and the Cailleach (as well as, in an epilogue, the modern figure of the Green Man).[49] Hutton shows that Christians in medieval Europe were able to construct and develop figures 'which operated outside of Christian cosmology' and were deeply transgressive, but they did not do so in opposition to Christianity. Ultimately, Hutton is drawn to conclude that 'the old polarizing dichotomy of Christian and pagan is no longer suitable' for describing popular medieval and early modern folk thought-worlds that are clearly neither survivals of ancient paganism nor ways of thinking that owe much to Christianity.

## The search for sources

The history of the 'pagan theme' in European history is vast, and this book does not attempt to examine it exhaustively. The book's primary focus is, rather, on those moments when the 'pagan theme' in culture spilled over into something approaching an attempt at a *religious* revival of paganism. Since most such revivals were undertaken by intellectuals, the writings of the protagonists (and the writings of others about them) are the principal sources. However, 'paganism' in post-antique Europe was by no means confined to learned elites—indeed, the vast majority of Europe's 'pagans' at any point up to the late fourteenth century were not intellectual dilletantes but ordinary people in Northern and East-Central Europe, and on remote islands such as the Canaries. Finding reliable evidence for the beliefs and practices of these 'ordinary' pagans is a much more challenging task. Pre-Christian religion cannot be reliably reconstructed from practices in Christianized societies that are simply assumed to derive from pre-Christian religion, since whether the practices recorded by nineteenth-century folklorists (for example) were deemed 'pagan' or not depended, in most cases, on little more than subjective intuition and personal prejudice.

The excesses of nineteenth- and twentieth-century British folklorists in identifying 'pagan survivals', often inspired by the writings of Sir James Frazer, provide a cautionary tale against fallacious lines of reasoning based on presumed survivals,[50] which often involve the enthusiastic exploitation of sources for their content with scant regard for their chronological priority or literary context. Thus the anthropologist Marija Gimbutas enthused in the 1960s about 'the folk religion which still lives in folklore in surprisingly pure elements going back to earliest antiquity'.[51] In reality, in the aftermath of conversion to Christianity 'pagan-seeming' practices can arise in a number of different ways, including complex processes of religious syncretism in popular Christianity, so that assertions of pagan survival can only truly be justified by historical rather than folkloric or ethnographic evidence.

A further obstacle to objectivity in perceptions of ancestral paganism is that the Bible supplies its own commentary on paganism—specifically, the pagan religions that surrounded the ancient Israelites—and Christian missionaries rooted in the Scriptures perceived and described ancestral religions through this Biblical lens, sometimes as a prescriptive model of what paganism should look like.[52] This means that we cannot necessarily rely on Christian accounts of pagan practices as reliable, since Christian commentators were often attempting to assimilate local practices to patterns of expectation based on Biblical narratives about idolatry. It is possible that this focus on Biblical models of idolatry also caused some missionaries to overlook local practices that did not clearly correspond to anything that appeared in Scripture. However, it is important to bear in mind that the authors of the New Testament belonged to a Hellenistic world that shared a widely accepted common conceptual language of demonology rooted in Platonic philosophy, which influenced the Jewish as well as the Greek and Roman worlds.

When it came to the pagan gods themselves, missionaries sometimes resorted to demonization (the attempt to convince people that the gods were evil) and sometimes to euhemerization (the ideas that the gods had once been human beings whom demons had tempted people to worship as gods). Both approaches had the effect of obscuring the genuine mythologies that underlay pagan cult, but euhemerization in particularly served an important evangelistic purpose in the northern world because it allowed veneration of the ancestors to continue without the contamination of idolatrous worship.[53] Advocates of euhemerization theory, such as Isidore of Seville, sought to portray the gods as mere human beings, and pagan worship as the misguided outcome of what were originally good impulses to venerate the mighty dead.[54] According to Alberic of London, writing in the twelfth century, some of the gods were originally nothing more than poetic names given to activities—Ceres to agriculture, Bacchus to viticulture, and so on—that superstitious people came to personify and worship as gods.[55]

As Barbara Newman and Ronald Hutton have shown, personification was an ongoing process throughout the Middle Ages that created fully autonomous culturally constructed beings capable of agency within the collective cultural imagination, and figures such as 'Mother Earth' could rise to a quasi-goddess-like status even within the Christian world.[56] The lesson is that what seems 'pagan' is not always a survival from the pre-Christian era; and yet, at the same time, we need not assume that cultural constructions assembled under Christian hegemony were always 'Christian'. Britain's fairies, for example, are in all likelihood largely a construction of the Christian period, but the extent to which they embody a fatalistic outlook on existence diametrically opposed to the providentialism of the Christian faith arguably makes them 'pagan' figures, perpetuating pagan outlooks in new, Christian-inflected ways.[57]

## Approach of the book

The subject of this book is the persistence and revival of paganism within European culture after antiquity, but it must begin with a survey of classical Graeco-Roman paganism, the best-attested form of European pagan religion. The first chapter then proceeds to consider in more detail the strand within classical paganism which has proved to be the most influential in later pagan revival movements: that is, the esoteric tradition, with its characteristic ingredients of Platonist philosophy, mysticism and magic. From this, the chapter moves on to consider the rise to dominance of Christianity in late antiquity. It gives special attention to the reign of the Emperor Julian, which represented the last serious attempt to reverse the process of Christianization; and it broaches the issue of where and when the classical pagan tradition finally died out as a distinctive religious movement.

The subject of Chapter 2 is the ways in which medieval Christians dealt with the pagan legacies of the ancient world, as well as the very living pagans who still existed at the frontiers of their world, whether in Scandinavia or the Baltic region. The chapter examines what we do and do not know about the religion of these medieval pagans, and the impact of living in proximity to living pagans on European Christian perceptions of the idea of paganism. Medieval Christian western Europe, as a society intellectually dependent on the writings of pagan Greek and Roman thinkers, was perpetually compelled to confront the problem of pagan authority: to what extent should pre-Christian authors be permitted to govern the thinking of Christians? This was a question that became ever more urgent with the recovery of many more Classical texts through contact with the Islamic world in the eleventh century. The chapter considers how the Christians of the medieval west dealt with their culture's pagan legacy, as well as assessing the complex issue of pagan survivals within Europe's Christian societies. The chapter argues that, while the concept of 'pagan survival' is not entirely useless, the nature of the survival of pre-Christian beliefs and practices in medieval Europe was complex, ambiguous, and often unexpected.

Chapter 3 considers revived expressions of paganism in the Byzantine Empire and in western Europe during the Renaissance. It notes that the Platonist version of classical paganism was never expurged from intellectual circles in the Greek East, but rather represented a source of enduring fascination for figures like Michael Psellus and George Gemistos Plethon. The revival of classical learning in fifteenth-century Italy is examined, specifically from the perspective of its religious dimension, which gave rise to an ambiguous literary and philosophical culture in which ancient paganism, Roman Catholicism and rationalism were mixed together in the lives and works of unorthodox scholars like Marsilio Ficino, Giovanni Pico della Mirandola and the members of the 'Roman Academy'. The chapter closes by considering the adaptation of 'pagan' as a polemical term in anti-Catholic discourse after the advent of the Reformation.

The fourth chapter picks up the story in western Europe in the eighteenth century, in the period after the Christian monopoly had been broken by years of sectarian strife and philosophical rationalism. The developing field of comparative religion allowed 'pagan' varieties of religion to be considered sympathetically and even admiringly. The chapter examines the pagan elements in the French revolutionary cults and other attempts from France to revive classical religious forms. It notes how Freemasonry represented a channel for the reintroduction of pagan ideas into European culture. Special reference is made to the first explicit modern pagan to appear in the historical record,

John Fransham of Norwich; and to his fellow English pagan, Thomas Taylor. The final part of the chapter traces the birth of Romantic paganism, with reference to phenomena such as the Druid revival, Francis Dashwood's 'Monks of Medmenham' and the pagan experiments of the circle around Percy Bysshe Shelley.

Chapter 5 examines the history of revived paganism in the nineteenth century. It identifies several distinct strands of contemporary pagan culture: the occultic paganism of Éliphas Lévi and the Golden Dawn; the late Romantic artistic paganism of Algernon Swinburne and the Decadents; and the more staid 'responsible paganism' of Edward Carpenter and others. Mention is also made of Charles Leland's *Aradia*, which was to become a key text in the witchcraft revival. Chapter 6 takes the story into the twentieth century, making reference to, amongst other things, the Woodcraft movement and the career of Aleister Crowley. The chapter goes on to consider the role of paganism in Europe's national revivals in the nineteenth and twentieth centuries, from the appropriation of pagan religion by the German far-right to the development of early expressions of 'native faith' movements in Central and Eastern Europe. The chapter ends with what may be regarded as the birth of the first enduring modern pagan religion: Gerald Gardner's Wicca. Finally, the Epilogue looks ahead to potential futures for pagan religion.

# CHAPTER ONE

# The First (and Last) Pagans: Ancient Greece and Rome

The first *pagani* were the adherents of the polytheistic traditions of the Roman Empire, who, as we noted in the Introduction, were given that name by their Christian neighbours. Our story therefore begins in the deceptively familiar world of Greek and Roman religion. This is a *familiar* world because it is still impossible, even today, to be socialized as a European or American without being significantly exposed to the ideas and symbols of classical paganism. This is so whether the exposure comes from the Farnese Hercules or the Disney *Hercules*; from reading *Ulysses* or from watching *Ulysses 31*. There is still enough classical literacy in mass culture that most people know who Jupiter, Athena and Apollo are. They could pick a temple out of a photograph, and they would be aware that sacrifices of animals were conducted there. They may even have some idea what an oracle or a Vestal Virgin was. Yet this familiarity is *deceptive*. We need to work hard to retain an appreciation of just how different pre-Christian European religion was from anything that lies within our experience of twenty-first-century Western society. In part, this is because of the general difficulty of stepping into a cultural universe in which religion was absolutely ubiquitous. Modern people, even those who happen to be religiously observant, struggle to appreciate what it means for an entire society to inhabit a world which is pervaded by invisible supernatural forces and populated by gods and spirits; and in which the very fabric of time and space is marked and divided by sacred places and rituals. There is another reason too for the gap in comprehension. Ancient paganism amounted to a way of being religious which in crucial ways does not fit with Christian assumptions; and those assumptions have to a large extent passed unchallenged into the post-Christian worldview, colouring the very essence of what we might perceive religion to be.

Classical paganism was first and foremost a religion of tradition.[1] Its practices and beliefs were handed down from generation to generation like so many cultural heirlooms. The individual did not practise their religion primarily because they were persuaded in their mind that its metaphysical claims were *true*, but because their parents and ancestors had done so since time immemorial. The emphasis was on performing the prescribed sacrifices and attending the customary festivals rather than on being taught from a catechism or believing in a creed. As the early modern French intellectual Bernard de Fontenelle put it, the rule was: 'Do what the others do, and believe what you wish'.[2] Put another way, Graeco-Roman paganism was a *religion*, but it was not a *confession*, in the sense of a collection of dogmas requiring intellectual agreement or self-conscious assent. Belief formed part of ancient religion in the trivial sense that the ancient Greek and Romans believed (probably, in most cases) that the gods to whom they performed rituals existed. But they did not believe, as Christians and Muslims later did, that correct religious belief was essential to their eternal spiritual destiny, or that the content of their beliefs needed to be strictly orthodox.[3] They had a 'noncompulsory theology, over which not a single religious war was ever fought'.[4] (Having said this, the Romans did have clear ideas about unacceptable religious practices—famously suppressing the Druids for their practice of human sacrifice, for example, and persecuting Christians for their refusal to sacrifice to the *genius* of the emperor.)

The purpose of maintaining the traditional religious observances was essentially practical. Religion was needed to make the world work properly. In the absence of modern agricultural techniques and healthcare, it was a matter not of spiritual exploration but of physical life and death. This was one reason why Christianity was so troubling: because it risked offending the gods by denying them their traditional worship. 'No rain because of the Christians', as the saying went.[5] One honoured the gods in the appropriate way so that they would bestow rewards and not punishments: it was not, for the most part, a question of personal salvation or self-realization.[6] In particular, relatively limited attention was given in Graeco-Roman religion to the subject of the afterlife. This life gave people quite enough to think about. Nor was paganism especially concerned with morality. There was a broad belief that some serious crimes were offensive to the gods; but there was nothing like the all-pervasive moral atmosphere of Christianity, in which sin and penance form part of the core of human experience and a silent thought can damn a person to hellfire.

There was therefore little room in paganism for concepts familiar from the Christian worldview such as personal faith, conversion and the salvation of one's soul. At the most, 'conversion' (in a sense) was possible if a person adopted a new set of customs on migrating to a different region or marrying into a foreign family. It has accordingly often been said that ancient paganism was not ortho*dox*—focused on right belief, like Christianity and Islam—but rather ortho*prax*—focused on right action. It was a matter of tradition and identity, not theology and metaphysics. The great pioneering scholar of ancient religion, William Robertson Smith, put it this way:

> [T]he antique religions had for the most part no creed; they consisted entirely of institutions and practices ... In ancient Greece, for example, certain things were done at a temple, and people were agreed that it would be impious not to do them. But if you had asked why they were done, you would probably have had several mutually contradictory explanations from different persons, and no one would have thought it a matter of the least religious importance which of these you chose to adopt.[7]

As a further point, it bears emphasizing that ancient paganism was fundamentally communal or civic in character. It was not a religion of the individual: the single soul who achieves salvation through an experience of spiritual rebirth. It was pre-eminently a religion of the *collectivity*, whether conceived as the family, the city or the Roman imperial state.[8] When religious decisions needed to be taken, they would be taken by the secular governmental authorities, just like any other important decisions affecting the life of the community. Priesthoods were filled by well-to-do citizens in roughly the same way as political offices; there was no separate class or vocation for religious professionals.

So much for what we might call the popular mainstream of classical pagan religion. It should be clear that we are dealing here with religion as an organic feature of the operation of largely rural premodern societies—rather than religion as a distinct and separable category of life, as it is in the modern West.[9] Ancient paganism was not simply a set of ideas about the gods and how to worship them: it was something that was deeply embedded in the social and cultural experience of the broad mass of the population. This had a consequence which is absolutely central to the study of pagan revival movements. Once paganism in the sense of the all-pervading religious dimension of ancient culture had been replaced by Christianity, it *became impossible to revive*, at least in anything like the same form. Once the altars were broken and buried, and the sacred fires extinguished, a thread was broken; whatever might emerge in later times would never be the unreflective, inherited civic cult that had gone before.

As we will see, post-classical pagan movements have generally been led by small groups of eccentrics, most of them educated and city-based. The argument of this book is that such people have had ample materials available to them because many elements of classical paganism persisted into Christian European culture, and this has made it easy for paganism to be repeatedly revived as a religious phenomenon. As we intimated in the Introduction, the elements of paganism in Christian culture have in effect been waiting for revivalists to reactivate them: they have been seeds waiting to be watered, organisms preserved in ice waiting to be melted. And indeed revivalists have succeeded in restoring major elements of classical pagan religiosity, such as believing in ancient polytheistic deities and worshipping them with authentically old texts and rituals. But revivalists cannot restore paganism as it was actually lived in antiquity—from fathers making daily offerings at the household shrine to state festivals with their complex civic and spiritual meanings—without also restoring an entire lost culture. Projects of restoring the old pagan socioreligious order in the face of increasing Christian dominance have occasionally been attempted: by the Emperor Julian in late antiquity (as we will see below), and by West Slavic and Baltic peoples in the Middle Ages (as we will see in Chapter 2). But one can never simply turn the clock back, and these projects tended also to include innovative and Christian-influenced components. Such projects are, moreover, wholly impractical once Christianity has won. After that point, there is no possibility whatever of revivalists being able to recreate pre-Christian society, and in practice they do not even try to do so. People like George Gemistos Plethon, Thomas Taylor and Aleister Crowley have made no serious efforts to persuade the mass of ordinary working people in their societies to return to the social existence of their pre-Christian ancestors, with the pervasive web of religious habits and assumptions that those people took for granted. Pagan revivalists tend to be intellectuals; and from this perspective they have tended to draw for inspiration on a very specific form of ancient paganism which lay outside the mainstream of popular religious practice.

In order to examine that specific form of paganism, we have to move away from the marble temples and state festivals, and focus instead on a rather different style of religiosity: a minority tradition which ran counter to the features of ancient paganism that we have been surveying. If popular mainstream paganism was conservative, civic and practical, this form of religion was radical, individualistic and focused on the care of the soul. It did not exactly *reject* the framework of mainstream paganism in the way that Christianity did; but it did generously add to, deviate from and reinterpret it.

This was the world of pagan esotericism and mystery cults: a world of mages, occult philosophers and private initiatory groups.[10] The mystery cults included, most notably, the mysteries of Eleusis, which were celebrated near Athens, and the cult of Isis, which originated from Egypt but spread elsewhere in the Mediterranean world. These cults have had a lasting impact on popular perceptions of ancient religion. Even today, the mysteries of Eleusis are remembered by people who otherwise know little about classical paganism. When in 1910 Aleister Crowley was looking for an evocative title for some occult rituals that he wished to stage in London, it is significant that he opted to call them 'The Rites of Eleusis', even though they had little to do with the ancient cult. The goddess Isis has likewise been remembered to some extent in popular culture, and the Isis movement has been influential for modern pagans and esotericists.[11] In antiquity, mystery religion offered what must have been an attractive prospect to people who were looking for a personal, devotional religious experience—although, perhaps inevitably, it also attracted charlatans. There is evidence that mystery initiators exploited their position both financially and sexually.[12]

The original esoteric mystery cults seem to have developed in the Greek cultural area—Greece and Greek colonies in Italy and elsewhere—in the sixth century BCE. They appear to have been centred on Orpheus, a legendary character who is said to have descended to the Underworld; and Dionysus, the god of wine. This 'Orphic' movement, as modern scholars call it, seems to have conceived of human beings as exiles from heaven who had become imprisoned in physical bodies. Adherents had an unusual concern for the fate of their souls after death, and at least some of them seem to have taken on board ideas that were circulating in Greek culture about reincarnation (or *metempsychosis*, to use the Greek term). The underlying purpose of being an Orphic initiate appears to have been to help one's soul to escape from its cycle of physical incarnations and to return to the divine: an idea familiar from other religious traditions elsewhere in the world, most obviously Buddhism.[13]

Among the surviving evidence on the Orphic movement, we find an interesting combination of the ascetic and the ecstatic: the themes of purity and remission of sins appear alongside Dionysian intoxication and revelry. What style of religiosity was this? Were these people monks or hippies? If only we had a cache of Orphic books, or a personal account from an initiate. But we do not. Scholars cannot even agree on how far the Orphic movement *was* a coherent movement with consistent ideas.[14] Few extended Orphic texts have survived into modern times, and most of those which have are late in date. For example, we have a body of 86 incantations to the gods known as the *Orphic Hymns*; but this collection, in its present form, comes from a late iteration of Orphism (second or third century CE?), and it can tell us little about the early movement. Nevertheless, the *Hymns* have proved to be a popular text among pagan revivalists, and we will be referring to them in later chapters of this book.[15]

One further feature of Orphic belief deserves special mention. The surviving Orphic texts bear witness to what might appear to be a tendency towards a kind of non-exclusive monotheism, focused on the chief Greek god Zeus. For example, one text which may be as old as the sixth century BCE states: 'Zeus is the head, Zeus is the middle, from Zeus all things are made.'[16] This is not strict, exclusivist monotheism of the sort familiar from Judaism, Christianity and Islam. Orphic initiates would almost certainly have continued to worship the other gods of the pantheon in the traditional manner. Yet we may see here the beginning of a tendency which would become fundamental to the ancient esoteric tradition, and which would reappear in later pagan revival movements. The idea was not so much that there was one true god as opposed to many false gods; but rather that one divine power came before and stood behind everything, including the gods themselves. This could be described as panentheism, in which everything subsists within God, or pantheism, in which everything equates to God. At any event, it is a conceptual framework which had the advantage of being intellectually credible as well as appealing to people of a mystical inclination. Popular mainstream polytheism might seem philosophically naïve, but a pantheistic or panentheistic philosophical model could accommodate polytheistic deities as expressions of particular forms of divinity within the ultimate ineffable Divine.

The Orphic movement might be regarded as the fountainhead of the esoteric component of ancient paganism. Another important early influence was the Pythagorean movement. The Greek philosopher Pythagoras, who was active in the decades around 500 BCE, seems to have combined interests in the metaphysics of numbers, asceticism and the fate of the soul after death. He founded a movement based on his ideas which went through several iterations and lasted for centuries.[17] Crucially, he influenced an Athenian aristocrat with an interest in philosophy by the name of Aristocles—or, as he has generally become known, Plato (428/7–349/8 BCE). A vast amount could be written about Plato's influence on the history of Western thought and culture, but for present purposes we are interested more specifically in the fact that his work had a profound influence on the ancient esoteric tradition. The mystical, nonrational side of Plato's writings is sometimes forgotten, but it is real enough. As the classical scholar Meric Casaubon wrote in the seventeenth century:

> The truth is, Plato's writings are full of Prodigies, Apparitions of Souls, pains of Hell and Purgatory, Revelations of the gods, and the like ... Indeed he hath many divine passages, yea, whole Treatises,

that can never be sufficiently admired in their kind; but too full of tales, for a Phylosopher, it cannot be denyed.[18]

Plato's writings are not systematic or consistent. As a very broad generalization, however, we might say that the basic premise of his thought is that there is more to existence than the things that we can see, touch and taste around us. His universe is essentially divided into two realms. The first is the ordinary physical world that we inhabit—this is a changeable place, a place of Becoming. The second is the world of changeless spiritual realities—the realm of Being. In discussions of Platonist philosophy, the physical world is referred to as the 'sensible' world, as we interact with it through our senses, while the spiritual world is the 'intelligible' world, as it is known through the mind or intellect. This is the context of Plato's well-known theory of the Forms. The objects that we can see around us in the sensible world have certain properties—blueness, health, 'tableness', 'swordness', and so on. These properties are the reflections of spiritual Forms which exist in the intelligible world—the Forms of Blueness, Health, Table and Sword. As Plato put it: 'beautiful things come to be beautiful by virtue of Beauty ... And are not big things big by virtue of Bigness ... and smaller things smaller by virtue of Smallness?'[19]

It is a fair generalization to say that Plato presents the sensible world of matter as a broken and imperfect reflection of the higher intelligible world. It is not evil, exactly, but it is an inferior sort of place. The Forms are both better and more *real* than the physical entities that we can see and touch:

> What if we were able to see Beauty itself—unmixed, pure and unalloyed, not filled with the flesh and colouring of human beings or any other mortal trash? What if we could look on divine Beauty itself in its simplicity?[20]

On the level of the individual human being, Plato believed that a sharp distinction existed between the body and the soul. The soul is spiritual and (at least in part) immortal. It is incarnated in a physical body, but it retains, to a greater or lesser extent, an attraction to the intelligible world. The human condition therefore presents us with a fundamental problem. The purity of the soul is sullied because it is joined to the body, and the body is not our friend:

> The body constantly disturbs us with its need for food. What is more, if we fall ill, we are obstructed from our pursuit of the truth. The body fills us with loves and desires and fears and all sorts of

folly and nonsense, so that (as they say) we are never truly able to think about anything ... In truth, we see that, if we are ever going to gain pure knowledge of anything, we must be released from the body and we must look at things in their reality with the soul alone.[21]

A philosopher should therefore prefer to be a disembodied spirit. For the same reason, death should not be feared, because it brings about a liberation of the soul from the body. Until that happy moment arrives, the philosopher should live an ascetic existence. In all, Plato's view of life is summed up in sentiments like this: 'we must try to escape from here to there as quickly as possible; and escape means becoming assimilated to the divine as far as possible'.[22] As for the afterlife, Plato famously taught the doctrine of reincarnation; although, as with other subjects, the views expressed about this in his writings are not entirely consistent.[23]

This overview of Plato's thought is sufficient to show how he drew on ideas from the Greek esoteric tradition, as represented by the Orphics and Pythagoreans, to fashion a vision of life and the world which differed in major respects from that of popular mainstream paganism. Yet Plato's works are lacking in one crucial respect. He was not fundamentally *religious*: at least, not in any practical sense. He did not give his readers any clear instructions on how to perform the task of escaping from the physical world to the divine realm. He conducted no rituals and performed no initiations. Some of his followers in later times would be rather more adventurous in this regard.

Having looked at the Greek roots of the ancient esoteric tradition, we turn now to a different source: Egypt. Egypt was, of course, a profoundly old religious civilization. By the time period in which we are interested (late antiquity), it had been colonized twice by foreign powers: by the Greeks in 332 BCE and then by the Romans in 30 BCE. The port city of Alexandria, founded by Alexander the Great, had become a multicultural melting-pot, a place in which Egyptian, Greek, Roman, Jewish and other influences mingled together. It was reputedly the location of the great Library of Alexandria, one of the outstanding intellectual institutions of the ancient world. More importantly for our purposes, the city also had a spiritually experimental side. It produced, amongst other things, an influential occult movement which is known today as Hermeticism.[24]

The Hermeticists helpfully left a body of writings behind them which set out what they believed. These writings purport to contain wisdom revealed by the gods, principally through a figure called Hermes Trismegistus

('Thrice-Greatest Hermes'), who was a combination of the Greek god Hermes and the Egyptian god Thoth. The Hermetic writings have deep and complex roots. They were mostly written in Greek, and their contents are indebted to the ideas from Platonic thought that we surveyed above, as well as to Greek Stoic philosophy. But they also show major influence from indigenous Egyptian religion, along with elements drawn from Persian, Babylonian and Jewish culture. Of particular interest for our purposes is a collection of 17 texts which is often referred to by the Latin title *Corpus Hermeticum* ('Hermetic Corpus'). The contents of the *Corpus* seem to date roughly from the first to the third centuries CE. It is likely that they were used for initiating neophytes into the Hermetic mysteries.[25]

The doctrine taught by the *Corpus* is not consistent across the various texts, or even necessarily within each text; but it can be summarized roughly as follows. There exists a transcendent, perfect God, beneath whom there is a descending hierarchy of other gods or spiritual entities. The underlying theology here can be described as essentially pantheistic or panentheistic:

> He is bodiless and many-bodied; or, rather, he is all-bodied. There is nothing that he is not, for he also is all that is, and this is why he has all names, because they are of one father, and this is why he has no name, because he is father of them all ... [Addressing God:] All is within you; all comes from you. You give everything and take nothing. For you have it all, and there is nothing that you do not have.[26]

This way of thinking provides the background for the key Hermetic idea that everything is one.[27] Everything in earth and heaven is connected together by mystical links or bonds of energy to make up a single entity. Sympathetic correspondences criss-cross the universe in invisible webs, linking together animals, plants, planets and the gods.

As for human beings, we have both a mortal, material aspect and an immortal, spiritual aspect. The Hermeticists essentially agreed with other ancient esotericists in drawing a distinction between spirit and matter, although the different texts of the *Corpus* vary in their level of negativity towards the material world, and it has been argued that it is a mistake to see Hermetic teaching as anti-physical.[28] The central promise of the *Corpus* is that we can transcend our normal earthly existence and be 'born again' so as to enter into divinity. The texts also refer to the doctrine of a cycle of incarnations and the need for humans to escape it. As to the means by which human beings might transcend ordinary mortal existence, it seems that one method employed was a ritual journey or ascent into the heavens involving altered states of consciousness. The Hermetic literature contains passages which seem to record genuine states of ecstasy, such as the following, from a dialogue between a teacher (Hermes Trismegistus) and his pupil. The 'eighth' and the 'ninth' are parts of the celestial realms; the ultimate transcendent God probably resides just beyond them in the 'tenth'.

> [Hermes:] 'My child, let us embrace in love. Be happy about this. Already from this, the power that is light is coming to us. I see, I see ineffable depths. How shall I tell you, my child? ... How [shall I tell you about] the All? ... I have found the beginning of the power above all powers, without beginning, I see a spring bubbling with life ... Language cannot reveal this. For all of the eighth, my child, and the souls in it, and the angels, sing a hymn in silence ...'
>
> When he finished praising, [the pupil] called out, 'Father Trismegistus, what shall I say? ... I see the eighth, and the souls in it, and the angels singing a hymn to the ninth and its powers. I see the one with the power of them all ...'[29]

The final link in the chain of ancient pagan esotericism that we need to examine is the philosophical school known as Neoplatonism. This was a new and distinctive iteration of Platonist philosophy which began in the third century CE. We have seen that Plato's cosmology worked on two basic levels—the intelligible spiritual world and the sensible material world—and that this two-tier model was also reflected in Hermeticism. The key innovation for which the Neoplatonists were responsible was to take this basic two-tier model and turn it into a more elaborate scheme consisting of multiple layers (which were known as 'hypostases'). At the top of the Neoplatonist cosmic hierarchy is a supreme spiritual principle—ineffable and perfect. This is sometimes called 'the One'. The One is a God, of sorts, but an utterly transcendent God. It is the ultimate source of everything, and everything subsists in it: we have here, again, a form of panentheism. Beneath the One there is a hypostasis called *Nous* or Mind (which is where Plato's Forms reside); then another hypostasis called Soul; and finally the sensible world. The whole structure emanates layer by layer from the One, like waters flowing out from a spring. To use a different metaphor, the Neoplatonists sought to identify and peel back the different layers of reality that go to make up the world that we live in.[30]

Like other ancient esotericists, the Neoplatonists taught that the human condition is characterized by a fall of spirit into matter. In spite of this fall, the human soul retains a natural attraction to and a desire to return to the One, the source from which it ultimately originates. The key religious question of Neoplatonism was how we might accomplish this return. Different Neoplatonic philosophers disagreed on this point. For the founder of the school, Plotinus (204/5–270 CE), the return to the One was a matter of personal purification and meditation. But others had an alternative route to spiritual enlightenment, one which came not through pure mental contemplation but through ritual. This route became known as 'theurgy' (literally 'god-work'). Theurgy involved practices which brought about personal encounters with the gods, who were invoked at different times into the theurgist himself, into other humans and into statues. It occupies an ambiguous space between magic and religion, two things which in later Christian and post-Christian thinking have tended to be kept separate. Not all Neoplatonists were enamoured of theurgy. Plotinus' pupil Porphyry (234–c.305 CE) seems to have broadly followed in his teacher's footsteps: his attitude towards theurgic practices was ambivalent at best. But Porphyry's own pupil Iamblichus (c.245–c.325 CE) believed that theurgy was an essential part of achieving communion with the divine. After Iamblichus, most Neoplatonists came to accept theurgy. It even ended up getting a foothold in the early Christian church.

No undisputed text of a theurgic ritual has survived from the ancient world, although this has not stopped scholars from attempting to reconstruct what theurgists did.[31] Interestingly, there is evidence from several different sources that theurgic practices involved inhaling sunlight.[32] One literary text tells us that certain 'theologians' used the following invocation to the solar deity Helios in their rites:

> Almighty Helios,
> breath of the world,
> power of the world,
> light of the world.[33]

The greatest gap in our evidence is the loss of the foundational text of the theurgic tradition: a collection of strange, complex poems known as the *Chaldaean Oracles*. This text, which survives only in fragments, was concerned in part with metaphysical philosophy and in part with magical ritual. It may have been compiled using what we would today call psychic mediumship: to that extent, it would contain supernatural revelations communicated directly by spiritual entities and would fall closer to the Qur'an or the Bible than to anything in mainstream ancient paganism.[34] A considerable number of rather baffling scraps from the *Oracles* survive, and, as we will see, they became influential among later pagan revivalists. The most complete work on theurgy that has come down intact to the present day was written by Iamblichus: its full title is *Reply of Master Abammon to Porphyry's Letter to Anebo and Solutions of the Questions Therein*, although it is more widely known as *On the Egyptian Mysteries*—a title that derives from Marsilio Ficino, a Renaissance intellectual whom we will meet in Chapter 3.[35] In general terms, this work may be seen as an attempt by Iamblichus to blend the Greek esoteric tradition with Egyptian spirituality, as the Hermeticists had done before him. He does not describe theurgic rites in detail, but he does tell us that certain stones, herbs, animals, aromatic substances and other material things were apt to serve as receptacles for the presence of the gods. This use of physical aids makes sense when we recall the theory of sympathetic correspondences that we met above in connection with Hermeticism. Iamblichus also put forward what was by now the very old esoteric idea that spiritual mastery involves becoming personally pure and transcending matter (although, as with the Hermeticists, it has been argued that we should not see his teachings as being anti-physical).[36]

One further resource which we have for understanding what theurgic ritual was like consists of the body of material known as the Greek Magical Papyri (*Papyri Graecae Magicae* or *PGM*). These are magical texts written on papyrus which have survived down to the present day due to the unusual climatic conditions of the Egyptian desert. The texts (as distinct from the papyri on which they are written) mostly date from the second to fourth centuries CE, although some of them seem to be much older. From what we can tell from our sources, many theurgical practices would have had similarities to some of what we find in the *PGM*. Scholars have therefore often used the *PGM* to cast light upon theurgy, although this must be done with caution. The *PGM* consist of a mass of heterogeneous material: spells for love, health and success at gambling; hymns and exorcisms; rituals for making magic talismans; and texts for use in scrying, necromancy and cursing. The cultural background of the *PGM* was eclectic. Like the Hermetic texts, with which they have some points of contact, they were the product of the encounter between Egyptian and Greek culture, the latter in the forms of both the Platonic philosophical tradition and popular mainstream religion. They also show Jewish influence.[37]

The best-known text from the *PGM* is the so-called Mithras Liturgy.[38] The physical piece of papyrus on which this text is written comes from the early fourth century CE, but the rite which it describes may be as much as two centuries older. It might be regarded as a theurgic rite, and it appears to echo the cosmology of the *Chaldaean Oracles*. The individual who went through the liturgy would undergo a spiritual ascent; they would be born again and would become immortal. The experience included receiving an epiphany of the sun god, who is described as 'Helios Mithras', and also an encounter with the 'Greatest God'. The text refers to herb-juices and drugs which may have been psychoactive; and the ritual seems to have involved the technique, which we mentioned above, of inhaling sunlight.

We may now draw the threads together. There was a distinctive esoteric tradition within ancient pagan culture, and this version of paganism contrasted considerably with the popular mainstream version. The world of initiatory cults, Platonic mysticism and theurgic magic offered believers the chance to transcend the physical limitations of the human condition and enter into divinity. This style of religiosity, which was by turns ascetic and ecstatic, did not reject the traditional polytheistic gods; but it did adopt an overall worldview which was pantheistic or panentheistic. The key point to emphasize from the point of view of our investigation into the persistence and revival of paganism is this: when people have sought to revive paganism in Christian and post-Christian times, it has tended to be *this* sort of paganism that they have revived. Not the popular religion of small farmers, the sacrifices at the local shrine, or the official cult of the emperor—but the kind of paganism that promised a personal experience of spiritual rebirth through meditation and ritual in a world pervaded by the divine. These were the elements of ancient paganism that revivalists have tended to reactivate—the seeds that they have sought to water—because the ancient mystery religions had the potential to be freestanding religious movements even within a society hostile to or uncomprehending of them, with a defined and self-selecting membership and a certain aura of intellectual prestige.

The story of the triumph of Christianity has been told many times, so many times that we tend to forget how strange and improbable it was.[39] Christianity was fundamentally unlike the indigenous polytheistic traditions of the Roman Empire and beyond. At its core, it preached an exclusive version of monotheism which left no room for acknowledging pagan deities except as devils—hence the pagan habit of describing Christians as 'atheists'.[40] To be sure, the transition to Christianity was smoothed to some extent by a tendency towards monotheism that became increasingly pronounced in the pagan culture of late antiquity. But this was *syncretic* monotheism in which worshippers were not required to deny a plurality of gods in favour of one true god. Rather, the pantheons of pagan gods were seen as being expressions of a single ultimate divinity, who was frequently linked with the sun.[41] This 'soft' monotheism was fundamentally different from the 'hard' monotheism that Christianity had inherited from Judaism.

That such a novel and uncompromising system as Christianity took on Roman society and state power and emerged as the victor is nothing short of extraordinary. The new faith required complete rejection of traditional religious observances, as well as adherence to a new and demanding code of morality. When pagans became Christians, they were explicitly detached from their previous religious identity. They spent a lengthy period of time in preparation before being initiated into a different religion and a different way of being religious. Their new faith required them not to preserve ethnic traditions but to profess revealed truths, and to do so to the point of martyrdom. These truths were accessed in ways that were highly unfamiliar to pagans: in part through written scripture, and in part through the authoritative teaching of a hierarchy of bishops who formed a 'state within a state'.[42] Moreover, Christians considered it a binding duty to make converts. They needed to persuade *everyone* to abandon their ancestral heritage on pain of eternal damnation. This whole style of religious life and practice had no parallel in paganism. In the end, Christianity could not coexist with the traditional Graeco-Roman forms of religion: it could only replace them.

It is possible that the outlooks of paganism and Christianity were so different, and so mutually incomprehensible, that many pagans were not hostile to Christianity but rather intellectually curious about it. This expansive and generous attitude may have contributed to the undoing of paganism. But other pagans, including members of the Roman ruling class, thought differently: some may have been imperialist patriots for whom Christians were subversives mounting an unthinkable attack on civilized culture; others may have been pious traditionalists who feared that the 'atheists' were offending the gods.[43] Accordingly, the pagans put up a fight. There were anti-Christian persecutions, although not on a large scale until the third century CE. And the battle between the two religious worlds was also fought using ideas, words and texts. In this regard, the combat was an unequal one. It was an encounter between a religious system which was based on claims of revealed truth and one which was based on loyalty to ancestral customs. Pagans were not well equipped to answer the Christian challenge that their religion was false, because explicit concerns about religious truth and falsity were a Christian novelty. 'How could tradition be true or false?'[44] It is significant that the persecutions sought not to force Christians to *believe* in the gods, but to *sacrifice* to them.[45] Some anti-Christian discourse was accordingly confined to the kind of crude smears that are always directed at stigmatized minorities: Christians were criminals who practised cannibalism and incest.[46] Nevertheless, a distinctive strand of intellectual anti-Christian apologetics, intended to persuade as well as denounce, did develop alongside the popular libels.[47] Some of the pagan intellectuals' criticisms of Christianity were based on unattractive Roman prejudices: God cannot have revealed himself to the Jews, of all people; Christianity is a religion for fools, slaves and women. Other criticisms were more theologically robust and challenging. The god of the Bible is a limited being, who cannot be equated with the transcendent deity of Graeco-Roman philosophy. The Bible itself is flawed, as is the Christians' interpretation of it. The Christians have rejected the Jewish law, and have therefore sawn off the branch on which they are sitting. Oddly enough, one of the anti-Christian apologists, the Neoplatonist philosopher Porphyry, promoted a version of the idea which has become popular in modern times that the historical Jesus was a praiseworthy teacher while the divine Christ is a self-interested construction of the church. The scene is an invocation of the goddess Hecate in a theurgic rite:

> When some people enquired whether Christ is a god, Hecate said to them: '... That soul belongs to a man of outstanding piety. People only worship him because the truth is alien to them.'[48]

As we now know, the pagans lost and the Christians won. But winning and losing in this context was not a straightforward matter. Having recapitulated the traditional binary narrative of Christians taking on and defeating pagans, we must now take a moment to remind ourselves that the complexities of human affairs rarely fit into simple dichotomies. Paganism and Christianity *were* fundamentally different and incompatible in principle; but there was more going on in the late Roman Empire than a battle between a monolithic pagan establishment and a unified Christian challenger. Paganism was inherently decentralized and pluralistic: a 'disorganized religion', as we might call it. Moreover, '[p]agans, in general, did not have doctrinal prohibitions or religious inhibitions';[49] and that potentially included inhibitions against taking up the language and ideas of Christianity for themselves. On the other side, Christianity evolved in the form of a number of different, and often mutually hostile, varieties. As David Petts has written in relation to the expanding Christian communion, 'the notion that there was ever an "essential" model for Christianity that held true across time and space is ultimately misguided'.[50] Not all Christians, moreover, were *radical*

Christians who were consistent in rejecting their pagan heritage. It may even be argued that paganism and Christianity occupied separate spheres which were often non-competing: while the church was concerned with matters of identity, eternal salvation and sacred authority, the cults and rites of the gods marked the ritual and agricultural years and were focused on ensuring equilibrium between the divine, human and material worlds and the continuance of natural cycles.

Even radical Christian zealots sometimes had their reasons for borrowing elements from the surrounding pagan culture. In a slightly later period, Pope Gregory I (reigned 590–604) wrote in a letter to a Frankish queen that 'many Christians both attend the churches and (it is abominable to say this) do not refrain from the worship of demons', meaning pagan gods.[51] But in another letter he advocated a compromise with Anglo-Saxon pagan customs:

> [Tell Bishop Augustine] that the temples of idols in that nation should not be destroyed, but that the idols which are in them should be destroyed. He should bless some holy water, sprinkle it around the temples, build altars in them and place relics in them. If the temples are soundly built, they must be converted from the worship of demons to the worship of the true God. When the people see that the temples are not being destroyed, they will put away their false beliefs from their hearts: they will recognise and worship the true God, and they will more readily gather together there because they are accustomed to do so. Also, because their custom is to sacrifice cattle in large numbers to the demons, a change should be made so that they have festivals of some sort adapted from this. They should ... celebrate festivals with religious feasts on the days when the temples are rededicated or on the birthdays of the holy martyrs whose relics are placed in them. They should no longer sacrifice animals to the devil: instead, they should slaughter animals to the glory of God for the purpose of eating them ... For there is no doubt that it is impossible for stubborn-minded people to abstain from everything at once: he who is trying to get to a high place must move up one step or pace at a time, not by leaps.[52]

This was an entirely typical attitude. The people who created Christianity made ample use, from the New Testament onwards, of the classical religious inheritance:

The 'basilican' shape of the first stone churches, and the use of candles, incense, wreaths and garlands, altars, formal liturgies, clerical hymns, vestments, choral music and sermons were all borrowed from paganism. Some of the iconography of Christian saints bore a striking resemblance to images of the former deities. Images of the Virgin drew upon some of the attributes of the chaste goddesses Artemis and Diana …

It is also well known that many Christian festivals were fixed, by Church Councils, upon dates already associated with major pagan celebrations.[53]

This is no more than a brief summary of the Christian church's debt to classical paganism: in Chapter 2 we will examine in more detail the role played by pagan elements in medieval Christianity. It is enough for the present to say that the victory of the church meant the transformation and repurposing of older pagan ideas and symbols rather than their obliteration—and this could be done quite knowingly. The persistence of paganism was Christian policy.

Quite why the Christian cause triumphed remains a matter of debate, and the unlikelihood of a despised sect achieving social dominance has come to be a Christian apologetic argument: 'surely God must have been on our side'. Secular explanations are also available, of course. In part, the victory of Christianity was probably due to sociological factors such as the Christian drive to proselytize, which created a demographic ratchet that was difficult to break. Without doubt, a crucial development in the story was the conversion of the Emperor Constantine (r. 306–337). Constantine is one of the more remarkable characters of late antiquity.[54] Even before his conversion, he seems to have participated in the contemporary trend towards solar monotheism, being a devotee of the sun gods Apollo and Sol Invictus. His decisive shift of allegiance to Christianity came during a period of civil war in 312, when he was said to have had a mystical vision from the Christian deity before a crucial battle. Constantine duly became a Christian. While this conversion had limited effects on his personal morality—and it cannot be proven that he ever attended a church service—his Christianity seems to have been sincere in its own fashion. To some extent he continued to go along with the old pagan ways, but he broke new ground by supporting the new faith with his patronage and applying its precepts in his legislation. In 324, he had his pagan co-emperor

Licinius executed, leaving Christianity unchallenged as the religion of imperial power. Rather suddenly, the Empire's pagan traditions found themselves on the wrong side of history.

The story of Christianization is not a straightforward one. A number of things stop the history of the fourth century from being a simple linear narrative of Christian triumph. There were bitter internal dissensions within the Christian camp: the Donatist schism in north Africa, for example, and the rise of the Arian heresy, which split the Christian world down the middle over the question of whether or not Christ is fully God. As we have intimated, doctrinal disputes of this kind did not and could not arise within the world of traditional paganism. One contemporary bishop saw such heresies as a tactic of Satan, who could no longer use the discredited method of paganism to seduce people.[55] But paganism was still a living reality, and another factor that complicates the simple linear narrative lies in the continuing 'tendencies to apostasy from [C]hristianity to the old religion'.[56] These tendencies are associated in particular with the reign of the Emperor Julian (331/2–363 CE), which saw the last revival of paganism before the onset of the era of unbroken Christian hegemony.

Julian was a pagan philosopher and theurgist who ended up on the imperial throne almost by accident. He was born in Constantinople, the great eastern capital of the Empire, at the moment when the centre of gravity in the Roman world was shifting from west to east. Christians have traditionally despised him: he was conventionally called 'Julian the Apostate' because he was brought up as a Christian and he consciously rejected the faith of his baptism.[57] There was little in Julian's background to suggest that he would end up as a champion of paganism or esoteric philosophy: he came from a family of soldiers, and he was the nephew of Constantine himself. It takes some explaining how a young man who was raised in the severely Christian and military environment of the fourth-century imperial house could end up writing lines like these:

> O mother of gods and men, you who share the seat and throne of great Zeus … Life-giving goddess, lady of good counsel and providence, creator of our souls … Grant to all humanity happiness, the greatest part of which is knowledge of the gods; and grant to all the Roman people that they may purify themselves from the stain of atheism … May the fruit of my devotion to you be to know the truth of the dogmas concerning the gods, to be perfect in theurgy, to have virtue and good fortune in all political and military works that I undertake, and to have a painless and honourable end to my life, together with good hope of journeying to the gods.[58]

Julian always seems to have been an unusual character. As a student, he cut an eccentric figure among his classmates.[59] It is clear that he was a secret pagan at least by his twentieth year, and possibly before that. A major influence on his embracing paganism was the Neoplatonist philosopher and magician Maximus of Ephesus (d. 370). Maximus was an unimpressive and avaricious figure, but he was nevertheless a pupil of a pupil of the great theurgist Iamblichus, and Julian can accordingly be seen as standing in the Neoplatonic line of succession. Julian's life changed for ever in 355, when he was suddenly transported from being a young philosopher to the position of 'Caesar', or deputy emperor. In this period of history, the Roman Empire was ruled by shifting combinations of senior emperors, 'Augusti', and junior emperors, 'Caesares'. Julian proved to be surprisingly good at the imperial work of soldiering and administration, although at this stage he shared his pagan views with only a few people. He even subscribed to a decree banning pagan worship.[60] In 360, his soldiers hailed him as Augustus; and civil war was narrowly averted when the incumbent Augustus, his cousin Constantius, conveniently died in 361.

After acceding to the imperial throne, Julian revealed his paganism openly. Temples were reopened and rebuilt. Sacrifices began again. The privileges of Christian clerics were revoked, and Christians were banned from teaching pagan literature. Julian did not, however, renew his predecessors' persecutions of Christians (although he did discriminate against them). Christian writers even complained that he had cleverly denied them the crown of martyrdom.[61]

Julian left more written works behind him than any other Roman emperor.[62] From the point of view of his paganism, his most interesting writings are two prose-hymns to the sun god Helios and to the Mother of the Gods (the quotation above comes from the latter). The *Hymn to Helios* is perhaps Julian's best-known production; he claimed that it was based on a lost work by Iamblichus. It may be seen as an example of the tendency for late-antique pagans to gravitate towards a 'soft' variety of monotheism focused on the sun. The text, which is not easy to interpret, speaks of several layers of reality within a Neoplatonic cosmological framework. The Sun-God is referred to as the 'King of the All': he proceeds from the transcendent godhead, and he is associated with Apollo, Zeus and other deities.

In Julian's time, the old pagan order was on the wane, but the border between Christianity and paganism still appears to have been somewhat permeable. This comes through from the story of Bishop Pegasius of Troas, the ancient city of Troy. In one of his letters, Julian remembered visiting the city before he became emperor. He noticed that altars were still burning and that a statue of the Trojan hero Hector had recently been anointed with oil. Julian asked Pegasius cautiously whether this meant that the people still engaged in pagan worship. The bishop replied, equally cautiously, by saying that it was surely appropriate that they would venerate a great man from their own city 'as we do the martyrs'. Perhaps sensing that he was dealing with a kindred spirit, the bishop then eagerly led Julian to a temple of Athena and showed him the statues there, which were in a perfect state of preservation. Julian noted that he did not make the sign of the cross in the typical Christian way as he did so. On another occasion, the bishop took Julian to the tomb of the hero Achilles, which he approached 'with great piety'. Julian further reports that Pegasius' enemies said that he used to pray to Helios the sun god. Whatever the truth of this, when Julian came to the throne, he rewarded him by making him a pagan priest. An encounter like this captures some of the spirit of the time; fourth-century pagans approaching potential kindred spirits with a mixture of eagerness and anxiety, a little like gay men in the repressive atmosphere of the 1950s trying to size each other up.[63]

A story like this indicates that Julian was not trying to resurrect a paganism that was already dead. But he *was* trying to do something quite strange. His intellectual, Platonist version of paganism should not be equated with popular mainstream observances: his project seems to have been innovative as much as it was restorative, in a way that prefigured later pagan revival projects. Ironically, it was also strongly influenced by the 'Galilean' enemy. Julian's response to the rise of the Christian church appears to have been to try to create a rival pagan one. Emperors had traditionally filled the office of *pontifex maximus*, or chief priest of the Roman pagan system—but Julian went further. He acted as a pagan pope, sitting at the apex of a polytheistic clerical hierarchy, embracing an ascetic celibate lifestyle, sending out encyclicals and preaching a gospel of adapted Neoplatonism. He was even prepared to learn lessons explicitly from the Christians. He accepted that paganism had failed the poor, and he resolved that his new pagan church would compete with Christianity in charitable works.[64]

Julian's instructions for members of his clerical hierarchy are particularly revealing of his agenda. Priests, he declared, should not go into taverns and theatres; they should not witness blood sports, and they should attend the sacred games only if women were not present. They should put on the appropriate vestments in the temples, but wear modest dress outside. They should not practise dishonourable professions. They should keep away from impure talk, and should eschew scurrilous poems, bawdy plays and love stories. Instead, they should study history and (the right sort of) philosophy. They should memorize hymns, and they ought to sacrifice to the gods two or three times a day. There was nothing new about pagan priests being treated as special members of society with specific duties and taboos, but something more is going on here. Julian was trying to create a priest*hood*: a sacerdotal fellowship whose members would be subject to rules requiring them to be personally pure and to separate themselves from unworthy worldly concerns and people. This was a recognizably Christian project. It is no surprise that his strictures resemble the canonical rules that were later drawn up for Catholic clergy.[65]

Julian died less than two years into his reign. Most of his time in power was taken up with military matters, and he died from a wound received in battle against the Persians. From one perspective, this poses one of the great 'what ifs' of history. What if Julian had lived to restore a pagan civic and religious order? It might be said that the year 363 is one of those world-historical years, like 1492 and 1789, in which the course of human affairs was permanently altered. Yet Julian was an eccentric figure, and his cause was not a popular one. That is why, by the time of his death, he had failed to build any serious movement that would outlast him. As one historian put it: 'The fanatic was gone, and there were few to regret him.'[66] Even if he had lived, Julian's endeavours might well have been too little, too late for the task that he set himself: by the 360s, Christianity was too powerful and resilient an opponent for the strange young philosopher-general.

Julian has become something of a symbol: an icon, both literal and metaphorical.[67] He has been written about, admired and condemned in a way that seems entirely disproportionate for a man who ruled for a period of 20 months. For Christians, 'Julian the Apostate' was a traitorous enemy who came to be seen as a precursor of the Antichrist. For more sympathetic observers, he has come to be an intriguing, even heroic figure: a geeky young man who accidentally turned out to be the 'last pagan'. He has caught the attention of later religious dissidents in Euro-American culture from Voltaire to Edward Gibbon to Gore Vidal; and he has acquired a small following among modern pagans and Platonists.[68] His supposed last words addressed to Jesus Christ—'Thou has conquered, Galilean'—were famously quoted by the Victorian philo-pagan poet Algernon Swinburne:

> Thou hast conquered, O pale Galilean; the world has grown grey
>     from thy breath;
> We have drunken of things Lethean, and fed on the fullness of
>     death.[69]

But Julian's ascetic Platonist world was pretty grey too, at least by the standards of a late Romantic rebel like Swinburne.

The break of 363 was not an absolute one: 'Roman paganism petered out with a whimper rather than a bang.'[70] The tradition of esoteric philosophy continued after Julian's time, and the line of Neoplatonist philosophers which culminated in Proclus of Athens in the fifth century formed a kind of alternative to the Christian apostolic succession of bishops, a 'golden chain' of pagan divine truth.[71] Among the Roman political élite, it has often been said that attempts at reviving paganism continued until 394, when the Christian emperor Theodosius I defeated the pro-pagan rebel Eugenius at the Battle of the Frigidus. This narrative has been seriously challenged, however, and whatever was going on in the 390s should probably not be regarded as a pagan revival.[72] The fact is that, after Julian's death, the Roman state broadly went back to Christianity-as-usual—not least because there were more than enough resources within Christianity to elevate, secure and glorify the imperial house as successors of Constantine the Great and 'equals of the Apostles'. Christianity was by now intimately associated with Roman power, with the sovereignty of God in heaven mirroring the supremacy of the emperor on earth. There was no campaign of anti-pagan persecution, but the cultural and material resources and freedoms available to the old religion steadily contracted. Major legal and financial measures against paganism were taken by the Emperors Gratian in 381–82 and Theodosius I in 391–92.[73] Elsewhere among the ruling class, the pagan old guard 'sometimes seemed as influential as the president of Polaroid in the age of the smartphone'.[74] Nevertheless, pagans must still have formed at least a significant minority of the population, and pagan rites continued to be practised to some extent. Religious traditions which had developed over millennia took a long time to die. Paganism survived into the fifth and sixth centuries, albeit not without state harassment, as the eastern part of the Roman Empire evolved into the Byzantine Empire.[75] Only around 529 CE was a law finally enacted imposing a blanket ban on paganism and requiring people to adhere to Christianity.[76] Writers who have wanted to find a neat cut-off point have often located the end of classical paganism in this legislation—the demise of the pagan tradition being (supposedly) symbolized by the closure of the Platonic Academy in Athens. As Alan Cameron wrote in a classic article: 'Scholars have credulously regarded the laws of 529 as the final victory of Christianity. Romantics have lamented the final suppression of the "Greek spirit".'[77] In reality, matters were not so clear-cut. There is evidence of paganism lingering on in the seventh and eighth centuries.[78] Indeed, indigenous pagan practices reportedly survived among some Greeks until as late as the ninth century;[79] and the 'survival' of elements of paganism at the level of folk customs and beliefs in medieval Greece will be examined in Chapter 3.

We may close this chapter by making mention of one candidate for the final home of the Graeco-Roman pagan tradition: a town in the south-east of modern-day Turkey called Harran (ancient name Carrhae). Harran was religiously conservative, and Julian himself visited the town and offered sacrifices there.[80] It was a geographically and culturally peripheral place: its location was near enough to the Empire's enemies to make it unwise for the central government to antagonize its citizens. More specifically, it has been suggested that the town became the last settlement of some Neoplatonist philosophers who left Athens when the Academy there was closed.[81] We do not know as much about Harran as we would like, but it seems to have remained a holdout of paganism—a combination of indigenous polytheistic cults and trans-planted Neoplatonism—after the rest of the Roman and Byzantine Empires had been Christianized. Certainly, enough pagans remained there by the late sixth century to prompt a persecution by the Byzantine authorities. The Arabs took the city around 640, and there is evidence that its paganism lingered on for some time after that. It appears that the Muslim authorities equated the pagans of Harran with the 'Sabians': a group who are mentioned in the Qur'an, together with the Christians and Jews, as having a protected status as 'peoples of the book'. The 'book' in this case seems to have been the *Corpus Hermeticum*; perhaps surprisingly, Hermes Trismegistus was traditionally equated with Moses. One celebrated Harranian mathematician and astronomer, Thabit ibn Qurra (d. 901) even established a 'Sabian' community following their native religion in ninth-century Baghdad, the heart of the Muslim world.[82]

The Arab conquerors seem to have allowed the local expressions of paganism in Harran to continue in existence until some point in the eleventh century.[83] So was it then that the ancient Graeco-Roman pagan tradition finally died out, in the unlikely location of the plains of Upper Mesopotamia? We cannot say that, because in truth it is impossible to set any such end point. Paganism persisted. The 'pagan theme' of classical culture was carried into all parts of the Christian world and continued a half-life under Christianity. Through the work of Augustine of Hippo, Neoplatonism was absorbed into Christianity, and thus paganism's final philosophical school might be deemed a victim of its own success: so intellectually all-pervasive that it ended up being co-opted by the Christian church it set out to resist.[84] But a very real pagan legacy nevertheless remained, and the next chapter will examine how Christians negotiated the potency of both living and dead paganisms in medieval western Christendom.

# Dealing with Past and Present Paganism in Medieval Western Christendom

In the summer of 1000 CE, when the Christian church was marking a millennium since the traditional date of Christ's birth, the lawspeaker of Iceland's Althing (an outdoor parliament), Thorgeir Thorkelsson, gave his response to the demand of Christian missionaries that the Icelanders adopt the Christian faith:

> And it now seems advisable to me … that we … do not let those who most wish to oppose each other prevail, and let us arbitrate between them, so that each side has its own way in something, and let us all have the same law and the same religion. It will prove true that if we tear apart the law, we will also tear apart the peace.

Medieval Iceland, unlike the Nordic nations from which its inhabitants had migrated, was effectively a republic and a direct democracy. While Denmark, Norway and Sweden had seen top-down conversions imposed by kings (as had the English kingdoms and many other early medieval polities in northern and eastern Europe), in Iceland Thorgeir's recommendation that the Icelanders adopt Christianity was a response to an incipient constitutional crisis. Iceland's Christians were refusing to recognize the 'pagan' laws of the Althing, and Iceland was rapidly dividing into two societies. Thorgeir's pragmatic solution was that everyone in Iceland should formally convert to Christianity and be baptised, so that everyone would be under the same law. He also insisted, however, that Icelanders should continue to be allowed to expose unwanted children and eat horse flesh, and '[p]eople had the right to sacrifice in secret, if they wished, but it would be punishable by the lesser outlawry if witnesses were produced'.[1]

Iceland's unusual character as a direct democracy meant that the sort of compromises tacitly accepted in other newly Christianized nations were set out in plain view. Historians have long been exercised over the question of whether newly converted societies like eleventh-century Iceland and seventh-century England (where according to Bede, King Rædwald of the East Angles continued to maintain altars to both Christ and 'devils')[2] were semi-pagan, still pagan in some sense, or essentially Christian. As we have seen in Chapter 1, Christianity and (ancient) paganism were not just different religions but different modes of religiosity—and modes of religiosity where it was not necessarily easy for Christians and pagans to talk to one another using a mutually comprehensible conceptual language. Furthermore, ancient paganism was embedded in society to the extent that once it was abandoned by the community as a whole, there is little point in speaking of lingering or surviving paganism—even if specific cultic and ritual practices sundered from the body of a living pagan faith might continue to survive. Once a *society* became Christian, even if it openly tolerated the persistence of certain pagan practices, then paganism as a coherent mode of religio-cultural life became difficult or impossible to sustain. On the other hand, if a society as a whole rejected Christianity after having once adopted it, a new kind of revived, self-conscious paganism became possible (albeit one which still had some degree of discontinuity with the pre-Christian past); we shall deal with such wholesale rejections later in this chapter.

Recognizing that fragmentary survivals of pagan cult and ritual in Christianized medieval societies do not represent the survival of paganism itself is important, because it puts to rest a discourse long popular in twentieth-century folklore and anthropology to the effect that Christianization was nothing more than the imposition of a Christian veneer on pagan societies, where the peasantry remained essentially pagan throughout the Middle Ages. This myth of the 'pagan Middle Ages', which inspired many authors and creative artists and remains popular in some quarters, has been thoroughly deconstructed by Ronald Hutton.[3] But it is also important to put to bed the myth of a medieval Christendom that was in some sense pagan or semi-pagan 'at heart', because there *were* pagans in medieval Europe outside of Christendom. By focusing our attention on non-existent paganisms in countries such as England, France or Ireland we are in danger of neglecting real people elsewhere who rejected and resisted the loss of their ancestral faiths.

The 'pagan Middle Ages' of barely Christianized peasants secretly creeping into the forests to worship the Green Man (or even the Fairy Queen) never existed. Yet there was another pagan Middle Ages that really did exist—more than one, in fact. One 'pagan Middle Ages' that really existed was a learned culture deeply saturated by pagan learning, which had to find ways to come to terms with its deep dependence on and reverence for the pagan thinkers of Greece and Rome. Another real 'pagan Middle Ages' was a post-pagan world in which pagan deities and pagan traditions continued to matter for the national self-understanding and legitimacy of Christian polities. And a third pagan Middle Ages was the continued survival of peoples and polities who remained resolutely unconverted to Christianity or rejected it, long after the rest of the Continent had accepted either Christianity or Islam. Most notably, the largest country in late medieval Europe was officially pagan until the end of the fourteenth century: the Grand Duchy of Lithuania. Even by the millennium of the Christian era, when distant Iceland submitted to the cross, Christianity was far from triumphant over Europe.

The subject of this chapter is the challenge posed by paganism in medieval Europe from around 1000 CE, as far as Christians were concerned—for it is largely from Christian writings that we know anything about medieval paganism at all.[4] That challenge was religious, political, military and intellectual, and was confronted as much in the halls of medieval universities by learned friars as it was on the battlefield by crusaders. By the beginning of the fifteenth century the pagan challenge had definitively passed as a genuine threat to the advance of Christendom, but the pagan legacy continued to matter in medieval Christian Europe. This chapter outlines the ways in which medieval Christians laid the foundations for the pagan revival of the Renaissance by wittingly or unwittingly conserving and transmitting neutral (or even positive) appraisals of pagan religiosity that subverted and ran counter to Christianity's foundational hostility to all things pagan. The chapter begins by examining the revival that occurred among West Slavic and Baltic pagans between the tenth and fourteenth centuries before turning to the subject of Christian intellectual engagement with the idea of paganism in the Middle Ages. Finally, the chapter considers the lingering importance of relics of the pagan world to medieval people.

No record has come down to us of what pagans thought of the spread of Christianity and Islam, other than what the proselytizers imagined they thought. Christian chroniclers sometimes put words into the mouths of real or imagined pagans: famously, Bede described the 'moment of epiphany' experienced by a counsellor of King Edwin of Northumbria, who compared the pagan view of human life to a sparrow flying momentarily into a warm hall and then out again into the cold, as well as the conversion of the pagan priest Coifi.[5] Coifi declares to King Edwin of Northumbria:

> For a long time now I have realised that our religion is worthless; for the more diligently I sought the truth in our cult, the less I found it ... Therefore I advise your Majesty that we should promptly abandon and commit to the flames the temples and the altars which we have held sacred without reaping any benefit.

Similarly, seven hundred years later, the Polish chronicler Jan Długosz imagined a Samogitian finally yielding to the conversion of one of Europe's last pagan territories by King Władysław II Jagiełło in 1413, after he witnessed Władysław's soldiers cutting down a sacred grove:

> On account of the fact that our gods, whose cults and rites we received from our ancestors, were destroyed by you and your soldiers, most serene king, and were defeated by the God of the Poles as if they were inert and powerless, we desert our gods and their rites, and adhere to your God and that of the Poles as stronger.[6]

Whether pagans really were convinced this easily of the inadequacy of their belief systems in comparison with Christianity as soon as they came into contact with missionaries is something we will probably never be able to know with certainty, but it seems rather unlikely. Coifi's attempted search for existential truth through the pagan religion of the Anglo-Saxons sounds very much like the imposition of Bede's Christian expectations on a religion that was in fact nothing like Christianity. Furthermore, not everyone was as pragmatic in their acceptance of Christianity as the Icelanders; pagans had proved reluctant to accept Christianity before, from the recalcitrant Norsemen to the Frisians who martyred St Boniface in 754. But the tenth century saw the first organized military resistance to Christianity from a pagan people, the Redarians, who resisted all attempts to convert or subdue them. The Redarians were pagan Western Slavs who lived in what is now the German state of Mecklenburg-Vorpommern, on the southern coast of the Baltic Sea—a group sometimes called the Polabian Slavs or Wends. The lands of the Polabian Slavs were attractive to the Christian Germans of Saxony, who began to settle in Slavic areas. However, when the Polabian Slavs revolted in 983 and formed a pagan tribal confederation known as the Luticians, Christians experienced a new kind of pagan violence which targeted churches and monasteries—not just for plunder, as the pagan Vikings had once done, but out of resentment for the growth and dominance of the Christian faith itself.[7]

Furthermore, some Slavs who had previously adopted Christianity now actively repudiated the faith and re-embraced their ancestral paganism. When the church arrived in a pagan land through the settlement of Christians, pagans faced a situation very different from the arrival of missionaries like Patrick in Ireland, Augustine of Canterbury in England or Boniface in Germany. They were not simply being given the offer of the Gospel, and invited to reorder their societies under the same rulers according to Christian rather than pagan understandings of authority and legitimacy; instead, they were being displaced by settlers who were already Christian. They were, in other words, being colonized. This new form of 'colonial Christianization' or Christianization-by-colonization was met with new iterations of pagan self-understanding. Indeed, it is possible that the advance of Christianity itself stimulated the transformation of Slavic paganism into something that provided structures of legitimation similar to Christianity itself.

The phenomenon of pagan religion being self-consciously revived in response to Christian hegemony was not, as we have seen, a new phenomenon in the early Middle Ages. It can be traced back to the Emperor Julian's efforts to reinvent a post-Christian Graeco-Roman paganism in the fourth century. In around 1005 Thietmar of Merseburg noted that the Luticians had constructed an enormous shrine called Riedegost served by a professional caste of priests which became the focus of the newly reconstituted Lutician nation.[8] Much later, in 1326 Peter of Duisburg described how the pagan Balts (the Prussians, Lithuanians, Latvians and other peoples) all came together to worship at a shrine called Romuva—which, even if untrue, demonstrated that Christian commentators were aware of the idea of 'national' pagan shrines among the unconverted peoples of Eastern Europe.[9] Some of the earliest evidence of Slavic and Baltic pagans focusing their cult on monumental sanctuaries and powerful anthropomorphic gods, in contrast to the nature worship that may have characterized earlier iterations of ancestral religion, comes from the tenth century onwards. In other words, just as churches, monasteries and cathedrals were central to Christianity, so the pagans responded with the construction (or re-imagining) of impressive sacred sites of their own.[10] However, while the state cult of the pagan grand dukes of Lithuania may have been influenced by Christianity—or developed in response to it[11]—some Christian chroniclers also deliberately portrayed pagan deities as the reinvented idols of apostates. Thus Helmold of Bosau claimed the three-faced god of the Rugians, Svetovit, was really St Vitus.[12] Such accusations allowed 'pagans' to be redefined as heretics or ignorant Christians who had fallen into error rather than apostates, since the possibility of apostasy suggested a failure of the reach of the Christian faith that few were willing to contemplate.

The religious 'arms race' between Christians and pagans in the southern Baltic gave birth to new and disturbing ideas about the relationship between Christianity and paganism. On 7 June 1066 Gottschalk, the Christian prince of one of the still largely pagan Slavic peoples, the Obodrites, was assassinated by one of his pagan subjects and anti-Christian violence spread throughout the southern Baltic region. The situation got so bad that in 1108 the bishops and nobility of eastern Germany addressed a plea to their peers in the rest of Germany as well as in France and Flanders complaining in lurid (and probably exaggerated) terms about the cruelty of the pagans:

> The cruel pagans, men who know not mercy and, in their evil, proud of their perversion, rebelled against us and won. They profaned the churches of Christ with their idolatry, demolished the altars and, though it be repulsive to the human mind to hear such things, they treat us with great cruelty. They frequently attack our region savagely and, sparing nobody, they pillage, kill, destroy and inflict sophisticated torments. They decapitate some and offer their heads to their demons. They rip the entrails out of others, cut off their hands and feet, tie them up and, to mock our Christ, they say: 'Where is your God?' Others are dragged to the scaffold and subjected to the worst torments, until they suffer a life more miserable than any death, when, still alive, they see themselves suffer until death by the mutilation of each of their members and finally, with their bellies cut open, they lose their insides in a horrible way. Many others they flay alive and, with the skin ripped off their heads, deformed in such a way, they expel them to the borders of the Christians and, pretending to be Christians, they pillage with importunity. The most fanatical of them say, whenever they wish to divert themselves at feasts, 'our Pripegala—they yell ferociously—wants heads, therefore must we perform sacrifices'. Pripegala, as they call him, is a lewd Priapus and Beelphagor. Thus, after slaughtering the Christians before the altars of their idolatry, they fill the basins with human blood and, howling with terrifying shrieks, say: 'Let us make this a day of joy, Christ has been vanquished, the victorious Pripegala has triumphed.'[13]

Whether West Slavic pagans really ever behaved like this or not, the so-called Magdeburg Letter is revealing of changing Christian perceptions of pagans as an active threat rather than just passive potential recipients of the message of the

Gospel. Furthermore, if pagans behaved this badly, there was a justification for setting aside the imperative of converting them in order to conquer, subdue or kill them. A dehumanizing anti-pagan discourse thus served the interests of the colonizer; conversion raised troubling questions of the equality of Christians before God, so if an agenda of prioritizing conquest and eradication could be justified, it was considerably more attractive to Christian rulers seeking to expand their territories to the east. On the other hand, Christian rulers were not averse to relying on the pagan Luticians for military assistance when it suited them; as Orderic Vitalis recorded, Luticians loyal to King Sweyn II of Denmark and 'still lost in the errors of paganism' sacked the English town of Ipswich and rampaged through East Anglia in 1069 before their defeat by Ralph de Guader near Norwich.[14]

The Magdeburg Letter seeded the idea that, if it was possible for Christians to wage a holy war against Muslims in order to gain control of the holy places in Jerusalem, perhaps it might also be justifiable to launch a crusade against pagans in Europe. In 1144, Pope Eugenius III launched the Second Crusade against the forces of Islam, and on 11 April 1147 Eugenius issued the bull *Divina dispensatione* ('By divine dispensation') at Troyes, at the urging of the Cistercian preacher Bernard of Clairvaux and Saxon princes, offering complete remission of sins to any Christian who went to wage holy war against the Wends.[15] The bull made clear that no tribute was to be extracted from the Wends while they remained pagans, and the Annals of Magdeburg further glossed the pope's intention: 'that [the crusaders] should either subjugate [the Slavs] to the Christian religion, or destroy them entirely by the help of God'.[16] While it might be anachronistic to refer to the Wendish Crusade as a planned genocide, it is possible to argue that the idea of genocide in European political culture can be traced back to documents like *Divina dispensatione*, which set aside the traditional justifications for crusade (such as the protection of pilgrims and the safety of the holy places in Jerusalem) and advanced a novel idea of conversion by warfare. We have no verbatim record of the diet at Frankfurt at which a crusade against the Wends was first decided, but it is possible that 'the campaign east of the Elbe River [was] ... nothing more than a continuation of the normal process of land acquisition under the novel rubric of crusade'.[17]

The crusade launched against the Wends in 1147 was not entirely unprecedented. In the summer of 1123 King Sigurd of Norway ('Sigurd the Crusader') had led a seaborne military expedition against pagans in the southern Swedish region of Småland, known in Swedish as the *Kalmare ledung*, since Kalmar was the principal city in the region. In Småland, as in other parts of Norse Scandinavia, Christianity had enjoyed considerable success in the deforested lowland areas, but paganism remained strong in the highlands and forests. The specific purpose of the expedition may have been to prevent a periodic sacrifice, which was due to take place in January or February 1124. By disrupting the cycle of seasonal sacrifice, Sigurd may have been hoping to prevent unrest fomented by pagans who were resisting to Christianization.[18] Once the pagan calendar was disrupted and the cycle of sacrifice broken, it was perhaps more difficult for people to return to the cult of the old gods.

The Wends and unconverted Norse were not the only pagan targets of crusaders. Hungary, formally converted to Christianity only after the coronation of King Stephen I in 1000 CE, was menaced by nomadic tribes such as the Cumans who threatened to draw the Magyar kingdom back into 'the nomad "pagan" world' from which it came.[19] The Cumans, otherwise known as the Kipchaks or Polovtsians, were a nomadic Turkic people who (like the Polabian Slavs) proved resistant to Christianization.[20] It was in order to deal with the Cumans that, in 1211, King Andrew II invited an order of crusaders from the Levant, the Teutonic Knights, to begin another crusade.[21] Here the Teutonic Knights began to seize Cuman territory, carving out a fiefdom for themselves—a policy they would bring to fruition further north, in Prussia, when invited to launch a crusade against the pagan Prussians by Conrad of Mazovia in 1226.[22] Owing to stiff Prussian resistance and a series of uprisings, it was not until 1274 that the Teutonic Knights established full control of Prussia; meanwhile another crusading order, the Livonian Brothers of the Sword (or Swordbrethren) established a territory known as *Terra Mariana* ('the land of Mary') or Livonia (the territory of today's Latvia and Estonia). The campaigns of these two crusading orders are conventionally known as the Baltic or Northern Crusades (although the term 'Northern Crusades' also has a more extended sense, referring to the Christianization of Finland and Catholic campaigns against Orthodox Christians as well).

In spite of their castle-building, heavy weaponry and mercenary support from the nobility of northern Europe, the Teutonic Knights and Livonian Swordbrethren were consistently unable to subdue the Baltic tribes east and north of the rivers Nemunas and Šešupė—the Samogitians and Lithuanians. If the history of pagans in medieval Europe is a narrative of decline, persecution and marginalization, the story of the Lithuanians resolutely defies it. Lithuania was, to begin with, a loose confederation of Baltic tribes speaking similar languages who were protected by the dense forests and marshes of their homeland from the Mongol raids that devastated the Orthodox principalities of Kyivan Rus' in the mid-thirteenth century. Capitalizing on Rus' misfortune, the Lithuanians burst out of the north and began to seize control of Rus' principalities, adopting a pragmatic approach to religion; Lithuanian princes who took over principalities in what is today Belarus converted to Orthodoxy and governed according to law codes written in Old Slavonic.[23] What resulted was a vast composite polity, the Grand Duchy of Lithuania, which was ruled by pagan grand dukes but whose dominant ethnic and religious group was Orthodox East Slavs, and where the official language of government was Old Slavonic.

Nevertheless, in spite of Lithuania's success the Teutonic Knights continued to threaten the nation in the west, and in 1253 the Lithuanian Grand Duke Mindaugas, who is usually credited with unifying Lithuania into a single coherent polity, agreed to be baptised and to cede Samogitia to the Teutonic Knights on condition that he received a coronation as king of Lithuania. Mindaugas reportedly founded a cathedral at Vilnius but his project of a Christian Lithuania was shortlived; in 1260 the Samogitians inflicted a devastating defeat on the combined forces of the Teutonic Knights and the Livonian Swordbrethren which stimulated a series of pagan uprisings in the Baltic which it took many years for the crusading orders to put down. In Lithuania, meanwhile, Mindaugas was assassinated (in spite of the fact that he may have renounced Christianity) and his successors were resolutely pagan.[24] In a dramatic example of the reversal of Christianity's ambitions in the Baltic, Mindaugas's cathedral in Vilnius was converted into a temple in honour of the thunder god Perkūnas. The cathedral's roof was stripped off so it was open to the sky and a six-sided altar installed along with six hearths which burned with sacred fires.[25] Such reversals of Christian progress were not confined to Lithuania; on the eve of St George's Day (22 April) 1343 Estonians revolted against their Danish overlords, overtly attacking Christianity by burning churches, massacring monks and clergy and restoring pagan cult, in a rebellion that lasted two years.[26]

Lithuania's Grand Duke Gediminas (r. 1315–41) made a virtue of Lithuania's refusal to adopt one of the monotheistic faiths of its neighbours—Catholicism, Orthodoxy or Islam—by playing off the country's neighbours against one another and opening residency in Lithuania to people of any faith—on the strict condition they made no attempt to proselytize the native people.[27] However, Lithuania's pagan stand and its peculiar brand of religious toleration finally fell victim to the geopolitics that had arguably allowed it to exist in the first place. In 1385, threatened by both Orthodox Muscovy and the Catholic Teutonic Knights, Grand Duke Jogaila accepted marriage to Jadwiga of Poland and the Polish crown, in exchange for baptism. The nominal baptism of Lithuania followed in 1387, although Samogitia's official conversion did not occur until 1413.[28] Indeed, Samogitia proved the most resistant region to Christianization, requiring a second attempt at baptism in 1417, and the final armed revolt by pagans against Christianity in Europe may have occurred in Samogitia in 1441, when a certain Daumantas was elected elder of Samogitia and rejected the Christianization of the duchy by the grand dukes of Lithuania.[29] The defeat of Daumantas's revolt marked the end of elite support for paganism anywhere in Europe. Thereafter, where aspects of pagan cult survived they were marginalized as peasant culture, and it is a contentious matter of interpretation whether they ought to be viewed as surviving paganism, deviant popular Christianity, or syncretism.[30]

The extirpation of pre-Christian religions as a political force in Europe was a process that lasted for most of the Middle Ages, with numerous reversals for the Christians, yet it has sometimes been portrayed as an inevitable triumph of Christianity over paganism. The continuity of paganism in Samogitia had important consequences, not just for Europe but for the world. In 1410, when the Teutonic Order was occupying Samogitia on the basis that its people were pagans and therefore lacked the right to determine their own political destiny, the Polish theologian Paweł Włodkowic (Paulus Vladimiri) advanced the case at the Council of Constance that pagans were, in fact, endowed with a natural right to sovereignty over their own land. Włodkowic's argument was politically motivated—the Samogitians preferred the rule of Włodkowic's master the king of Poland over the Teutonic Knights—but the basic idea that pagans might be endowed with some natural rights anticipated later debates about the rights of Indigenous peoples in the New World in the sixteenth century.[31]

In addition to reckoning with the pagans at its borders, medieval Christendom was forced to reckon with its own pagan roots and the pagan influences on its intellectual life. The full-throated denunciations of pagan learning attempted by some of the Church Fathers in late antiquity—even if they omitted to acknowledge their obvious debt to Neoplatonism—became unsustainable as the intellectual life of Latin Christendom increased in complexity in the High Middle Ages. The medieval 'Problem of Paganism', as John Marenbon has called it, was multifaceted, but was essentially a form of cognitive dissonance: the problem of how to balance the awareness that the pagan outlook was theologically incorrect with the reality of pagan achievements and, indeed, the reality of pagan virtue.[32] The problem is crystallized most memorably in literary form in Dante's *Inferno*, where the poet struggles between his admiration for the Roman poet Virgil and his knowledge that Virgil, as a pagan, can never enjoy the bliss of heaven. While it had been possible for early Church Fathers such as Augustine to distance themselves unambiguously from the pagan past, ironically that distancing had only been possible because they themselves existed in and benefitted from a Roman society derived from the pagan world. As the Roman Empire disintegrated in Western Europe in the fifth century, Christians were faced with the question of what they should keep and what they should leave behind from the pagan Graeco-Roman world, and it is thanks to most learned Christians adopting a fairly maximalist approach in the preservation of ancient texts that so much has come down to us from the Greek and Roman worlds.

Awe at the achievements of the classical world, combined with reverence for the principle of authority (the idea that authoritative knowledge was to be derived from ancient authors) ensured that some unlikely products of the pagan world were sedulously copied and preserved by Christian scribes. One famous example is Apuleius of Madaura's second-century novel *The Golden Ass*, which extolled the cult of Isis, but was upheld by some medieval authors as evidence that magic could transform people into animals—overlooking the possibility that Apuleius might have intended the transformation of Lucius into an ass as a literary conceit, and indeed the fact that *The Golden Ass* is a work of fiction.[33] Christian authors of the early Middle Ages were at ease with the legacy of the pagan ancient world, to the extent that questions about the validity and value of pagan knowledge were seldom posed.[34] The idea that divine providence prepared the Roman Empire to receive the Gospel (*praeparatio evangelica*) and then become its propagator had the effect of 'sanctifying' the *Romanitas* that so many early medieval rulers craved in the wreckage of the Western Empire, and in the first stage of Europe's Christianization, conversion went hand in hand with cultural 'Romanization' like the introduction of Latin as a learned *lingua franca*, even in territories like Ireland that lay beyond the limits of the actual empire. Even in the second stage of Christianization, involving the conversion of peoples such as the Anglo-Saxons and Frisians, there was little need for missionaries to engage with pagan ideas or practices because conversion was both rapid and attended by the prestige of association with *Romanitas*.[35]

One area in which medieval Christians were particularly admiring of pagan achievements was philosophy; and, indeed, such Christian admiration reached back into late antiquity and was itself a Christian tradition. Augustine of Hippo was eager to excuse the ancient philosophers from being pagans in the sense of being idolaters, suggesting that they did not really believe in polytheism, or even that some of the gods they venerated were actually angels rather than demons.[36] In the early thirteenth century the re-discovery of the works of Aristotle, first in Arabic and later in Greek (as a result of the Christian recapture of Toledo from the Muslims) created a new Aristotelianism in the Latin west that sought to harmonize Aristotle and Christianity—indeed, the effort to reconcile discrepancies between Aristotelian thought and Christian doctrine was arguably the central preoccupation of high medieval philosophy. Philosophy created an alternative space to theology or apologetics for the evaluation of pagan wisdom, which was less concerned with pointing out pagan errors and more concerned with finding common ground and a identifying a shared rationality.

But while the schoolmen of Paris, Bologna and Oxford debated the propriety of pagan philosophy written by long-dead Greeks, the seemingly unstoppable process of Christianization was hitting the buffers at the frontiers of Christian Europe—and especially at its eastern frontier. Missionaries were forced to pose searching questions about the pagan peoples they were seeking to convert. As we have already seen, this third stage of conversion, the Christianization (or attempted Christianization) of the Slavic and Baltic peoples, met significant resistance, to the point that pagans redefined their own religious practices in response to Christianity and converts backslid from previous commitment to the new faith. Some Christian authors responded to these developments with dehumanizing invective and calls for ever more anti-pagan violence, which groups like the Teutonic Knights certainly did their best to deliver. Yet this was by no means the only approach. For as long as the annihilation of recalcitrant pagans remained unrealistic or undesirable, their conversion remained the priority; and if people are to be converted to a faith which requires assent and belief, they must first be deemed human. Accordingly, some Christian authors fostered a 'proto-ethnographic' interest in pagan religiosity, enquiring into how the pagans had come to be deceived about religious truth.[37]

Grounded in the words of Psalm 96:5 ('All the gods of the nations are demons'), one of the basic strategies of the missionaries was to persuade pagans that the gods they were worshipping were in fact evil demons: the process of demonization.[38] Demonization did not technically deny the reality of the gods—and indeed such an ontological denial would almost certainly have been incomprehensible both to pagans and, in all probability, to many of the missionaries themselves; for one thing, the involvement of demons explained the wonders pagan magicians could supposedly perform.[39] It was a standard argument of the Church Fathers, and notably Augustine, that various groups of human ancestors fell into idolatry after the Flood when demons appeared to them masquerading as deities. Over time, all the elaborate panoply of ancient pagan cult came to be built around these original cults of demons.[40]

An alternative model to demonization, for those missionaries who preferred it, was euhemerization; the argument that the pagan gods had once been exalted human rulers who came to be worshipped as gods after their deaths through a combination of ignorance and idolatry.[41] Euhemerization could even be combined with demonization: cults originally focused on commemorating great men and women were hijacked by demons who pretended to be those original heroes who inspired the cult. In contrast to demonization, euhemerization left open the possibility that the original mortals who had been mistakenly venerated as gods could remain as venerated ancestors. Thus many Anglo-Saxon monarchs continued to claim descent from Woden in their royal genealogies centuries after the conversion of England, perpetuating a kind of limited 'ancestor worship' in a post-pagan context.[42] In the Norse *Prose Edda* Snorri Sturluson (1179–1241) made one of the most thorough attempts at euhemerism beyond the former Roman world by identifying the Norse gods as misremembered Trojan heroes—an elegant hermeneutic solution which allowed tales of the pagan gods to be told and re-told in medieval Iceland without religious complications.[43]

The role played by the pagan gods in medieval Ireland is perhaps even stranger than the case of Iceland, since Ireland had been converted to Christianity half a millennium before the Scandinavians, yet tales of pagan gods retained an important place in Irish literature. In Ireland, as elsewhere, the usual process of demonization of pagan gods initially took place,[44] but some deities were later revived in a form suitable for a Christian Ireland that nevertheless rested on pre-Christian political concepts. Thus the god Lugus (later Lugh) was reinvented as a royal ancestor, a literary character, and an embodiment of ideal Irish kingship in an early medieval world where Irish kingship was an amalgam of Christian and pre-Christian ideas. The latter included the idea that the king's righteousness determined the success of the reign (with disasters like a bad harvest taken as evidence of his unrighteousness), and the need for the king to avoid certain ritually prohibited acts (*gessi*).[45] Furthermore, medieval Irish writers re-envisioned their Christian past as a local version of the Old Testament, presenting ancient Ireland as a culture providentially prepared by God to receive the truth of the Gospel (the idea of *praeparatio evangelica*). The euhemerized old gods and heroes thus became potential moral and theological exemplars.[46]

The partial preservation of knowledge of Ireland's pre-Christian deities in literature written by medieval Christian writers—if it can be taken as in any way reliable—may be down to Ireland's early conversion, and the fact that Ireland's conversion lay largely outside the turmoil of international politics and colonization which often marred later conversion processes. There was no incentive for missionaries or evangelists to suppress Ireland's distinctive culture, and the completeness and rapidity of Ireland's Christianization may have contributed to a feeling of cultural security among Christians making use of pre-Christian themes. There was little danger of backsliding since the pagan threat lay solely in the past. Furthermore, Ireland developed a vernacular literature centuries before most other European nations, with the result that its mythology was recorded much earlier than elsewhere—even if we must be wary of ascribing pre-Christian origins to a mythology codified in the light of Christianity.

*Interpretatio Romana* allowed one god to be easily replaced at will by another, such as calling Woden Mercury—in part, because it did not matter to Christians which gods the pagans worshipped.[47] But *interpretatio Romana* also reinforced the idea that the gods of the pagans were real demonic beings: fixed realities whose identities could be discerned across different cultures. Wherever missionaries went, they could expect to see evidence of deities such as Jupiter, Mercury and Venus. While it is true that Christian knowledge of paganism, however deep it went, usually served only the purpose of refuting paganism, the more deeply Christian writers examined the pagans, the more human they seemed. Thietmar of Merseburg praised the morality of the Slavs, for example. Pointing out the virtue of pagans also served the double function of ingratiation—enticing the pagans to conversion by praise—and shaming Christians by contrasting their immoral ways with those of pagans who knew no better.[48]

Even a statement as ostensibly antagonistic towards paganism as 'All the gods of the nations are demons' was capable of more sympathetic interpretation; after all, the word 'demon' was adopted by Christianity from Platonism, and referred originally to any kind of spiritual being dwelling beneath the sphere of the moon, regardless of moral status.[49] While the Fourth Lateran Council (1215) formally defined the devil as an angel who fell as a consequence of rebellion against God, cementing a theology of demons as fallen angels, older ideas of demons as aerial spirits midway between heaven and hell lingered, especially in folklore. As Richard Firth Green has noted, it was not until the late Middle Ages that the church became concerned about belief in fairies—which, while not truly 'pagan', was hardly Christian either.[50] In the thirteenth century Caesarius of Heisterbach recounted a series of tales which portrayed some demons as filled with regret for their rebellion against God, and eager to help Christians, insisting that 'not all demons are equally bad',[51] and Coree Newman has shown that an unorthodox tradition of 'neutral' angels (angels who had remained neutral in the primordial battle between God and Lucifer) persisted throughout the Middle Ages. These 'neutral angels' or 'good demons' might perform roles similar to fairies or even pagan deities.[52]

There is no compelling evidence that anyone ever identified specific pagan gods with 'neutral angels', but the fact that fairies sometimes took the place of ancient deities in medieval stories—such as the substitution of the Fairy King for Pluto[53]—suggests that medieval authors were reaching for an evaluation of pagan deities that went beyond mere demonization. Dante went a step further by denying the traditional identification of gods with demons altogether, identifying them instead with the celestial 'intelligences' of Arabic Aristotelianism and identifying these intelligences as angels.[54] Similarly, in *The Knight's Tale* Geoffrey Chaucer presented the Olympian gods as real but identified them as planetary influences rather than demons—and therefore as beings morally neutral in and of themselves.[55] At both ends of the spectrum of learning—learned and popular—medieval Christians tested the limits of what could and could not be said about the pagan gods, and the development of vernacular literature seems to have encouraged such speculations. After all, the literary inspirations of authors like Dante and Chaucer were the great pagan poets of Rome.

Missionaries who routinely came into contact with pagans generally had a less stereotyped view of them than other Christians,[56] but some commentators went further and practised a kind of 'incommensuration', whereby they kept their assessments of pagans within a different sphere of judgement from that which they might apply to Christians.[57] Thus Sir John Mandeville, whether or not he actually visited any of the countries he claimed to, made sense of the alleged cannibalism of some distant peoples by redefining it as an act of mercy towards the sick and dying.[58] While Mandeville might be an extreme example (and he was not a missionary), this relativist tendency emerged from a genuine yearning to understand the humanity of pagans. When it came to the 'civilized' pagans of the past, Christians were even more likely to be sympathetic, and influential theologians such as Thomas Aquinas, Henry of Ghent, John Duns Scotus and William of Ockham all affirmed (contra Augustine) that it was possible for pagans to display genuine virtue—and even heroic virtue, in Ockham's view.[59]

Dante, famously, went even further and claimed that God made special provision to ensure that three pagans (the Trojan Ripheus, Cato, and the Emperor Trajan) were saved and now enjoyed the beatific vision.[60] Indeed, Christian speculation about the possibility of pagan goodness tended not to focus on the gods or on contemporary pagans but on the virtue of ancient philosophers, which reached fever-pitch in the pseudo-Aristotelian *Secret of Secrets*, an Arabic work translated into Latin in the thirteenth century which claimed God called Aristotle an angel rather than a human being and allowed him to ascend to heaven in a column of fire.[61] While they were by no means uncritically received by medieval Christian thinkers, works like these did not so much rehabilitate the old pagan gods as make new gods out of pagan philosophers, and at the fringes of both Arab and Christian Aristotelianism Aristotle was virtually worshipped. Boethius had already claimed that the soul of the Christian could become a god,[62] and when coupled with adoration of the pagan dead the Christian idea of 'divinization' could take on a very pagan-seeming character indeed.

In the late fourteenth century the Dutch Dominican friar Dirc van Delf drew a 'Table of the Christian Faith' which, despite its name, paid notable attention to exalting pagan virtues. Dirc even listed 'the five pagan commandments' alongside the Ten Commandments of Scripture: fear one God; grant your fellow man the same as you do to yourself; do not judge a fellow man; avoid stupidity, evil thoughts and abominable deeds; and profess the truth in all things.[63] Dirc effectively identified the gods of the ancients as personifications of virtues, declaring: 'The pagans determined that there were as many gods as there were virtues, which gods they called and to which they appropriated the virtues.'[64] This was an attitude that opened up the possibility of considering the enlightened ancient pagans as proto-deists who understood the gods were mere allegories, while the ignorant people of the ancient world remained mired in idolatry. The idea of the gods of the ancients as personifications was not a new one; in around 1160 Alberic of London, a canon of St Paul's Cathedral, had made the same argument in his *Liber imaginum deorum* ('Book of the Images of the Gods').[65]

One of Dirc's influences was the brilliant 'classicizing' English Dominican Robert Holcot,[66] who died of the Black Death at Northampton in 1349. Holcot had gone well beyond the celebration of pagan virtue, especially in his *Liber moralizationum historiarum* ('Book of the Moralizations of Histories'), which 'offends and insults modern sensibilities' by treating the writings of the ancients as a subject for exegesis for the Christian message, much like the Old Testament.[67] Robrecht Lievens has argued that Holcot belonged to a 'classicizing' intellectual school of mendicant friars teaching at Oxford and Cambridge along with John of Wales, John Ridevall, Thomas Waleys, and Nicholas Trevet who were comfortable with applying Biblical styles of exegesis to classical texts and drawing moral lessons from the pagan ancients, without sharply differentiating between pagan and Christian virtue.[68] Holcot and his colleagues stood in the 'pagan-friendly' Christian tradition of Justin Martyr and Origen, which was open to pagan wisdom as the 'despoiling of the Egyptians'—as Origen put it, referring to the ancient Hebrews taking the gold of the Egyptians in the Book of Exodus.[69] Already in the twelfth century, John of Salisbury had presented Plutarch's guidance on the proper worship of the gods as a model for Christians, provided 'God' was substituted for 'the gods'—a bold attempt at upholding the unity of religious wisdom and knowledge, regardless of a thinker's pagan or Christian background.[70]

As Sarah Salih has argued, the imagined pagan was 'good to think with' in theological and philosophical 'thought experiments' that explored the distinction between grace and nature in the human soul.[71] More often than not, this imagined pagan was a virtuous and admirable figure of the ancient past—after all, the pagans of the present were often portrayed as a barbarians, and lay not only outside the Christian faith but also outside the civilized world. Ancient pagans were unchristian, yet civilized. But did the sympathy of some medieval Christian writers to pagans ever cause them to cross the Rubicon of portraying *present-day* pagans in positive terms? As we have seen, Peter of Duisburg's portrayal of Romuva, the great shrine of the Balts, might be considered one example—apart from the likelihood that Peter's account of Baltic pagans was also fictional. Fictional or not, however, Peter's account did spring from a genuine cultural development in the Baltic region, whereby the geographical and cultural proximity of the Teutonic Knights and their allies to a pagan society resulted in a kind of grudging respect between the two cultures, not dissimilar to the respect crusaders sometimes had for their Muslim foes.[72]

In the late Middle Ages, diplomatic contacts between Christian courts and the Mongols encouraged a strand of favourable perception of non-Christians.[73] It is noteworthy that when Portuguese sailors first encountered a pagan society previously untouched by contact with Christianity when they landed on Gran Canaria in 1341, the Portuguese took the idols of the Guanches back to Lisbon, but regarded them with curiosity rather than horror.[74] Similarly, captured pagan Lithuanians were regarded with great curiosity at the courts of Christendom,[75] and when Polish Franciscan friars destroyed the shrine of Perkūnas in Vilnius in 1387 they kept the idol as a trophy in their dormitory for centuries, showing it off to visitors as a curiosity, rather than destroying it.[76] It was perhaps because living paganism was a phenomenon rarely encountered by Christian Europeans before 1492 that curiosity was a more likely response to it than abject horror. Furthermore, when late medieval Christians did denounce paganism, what they were usually denouncing were not the practices of 'pagans proper' (that is to say, the unbaptised or open apostates) but rather the folk religion and non-standard beliefs and practices of people who were baptised Christians.[77] 'Paganism', as always, was in the eye of the beholder.

Medieval Europeans often lived amid the physical wreckage of a former pagan world, and pagan buildings and objects could sometimes come to be endowed with significance. The earliest European Christians also lived amid the cultural and religious detritus of paganism as a thought-world, although Mark Williams has argued that the public worship of pagan deities usually disappeared in a society within forty or fifty years of the conversion of its rulers, including a brief period when paganism co-existed with Christianity.[78] On the other hand, conversion could also be a slow process, because some peoples took longer to reach than others—thus it was the geographically remote Isle of Wight which became, in around 680, the last part of England to formally receive the Christian faith—over eighty years after Augustine of Canterbury's mission to Kent.

The historiography of the 'survival' of paganism into the Middle Ages in Britain and Ireland is a very well-trodden field, and Ronald Hutton can perhaps be allowed a last word on the subject: 'the answer to the question [of whether paganism survived] is now generally assumed to be obvious, and firmly negative'.[79] There is simply no evidence to support the survival of pagan cult in medieval Britain beyond the tenth century, when the last Scandinavian stragglers received baptism. In two solitary reported cases of medieval priests turning to idolatry, the insanity of the protagonists seems to be implied,[80] and there is no indication they were perpetuating any pre-existing tradition. Supposed instances of pagan survival in Britain have a tendency to vanish, like phantoms, when they are inspected in detail—allegations of the worship of sacred trees in medieval England are a case in point.[81]

In the 1990s Eamon Duffy took to task Jean Delumeau's characterization of medieval peasants as 'polytheistic and deeply magical', showing that charms and protective invocations such as the Charlemagne prayers appeared in elite as well as popular sources and were widespread through society.[82] Popular Christianity was more than capable of developing its own forms of magical thinking without the need to appeal to a kind of paganism surviving within it; and indeed Delumeau's attitude was redolent of anti-Catholic polemics which sought to discredit Catholic practices as not Christian at all, but relics of paganism (see further Chapter 3 on this). There is nothing uniquely pure about Christianity (or any other religion, for that matter) that insulates it from the development of popular beliefs and practices more akin to magic than religion—and the attempted externalization or othering of such things as 'pagan' does a disservice to the complexity of the Christian tradition, and encourages a facile understanding of medieval Christianity.

The question of 'pagan survival' has been more thoroughly explored in relation to Britain and Ireland than any other region, but similar principles can be applied to numerous other Christianized European societies where there was a fairly swift conversion of ruling elites who saw advantages in allegiance to the new faith. Where the examples of Britain and Ireland break down as useful 'type-specimens' for a pagan society's conversion to Christianity is where conversion was a very different process, and took place under the pressures of systematic colonization and crusade. If we cannot speak meaningfully of pagan survival into the Middle Ages and beyond in Britain and Ireland, it is far less clear that this is true of Estonia, Latvia, Sápmi or Finnic peoples inhabiting the north bank of the Volga, where resistance to a Christianity imposed by German, Danish, Swedish and Russian overlords continued for centuries. However, it is also far from clear whether we should refer to religiously recalcitrant Estonians, Latvians, Sámi, and Mari, many of whom had been baptised, as 'pagans', or even as 'syncretists' who followed some sort of dual-faith observance. As Marenbon notes, it is possible for people to inhabit more than one tradition or conceptual scheme without synthesizing them,[83] and we should not be tempted to apply excessively neat categories to people at the fringes of medieval and early modern Christendom.

Ramsay MacMullen, in his influential survey of the relationship between Christianity and paganism between the fourth and eighth centuries, argued that '[t]he triumph of the church was not one of obliteration but of widening embrace and assimilation'.[84] In other words, the church only vanquished paganism by accommodating, tacitly or otherwise, a number of pagan practices (such as amulets and phylacteries); and the church was thus reshaped in the likeness of paganism.[85] The difficulty with this argument is that it assumes that practices such as the making of phylacteries or hanging petitions from trees could remain in some sense meaningfully 'pagan' long after they became dissociated in any way from pagan cult. There is a persistent danger in the history of religion of historians seizing upon any practice deemed strange, unusual, or vestigial and identifying it as a survivor of some pagan religious substratum on which Christianity was later imposed. But just because a practice such as the making of phylacteries existed in both the pagan and the Christian era, this does not mean it is meaningful to describe phylacteries as 'pagan'. Once the 'pagan system' (as MacMullen called it) is gone, it is difficult to see how practices only tenuously related to pagan cult can remain pagan; they simply drift into the common currency of popular religion, and will be expressed in Christian ways in a Christian society, or in Islamic ways in a Muslim society.

Bernadette Filotas paints a picture of the decaying pantheon of late antique Gaul and Iberia, where rustics still venerated Jupiter, Mercury (sometimes identified with the Archangel Michael), Minerva and various manifestations of Diana at shrines in fields or hidden inside barns.[86] New deities seem to have come into being, like the mysterious figure Geniscus (who may have been linked with the *genius*),[87] and the strange air-dwelling *mavones* (perhaps linked to the *di manes*, the spirits of the dead).[88] Yet the idea that the persistence of the names of pagan deities means that they were worshipped long after Christianization is absurd, since the later application of those names bore little or no relation to the original character of the deity from whom they derived. Consider the French *lutins*, dwarf-like beings whose name can be traced ultimately to the name of the god Neptune.[89] Deities and spirits are culturally constructed beings, and we cannot expect their names to remain stable in meaning and reference over time.

One area of the material world where very obvious reminders of paganism survived was in the ongoing popularity of Roman cameos, intaglios and engraved gems in the early medieval world, which often depicted pagan themes. These intaglios were often set into reliquaries, crowns and jewellery—sometimes in the belief that their pagan iconography increased their apotropaic power.[90] Intaglios also became popular as a component of personal signet rings—such as the seal of Archbishop Thomas Becket, which featured a helmeted figure who might be Mars or Perseus.[91] While some images, such as Perseus holding the head of Medusa, could be reinterpreted in Christians terms (as David holding the head of Goliath) this was less straightforward for other images.[92] Acceptance of amulets was an early Christian concession to pre-Christian practice,[93] but the continued popularity of pagan intaglios is harder to square with the new faith. It seems unlikely that such items were valued purely as antiquarian relics of the prestigious civilization of Rome, yet the presence of tiny images of pagan deities on intaglios attracted none of the opprobrium of large, freestanding statues of the gods—as if people were more willing to accept that the imagery on intaglios was merely decorative, since no-one had ever worshipped an intaglio. However, the sacred and highly personal uses to which medieval people put ancient intaglios (whether adorning reliquaries or forming part of seals) suggest they were more than merely decorative, and were imbued with some kind of desirable spiritual power which surely lay beyond Christian orthodoxy.

In Ludo Milis's view, elements of paganism lingered in order to 'fill the gaps' in people's spiritual needs left by Christianity, an otherworldly religion focused on escaping this world.[94] While there may be some truth in this argument, it overplays the otherworldliness of Christianity and the capacity of popular Christianity to fill those gaps even once lingering traces of paganism were forgotten. The tendency of earlier scholarship to interpret anything unexpected or unusual about medieval religious behaviour as 'pagan' was a regrettable one, and misconceptions still abound—such as the notion that witchcraft was somehow linked with paganism. Belief in witchcraft in its malefic form only emerged at the end of the Middle Ages, and demonologists of the period like Heinrich Institoris (the author of the *Malleus maleficarum* or 'Hammer of Witches') sought to distinguish the witches of their own time—who they believed to be devil-worshippers—from the worshippers of Diana described in the tenth-century *Canon Episcopi*.[95] The reason for this was that the old canon dismissed women who believed they flew at night with Diana as deluded; Institoris was unable to reject the canon, and therefore he needed to show that the witches of his own time were *not* pagans, but rather diabolists. In other words, witches were heretics whose cosmology was a Christian one, but who chose to worship the devil instead of Christ.

The Middle Ages did not keep paganism alive. As Ludo Milis put it: 'Important but loose elements [of paganism] survived in the Middle Ages … But the structure had gone. All the pagan beliefs were beaten, systematically, oftentimes violently, often parallel with territorial conquests and new regimes.'[96] No pagan polity survived the period of Christendom's expansion (even if the Grand Duchy of Lithuania came close), and by 1500 there were few people in Europe who had not been exposed to proselytizing monotheism, with the consequence that their pre-monotheistic worldviews were in some way disrupted; the Sámi of northern Scandinavia were perhaps the least affected. Attempts to deny the reality of Christianity's obliteration of traditional pagan religions by speciously interpreting the historical evidence are misguided. This does not mean, of course, that the Christianization of Europe was entirely completed in this period—far from it. Various forms of syncretism and compromise with pagan legacies lingered long into the early modern period. But medieval Christians were more likely to engage with imaginary pagans than they were with real practitioners of pre-Christian cults. It is therefore within Christianity itself, and within the range of attitudes to paganism that existed inside it, that the seeds which germinated into pagan revivals were created.

For most medieval Christians who thought about it, the gods of the pagans were real, albeit as malevolent demons. Paganism was thus a real threat; it was not merely error, but error super-charged by the assistance of ancient, malevolent entities who were intent on ensnaring human souls and masqueraded as gods. Medieval Christians were more likely to respond to paganism with horror than with ridicule. But this was not the only face the pagan gods wore in the Middle Ages, and some authors were quite willing to make more positive use of the pagan gods in order to underpin moral allegories. Whether the pagan gods were to be considered embodiments of evil or morally neutral symbols depended, essentially, on context. As Marenbon puts it, in the Middle Ages 'a pagan vision is given the space to be taken seriously, even though it is recognized to be false'.[97] There was not one 'pagan Middle Ages', but rather a multitude of trajectories taken by the detritus of paganism in the medieval world. And that detritus, as we shall see, had more than enough potential to be re-assembled into something like a functioning revived paganism as the Renaissance glimmered into view.

# CHAPTER THREE

# Pagan Renaissances

If any period of European history has a reputation for attempting to revive paganism, it is the Renaissance. There is an enduring popular image of 'Renaissance men' as religious mavericks who borrowed indiscriminately from the corpus of official Catholicism and from the persisting ideas and symbols of classical antiquity: 'They carved Madonna and Adonis on the self-same shrine; they confused the mythology of Olympus with the persons of the Trinity, the oracles of alchemists and necromancers with the voice of prophets, the authority of Virgil, Ovid and Euripides with that of David and St Paul.'[1] There is much truth in this stereotype, but the story of Renaissance paganism is more complex than is usually realized. It is a tale of pagan persistence and revival whose roots lie deep in earlier history. Part of that history has been recounted in the previous chapter; and to tell the rest we must turn our attention to the world of medieval Byzantium. To reiterate a couple of metaphors that we have been using, some of the desiccated seeds had already been watered there, and some of the ice had already been melted.

In the Middle Ages, the name and legal forms of the Roman Empire were inherited by the Byzantine Empire. Greek in language and culture, the Byzantine state was ruled from Constantinople, and its heartlands lay in modern Greece and Turkey. It went through a thousand eventful years of history, marked by wars, plagues and court politics, until it finally succumbed to the Muslim Ottoman invaders in 1453. The Byzantine Empire tends to be remembered as a very Christian place indeed: a world of icons, monks and the Hagia Sophia. And Byzantine culture *was* profoundly Christian, not to say clerical, in character. More specifically, the Byzantines practised the Eastern Orthodox variety of Christianity, which was at odds with that of the Catholic west. The decisive breach between the pope of Rome and the patriarch of Constantinople is generally dated to 1054, although that breach was part of a longer history of discord. All this meant that the religious politics of Byzantium were very different from those of the original Roman Empire. The Orthodox Byzantines' religious enemies were not polytheistic pagans, but rather Catholic crusaders from the west and Muslims from the east and south.

Yet even in this conspicuously Orthodox Christian world, the continuing influence of the classical pagan legacy ensured that the old pre-Christian ways would continue to resurface in certain forms and in certain quarters; and, since the Eastern Roman Empire did not undergo the same process of disintegration and cultural reconstitution as the Latin west, Byzantium's relationship with the legacy of its pagan past was rather different from that of western Europe. A key driving force of this relationship was Platonist philosophy. We saw in Chapter 1 how currents of thought and practice deriving from Plato occupied a distinctive place in ancient Graeco-Roman pagan culture, and how they had important esoteric elements. Plato had been influential among Christians too. The Church Fathers had drawn on Platonist thought, and Augustine of Hippo famously commented that Plato's philosophy was the closest pagan system to Christianity.[2] But Byzantium was not necessarily a hospitable place for Platonism. This was a world in which mentioning Plato's name could be enough to make monks cross themselves in horror and utter curses against the Greek Satan.[3]

It might be argued that there was never a period of Byzantine history in which paganism was wholly replaced by Christianity. We noted in Chapter 1 that the last surviving organic remnant of pagan religion in Greece seems to have been extinguished in the ninth century. Yet at that same time there also seems to have been something of a revival of paganism (notably, in its Platonist form), at least among the élite.[4] Similarly, in the eleventh century, at the very time that the lingering vestiges of the ancient pagan tradition were being eliminated in Islamic Harran, that tradition was being reignited by Byzantine Greeks a relatively short distance to the west. This eleventh-century pagan revival merits special attention. Its central figure was a clever and duplicitous man by the name of Michael Psellus (1018–c.1078).

Psellus was a number of things: a politician, an academic, a Platonist philosopher, a historian, a civil servant, and for a short time a monk. He was outwardly an Orthodox Christian. Indeed, he did not shrink from positioning himself as a persecutor of pagans in the name of the true faith. He composed a remarkable speech of denunciation in which he alleged that the head of the Orthodox Church, Patriarch Michael I Cerularius, had fallen into heresy, paganism and occultism together with two monks and a supposed prophetess called Dosithea (Michael died before the speech could be delivered).[5] The evidential basis of these charges remains uncertain, but they were probably not without foundation. Yet Psellus was a slippery character. He was suspected of heresy in his lifetime, and beneath his pious public persona he appears to have had an attachment to pagan ideas.[6] In particular, it is noteworthy that he made the *Chaldaean Oracles*, the old sacred text of the pagan Neoplatonists, a pillar of his philosophy.[7] He assembled a collection of 42 fragments of the *Oracles*—the first such collection ever to be made—and wrote influential commentaries on them.

On one level, Psellus's attachment to paganism was intellectual. But he also seems to have had an interest in practical magical techniques of the kind that we have seen were bound up with the ancient Platonist tradition. Psellus explicitly condemned this aspect of paganism, but we should probably not take his condemnation at face value. For example, one of the *Chaldaean Oracles* contains the enigmatic advice, 'Work around the *strophalos* of Hekate', in reference to the Greek goddess of witchcraft. But what is a *strophalos*? Psellus is on hand to explain what he happens to know about this pagan magical implement, so that his readers will understand just how devilish it is:

> The *strophalos* of Hekate is a golden ball, with a sapphire embedded in the middle of it, which is whirled around using a bull's hide. It has characters written all over it. People whirl it around while making invocations. They generally call such objects *iynges*: sometimes the object in question is spherical, sometimes it is triangular, and sometimes it is another shape. People spin them around, beating the air with them, while laughing and making unintelligible or animal-like noises. The oracle teaches that the ritual is accomplished by whirling this *strophalos* around because it has some unspeakable power. It is called the ball 'of Hekate' because it is dedicated to Hecate. Hecate is a god of the Chaldaeans, who holds the wellspring of virtues in her right hand and that of souls in her left. This oracle is complete nonsense.[8]

Well, possibly. Psellus did not keep his paganizing views to himself. He had a pupil, John Italus, whose name derives from his origin in the historically Greek part of southern Italy. Unlike Psellus, John reached the point of being formally charged with heresy and was forced to retract. He also had his own followers, including a man named Serblias who reportedly called on the god Poseidon as he drowned himself in the sea.[9] John has been immortalized in the Christian liturgy, as an official denunciation of his ideas was incorporated into a document known as the Synodikon of Orthodoxy, which is read to this day in Orthodox churches on the first Sunday of Lent. The Synodikon explicitly repudiates Platonic theories; and the second and seventh condemnations laid against followers of John's ideas are particularly interesting:

> To those who profess piety yet shamelessly, or rather impiously, introduce into the Orthodox and Catholic Church the ungodly doctrines of the Greeks concerning the souls of men, heaven and earth, and the rest of creation—Anathema, Anathema, Anathema!
> . . .
> To those who not only undertake Greek studies for purposes of education but also follow after their vain opinions, and are so thoroughly convinced of their truth and validity that they shamelessly introduce them and teach them to others, sometimes secretly and sometimes openly—Anathema, Anathema, Anathema![10]

The ideas espoused by Psellus, Italus and their followers did not die with them. In the centuries that followed, the threat posed by the revival of pagan and Platonist ideas, mixed in with rationalism, continued to be a live issue in Christian Byzantium.[11] A crucial development came in the fourteenth century, with the rise of a humanist intellectual movement: humanist in the sense that it revered ancient Greek learning, including Platonist philosophy. There are parallels here, of course, with the later Italian Renaissance. This movement came into conflict with a form of monastic Christian spirituality known as Hesychasm, which promoted transcendent experience of the divine through prayer. It bears noting that Hesychasm itself was sustained by an interpretation of pagan Greek philosophy (in particular, Gregory Palamas's conception of the divine *energeia*, which was rooted in Aristotelianism).[12] All strands of Byzantine theology were indebted in some way to the pagan philosophical tradition; and to that extent it could be said that the classicizing interests of the humanists were not strange or subversive in themselves. Nevertheless, the conflict between humanism and Hesychasm was irresolvable at its heart. The mystical Hesychasts could never be reconciled with the Platonist philosophers, for whom union with the divine came through the intellect rather than through ineffable contemplative experience. Ultimately, it was the Hesychasts who won. For our purposes, it is sufficient to note that there is evidence of what one might at least call paganizing *tendencies* on the anti-Hesychast side. Two anti-Hesychast leaders, Barlaam and Akindynos, ended up being condemned alongside John Italus in the Synodikon.[13]

The triumph of Hesychasm, and the monastic interests associated with it, was not the end of the story. Byzantine humanism did not die out: indeed, its final flowering was yet to come, in the form of an intellectual by the name of

Georgios Gemistos (1355–1450/52), who in homage to Plato took the name 'Pletho' or 'Plethon'. Born in Constantinople, Plethon's unorthodox ideas got him exiled to the semi-autonomous state of Mistra in Greece, a place which had come to serve as a kind of refuge for anti-Hesychast intellectuals. Plethon was an imperial adviser and diplomat, and he stands out as an unusually radical thinker. He has been seen as a precursor of nationalism, socialism and totalitarianism before those concepts existed. Mostly, however, he is remembered for his unconventional religious views. Scholarly opinions on Plethon's religious position have differed, and outwardly he was an Orthodox Christian. But in reality it is very likely that he was a Platonist pagan.[14] His pagan convictions were expressed most clearly in a work called the *Laws*, which survives in fragments. In this text, which was plainly modelled on Plato's *Laws* and *Republic*, he set out a constitution for a utopian pagan city-state. After Plethon's death, the manuscript of the work was burned by Patriarch Scholarios, together with other writings of his. But by that time his ideas were already loose in the world and spreading. He continues to have influence today: a modern pagan writer has recently published a guide to his ideas, including the surviving contents of the *Laws*, for the benefit of other modern pagans.[15]

Plethon's religious system was recognizably pagan. He wrote of a hierarchy of polytheistic gods under the supreme deity, Zeus, and his eldest son Poseidon. He retained the nomenclature of the old Greek pantheon, albeit with a view to advancing his own philosophical agenda rather than indulging the 'distortions of poets'.[16] He even wrote hymns:

> King Zeus, you are Being itself, Unity itself and Goodness itself: you are great, great in being, and surpassingly great … You have existed in yourself since time before time. Alone of all things, you are wholly and entirely unbegotten … Through you and from you everything exists, is born and is established …
>
> O Zeus, greatest and most exalted of the gods, o Father who are your own father, o eldest creator of all things in the world, o emperor and mighty ruler of existence, from whom all other power and authority over all other things is established, directed and rightly applied under you and your might—o Lord of lords and most merciful Master, whom all things serve in strictest justice and for their own good—from you all things are generated and exist.[17]

Nevertheless, Plethon's paganism was not especially *devotional*: it was intellectual and philosophical. Plethon rejected not only Orthodox Christianity but also the ritualistic and spiritual versions of paganism and Platonism. He believed that the divine is knowable: he left no room for mysticism. One scholar has even suggested that he embraced 'a proto-deistic natural religion'.[18] He conceded that pagan rituals had a valid function, but not as objects of religious duty or methods of theurgical enlightenment: rather, they were tools for encouraging social stability and moral behaviour.[19] It is worth noting that Plethon, like Psellus, was particularly interested in the *Chaldaean Oracles*.[20] He drew on Psellus' work on the *Oracles*, although he was willing to make what he considered to be improvements to it, and he produced his own commentaries on the text. Plethon's approach to the *Oracles* was essentially rationalistic: he wanted to present them as philosophically credible, untainted both by Christianity and by the theurgic form of paganism.[21] Significantly, he removed or reinterpreted the fragments collected by Psellus which appeared to mention practical magic.[22]

One of Plethon's theories went on to have considerable importance in the history of post-classical paganism and esotericism. This theory—which is often referred to by the Latin term *prisca theologia*, 'ancient theology'—claimed that a pure primitive wisdom had been handed down to humanity by ancient sages such as Plato, Pythagoras and the Persian prophet Zoroaster. The concept of *prisca theologia* went on to be highly influential in the Renaissance and later.[23] It was an essentially subversive idea, as it represented a pagan alternative to the claim made by Christians and Jews that Moses was the fountainhead of divine revelation.

Plethon had high hopes for a revival of paganism. A devout Christian enemy of his, George of Trebizond, claimed to have heard him predict that in a few years the whole world would become pagan.[24] In the event, of course, there was no such mass conversion; but Plethon did influence a number of people, both during his lifetime and after it. A group of pagans who followed his ideas appear to have been operating in his part of Greece in the early 1450s. It included apostate monks and nuns: one of its members was a former monk called Iouvenalios who ended up being tortured and killed, and reportedly saw himself as a martyr for paganism.[25] But Plethon's impact on post-classical paganism extended much more widely than this. He stood at the centre of a web of pagan and philo-pagan figures whom he taught, met or influenced— figures who went on to spread paganizing ideas not only in Greece but also in Italy (in particular, Rome and Florence), where several of them migrated for reasons connected with the Ottoman capture of Constantinople in 1453.

We will meet several of these figures in the later part of this chapter, but it is worth mentioning a few of them here. There was Plethon's follower Michael

Apostoles, an apparent admirer of paganism who lived in Italy and campaigned for foreign intervention against the Ottomans.[26] There was Demetrius Raoul Kabakes, another intellectual who migrated to Italy, who regarded the sun as divine and whose influences included both Plethon and the Emperor Julian (although he did not adopt Plethon's Neoplatonic philosophical system). We might mention in passing that Kabakes was connected with the circle of Pomponio Leto, a Roman with pagan revivalist inclinations whom we will meet shortly.[27] Then there was Plethon's pupil Laonikos Chalkokondyles, who may also have been an *émigré* to Italy; he was a historian who embraced a pagan identity.[28]

Finally, for now, we may mention in this connection the soldier-poet Michael Tarchaniota Marullus (*c.*1454–1500).[29] Marullus appears to have been another figure of the age who was influenced by Plethon, although whether he can be called a follower of his is more doubtful. He spent most of his life in Renaissance Italy, and his associates included Kabakes's son, Pomponio Leto and Giovanni Pico della Mirandola, another figure who we will be meeting soon. Marullus's life and work bear witness to an exile's nostalgia for Greek culture, a longing for the liberation of his native land from Ottoman rule, and an attachment to pagan religion. This attachment led him to write a remarkable series of hymns to classical deities, such as Jupiter, Athena and Mars, and to other cosmic powers. This passage, for example, is from a hymn to Pan:

> But, when resplendent Hesperus has raised his holy
> face from the waves of his mother Tethys,
>     and Night, veiled in darkness, has spread
>         Lethean sleep throughout the world,
>
> Then Father Jupiter reveals himself to the powers of heaven
> in full glory, riding on his swift chariot, now here, now there,
>     travelling around, blessing and
>         nourishing every place under heaven!
>
> Behind him in a long train
> follows a great chorus of gods,
>     ranked under the eleven chiefs,
>         while only good Vesta remains in her temple,
>
> Until they arrive at the sacred heights
> of serene Olympus, their bodies tired by

the journey and the jolting of the chariots,
     and they refresh themselves with banquets of ambrosia.

There by turns they occupy their days
in feasting, free from the savage attacks of
     troubles and sleepless complaints,
          and in refilling their capacious goblets,

And, given strength to sing lovely songs by the abundant
nectar, they sing of you, the father
     of the Earth and of the windy Sea,
          and of the fertile Air—good Pan[30]

Marullus was a keen student of the ancient esoteric tradition, although he also bore the influence of the great Roman materialist philosopher Lucretius. Whether he was a committed pagan is a matter of debate, although one person who claimed so was George Eliot, in her novel *Romola*.

The foregoing survey serves to cast light on some of the continuing manifestations of paganism which periodically appeared in the bosom of Byzantine Christianity. Even as it loudly professed its allegiance to the gospel of Christ, medieval Greek society saw repeated attempts to revive pagan ideas, mainly under the inspiration of Plato and the Platonist tradition. We have been focusing hitherto mainly on the intellectual and social élite, but persisting pagan ideas were also evident in different forms among the ostensibly Orthodox ordinary people of the Byzantine Empire—and that brings us to our next area of enquiry.

As we have seen in earlier chapters, the idea of searching for 'pagan survivals' is a perilous one, and it was possible for the outward husks of pagan deities to survive as characters in folklore while their religious meaning was entirely hollowed out. The echoes of pre-Christian religion should not be mistaken for fully fledged worship of pagan gods. Yet as one scholar observed, the people of the late antique Mediterranean were open to syncretic understandings of Christ as one god among many, while Christian missionaries themselves sought not to deny the existence of the pagan gods but rather to discredit and demote them to the status of *daimonioi* (a word which, as we intimated in Chapter 2, did not necessarily have the exclusively negative connotations of our 'demons').[31] The combination of ready syncretism on the part of the converts and a strategy of demotion of deities on the part of the missionaries was hardly a recipe for the abrupt eradication of all traces of paganism, and sure enough they survived in Greece, both in folk religion and in magic.

The pattern followed by the displacement of paganism by Christianity in Greece resembled what occurred elsewhere in European pagan cultures, where the Christian god assumed celestial sovereignty. The Christian god replaced the senior Olympians, but the 'godlings' of rural worship (in Greece the nymphs and satyrs) continued to enjoy a folkloric existence, partly because Christianity offered nothing quite like them to replace their function as highly localized guardians of specific features in the landscape. However, the tendency of earlier scholars to identify continuities between modern Greek folklore and ancient Greek religion is now controversial. The search for continuities often involved a patronizing attitude to Greek Orthodox Christianity, where people supposedly replaced the gods with saints without understanding the difference, and scholars who confidently asserted continuities were often unable to back up their claims with evidence. The possibility that Christianity might produce its own eccentric folk-religious practices, entirely separately from relics of paganism, was barely considered.[32]

While some of the beings of Greek folklore, known as *exotika*, are indeed of Classical descent, they are often heavily demonized from their contact with Orthodox Christianity. Thus the *nereïda*, who are apparently the descendants of the nymphs, are usually portrayed as sources of misfortune in contrast to the nymphs of pagan Greece.[33] The nymphs of Greek folklore of the Christian era are broadly equivalent to the child-abducting fairies found in many European countries,[34] and in Greece as elsewhere it is largely the 'small gods' of nature and the household that have endured in folklore.[35] While ancient sacred sites such as the sanctuary of Aphrodite in Paphos remained the focus of popular religious activity such as the hanging of rags from sacred trees,[36] it is difficult to characterize such practices as *pagan*, any more than it was pagan for Cornish parents to pass their children through the circular standing stone at Mên-an-Tol. Sacred sites in the landscape attract attention and are selected for pilgrimage throughout the ages because they are physically remarkable, and not always because any memory of their original sacred function lingers. Describing practices of popular religion performed at pre-Christian sites as 'pagan' immediately imposes a particular interpretation on Christian popular religion as a thinly veiled pagan survival, which falls down when it becomes apparent that the same practices also occur on Christian sites with no pre-Christian connection. On the other hand, animal sacrifice remains part of some modern

Greek festivals, although the sacrifice is offered to a saint rather than to a god.[37] Thus while elements of pagan cult are detectable in modern Greek culture, 'pagan survivals' is perhaps too strong a term to use.[38]

Just as pagan traces can be detected in Greek folklore, so they can be found in the magical traditions of the Byzantine world. The San Marco Cup, described in the Introduction above, is one object that testifies to the importance of such traditions.[39] The combination of both pagan imagery and allusions to Islam on the cup suggests an attempt to convey the forbidden and transgressive nature of what the magician was attempting in lecanomancy—comparable, perhaps, to the showmanship of later service magicians who sought to convey their learning by displaying 'forbidden' books. Yet lecanomancy was not the only form of magic practised in the Byzantine world. The disfigurement of statues (usually of pagan gods) in order to draw on their occult powers was known as *stoicheiosis*, and considered a black art.[40] Such a practice implied, of course, that statues of the gods remained powerful and therefore hinted at pagan belief. However, while the distinction between religion and magic is always a difficult one to negotiate, it is perilous to draw conclusions about religious beliefs from magical practices. From the Greek Magical Papyri onwards, there is a long history of people freely drawing on the magical power of gods and entities from a range of religious traditions in transgressive rites of ritual magic; and none of this can be adduced as evidence for what those people themselves believed, because such behaviour is part of the rhetoric of magic. Thus the persistence of the pagan gods in magical practices is evidence of their ongoing cultural importance, but it is problematic to draw on the world of magic for evidence of pagan religiosity in any shape or form.

We now take our leave of medieval Greece and shift focus to western Europe. As we acknowledged at the start of this chapter, a major episode in the revival of pagan ideas in the Catholic west came with the unfolding of the cultural movement known as the Renaissance. This is a period which tends to be remembered as a time of art, learning, banking and war; a time of increasing wealth and expanding science; a time of burning heretics, burning Talmuds, colonialism and gunpowder. Yet it has become unfashionable to point to the Renaissance as a true intellectual and cultural 'rebirth'. This is not *purely* an academic knee-jerk against a received idea: the term does implicitly belittle the vitality of the Middle Ages and risks obscuring the importance of earlier 'renaissances' such as those of the ninth and twelfth centuries. Nevertheless, the period from the fourteenth to the sixteenth centuries unquestionably saw momentous changes, beginning in Italy and spreading elsewhere through Europe. In particular, the scholars and artists of the age were deeply attached to the classics—not from an instrumental perspective, but for their own sake—and in recovering as much from the ancient world as possible. Medieval culture had been happy to plunder the riches of ancient pagan civilization; but Renaissance culture wanted to mimic it down to the last detail.

This obsession with the classics provided a major stimulus for contemporary figures to experiment with reanimating classical pagan religion. But there was also a deeper history at work here. Against the background that we have sketched out, it will become apparent that the pagan revivals of the Renaissance developed out of trends which had been in progress for centuries in the Byzantine world and were spread westwards by men like Plethon and his sympathizers. Renaissance paganism was one episode in a much longer, interconnected history of post-classical pagan persistence and revival. It did not spring fully formed like Athena from the head of Zeus.

The Renaissance movement for the study and recovery of classical culture is generally referred to as humanism, a term which we have already used in relation to the equivalent phenomenon in Byzantium. Renaissance humanism was not necessarily pagan: it could be very decidedly Christian. It could also be subversive of all religion, under the influence of the rationalist Roman philosopher Lucretius, who was rediscovered in this period (we referred earlier to his influence on Michael Marullus). Alternatively, humanism could promote an eirenic rethinking of the relationship between different religions. Exemplary here is a German churchman and intellectual, Cardinal Nicholas of Cusa (1401–1464). Distressed by the conquest of Christian Constantinople by the Muslim Ottomans, he wrote *De pace fidei* ('On the Peace of Faith', 1453), in which he argued that all religions have a common foundation. Muslims, pagans and others are in some sense fundamentally Christians without knowing it. Another example of the sort of benign ecumenism which could be found in this period is provided by the writings of the merchant and diplomat Cyriac of Ancona (1391–1452). An antiquarian who knew Plethon and Kabakes, Cyriac cheerfully mixed together the language of Christianity and Roman paganism, referring to Jesus Christ as *Jupiter humanatus*, 'Jupiter incarnate'. He also wrote of his divine protector, Mercury, and of the Muses and the Nymphs.[41]

It is well known that pagan ideas and allusions are a recurring feature of Renaissance literature. A remarkable example of this is *Hypnerotomachia Poliphili* ('Poliphilo's Strife of Love in a Dream', 1499), a long novel which is believed to have been written by a Dominican priest named Francesco Colonna. The novel tells of the eponymous Poliphilo's dream-world quest for Polia, the woman whom he loves. He comes to be married to her by a high priestess in a temple of Venus using rites which draw on Christianity and Roman paganism (the Radcliffe Camera in Oxford is an attempt to recreate the temple). The work is susceptible of Christian interpretations, but it also features nymphs, Cupid and the phallus-god Priapus, and it celebrates love and sexuality in a rather un-Catholic way. Venus appears as a divine creatrix, her consort being Mars. This is paganism persisting with a vengeance: the free usage of the resources of classical pagan culture in parallel with those of contemporary Christianity.[42] Such paganizing soon spread well beyond Italy, and in general the poetry of the Renaissance is remarkable for its willingness to mingle pagan and Christian themes. The early Polish Renaissance poet Jan of Wiślica (c.1485–1520), for instance, included a lengthy prayer to the Virgin Mary, a vision of the god Apollo, a vision of St Stanisław, and a full scale 'council of the gods' in an epic poem about Poland and Lithuania's victory at the Battle of Grunwald in 1410,[43] without stopping to offer any explanation of a poetic cosmology that would allow gods and saints to exist within the same mythological world.

Girolamo Fracastoro (1478–1553), who was both a poet and a significant figure in the history of medicine, wrote Latin verse that explicitly deploys the language of pagan polytheism, including an epic poem on syphilis. In a remarkable poem to Cardinal Alessandro Farnese, he promised to found a festival for the latter at Caphi near Verona:

> Meanwhile, since you will always be a God to me,
> I will build sacred altars to you in the mountains
> of Caphi ...
> Here I will establish a feast day to you, called by
> your name, with sacred rites to be performed every year.
> There we shall have roses, violets, purple
> hyacinths and vervain; old men shall weave flowers,
> and place crowns of green on their grey-haired heads,
> and spend the long day in joy with much Bacchus [i.e. wine],
> cheating their age and driving cares from their heart.
> Perhaps one of the Muses, and your patron Apollo,
> will give me a lyre and plectrum; the God himself shall
> lead my song all through your life and deeds of honour.[44]

One has to stop for a moment and contemplate the fact that Renaissance Italy was a world in which a major scientist could compose such a poem for a prince of the church. Other examples of the same paganizing tendency could be multiplied. For instance, an associate of Fracastoro, the poet Nicolò d'Arco (1492–1546), described the physician Marcantonio della Torre as praying on his deathbed to the gods (*Dii*) for the sake of his soul (*meos Manes*, a pagan Latin term). D'Arco added his own prayer to Jupiter to be gracious, and declared that the deceased was now among divine beings (*divos*), in the company of Venus and the Loves (*Amores*).[45]

Quite how this sort of thing should be interpreted is open to debate. The pagan elements can be explained away, if one wishes to do that. In the quotation above from Fracastoro, the word translated as 'God' is *Divus*, which was also applied to saints and other exemplary human beings; using 'Bacchus' for wine is a standard poetic metaphor; referring to Apollo as god of poetry and song is a colourful scholarly allusion; and so on. There is probably no amount of literary paganism that cannot be neutralized by means of phrases such as 'intellectual exercise' and 'literary device'. But applying such an approach to Renaissance culture fails to grasp the significance of what was going on. Contemporary intellectuals, particularly in Italy, were consciously recovering classical patterns of thought as a means of identifying themselves with the legacy of ancient Rome. They were not literally practising the old religion; no-one suggests that Fracastoro built physical altars at Caphi in order to make sacrificial offerings to Cardinal Farnese. But such people *were* fashioning an identity for themselves as the heirs of the ancient Romans, and pagan religion was integral to the Roman heritage that they claimed. We are not dealing here with a mere literary conceit. Religion is nothing if not a matter of identity. These were people who learned and used, fluently, the idiom of classical polytheism as a means of expressing who they were.

Some Renaissance figures went even further in their admiration for paganism. This strand of humanism could have a decidedly anti-Christian slant. Isaac Disraeli, the writer and father of British prime minister Benjamin Disraeli, captured something of the mood of the time:

> The classical purity of Cicero was contrasted with the barbarous idiom of the Missal; the glories of ancient Rome with the miserable subjugation of its modern pontiffs; and the metaphysical reveries of Plato, and what they termed the 'Enthusiasmus Alexandrinus'— the dreams of the Platonists—seemed to the fanciful Italians more elevated than the humble and pure ethics of the Gospels ... Touched by this mania of antiquity, the learned affected to change their vulgar Christian name, by assuming the more classical ones of

a Junius Brutus, a Pomponius, or a Julius, or any other rusty name unwashed by baptism. This frenzy for the ancient republic not only menaced the pontificate, but their Platonic or their pagan ardours seemed to be striking at the foundation of Christianity itself.[46]

So it was that, for instance, Niccolò Machiavelli (1469–1527) could look back to ancient paganism as more vigorous than insipid Christianity. Why had the ancients been more willing to fight for their freedom? Machiavelli had the answer. The Christian faith, to be sure, had shown people the true path; but it had also led them to look down on worldly glory. The pagans, by contrast, had regarded the glory of this world as the highest good, and this had led them to be more ferocious. Their religious ceremonies were not only magnificent: they included the violent, bloody act of sacrifice. The sight of animals being killed was terrible, and it made the worshippers terrible too. Machiavelli added that paganism only celebrated men who had achieved worldly honour—great warriors and rulers of states—while Christian heroes were men of humility and prayer.[47]

Machiavelli was Machiavelli, and not everyone shared his perspective. But some certainly did. One person who combined a love of worldly glory with a paganizing classicism was Sigismondo Malatesta (1417–1468), the lord of Rimini.[48] An aristocratic warrior and patron of the arts, Malatesta is the only person in history who has been personally damned to hell by a pope. He is said to have been a tyrant and a murderer, although it is not clear how far this reputation was manufactured by his enemies. He was also accused of being an atheist; but there are indications that he had pagan sympathies. Like his contemporaries, he was preoccupied with the ancient Graeco-Roman past, and he was associated with a couple of the characters whom we have already met: he appears to have known Cyriac of Ancona, and he offered Plethon a place at his court (Plethon declined). He famously had a local Franciscan church restructured into a kind of quasi-pagan temple, complete with images of polytheistic deities; and he ended up bringing Plethon's remains from Greece in 1465 and placing them in this edifice. His court literature portrays him as praying and sacrificing to the gods, conducting pagan divination rites and believing in reincarnation.

How much of this is to be taken at face value is open to debate. The literature that we have referred to also contains Christian elements; and Malatesta was certainly an outwardly conforming Catholic. To this day, masses continue to be celebrated in his temple, the 'Tempio Malatestiano', which remains a tourist attraction in Rimini. Yet the warlord's Catholic piety did not serve to dispel doubts about his loyalties. It cut no ice with Pope Pius II, who wrote of him: 'He built a noble temple at Rimini in honour of St Francis, but he filled it with pagan artworks, so that it seemed like a temple not for Christians but for demon-worshipping infidels.'[49] In similar vein, a nineteenth-century art critic wrote that the building's interior 'has so heathen an aspect, that we involuntarily look towards the altar for a train of chaplet-crowned priests and augurs, about to offer a milk-white heifer in sacrifice to the god and goddess of Rimini'.[50] This reference to the 'god and goddess' alludes to another possibility: that the temple should really be interpreted as a shrine to Sigismondo, his wife Isotta and his family.[51] Such are the ambiguities of interpreting the ambiguous works of an ambiguous man in an ambiguous age.

At this point, we may go back to the quotation from Isaac Disraeli above, and his mention of Italian intellectuals adopting paganizing names like 'Pomponius'. This is an allusion to the humanist academic Julius Pomponius Laetus, who is generally known by the Italian form of his name, Giulio Pomponio Leto (1428–1498). Leto started a private circle of humanists known as the 'Roman Academy'. The activities of this Academy had anticlerical and homoerotic overtones, and Leto did indeed encourage its members to adopt pagan Roman names: his own real name was Giulio Sanseverino.[52] As one might expect, the Academy ran into serious trouble with the authorities. Pope Paul II ordered the arrest of its members for conspiring to assassinate him.[53] The men were duly imprisoned and tortured. One of them, Bartolomeo Platina, later recounted how they were personally interrogated by the Pope. Platina's account is a remarkable document. It captures something of the special atmosphere of Renaissance Italy, and how it could serve as a site of ambivalence and conflict between Christianity, paganism and outright irreligion:

> [Paul II] hurled many accusations at us: in particular, that we made a practice of debating whether or not the soul is immortal, and that we adhered to the philosophy of Plato (which St Augustine considers to be the closest to the Christian religion). 'Cicero rightly calls Plato a god [deum] among philosophers,' said Aurelius [an Academy member], 'Without doubt, he excelled all the others in talent and wisdom.' … 'Through your debates,' said Paul, 'you call the existence of God into doubt.' …
>
> [I said:] 'I have lived as a Christian should. I have never missed going to Confession or Communion at least once a year. I have said nothing that is against the Creed or is suspect of heresy …'
> Paul also laid the charge against us that we were too fond of pagan

culture [*gentilitatis*], although no-one was more devoted to it than he was. At that time, he was taking ancient statues from all over the city and gathering them together in that famous palace of his which he was building under the Capitoline Hill … What is more, without any authorisation from the Senate, he placed an enormous number of gold, silver and bronze coins, stamped with his image, in the foundations of buildings which he constructed, in accordance with ancient custom.[54]

Not even popes, it seems, were immune to paganizing temptations. We might also mention in this connection Julius II's continuing experimentations with pagan statuary, which scandalized the fundamentalist Catholic Gianfrancesco Pico della Mirandola.[55]

The references to Plato in Platina's account highlight an important point. It was in the sphere of Platonist philosophy that Renaissance philo-paganism had its most lasting impact. It is sometimes said that Platonism was rediscovered in western Europe at the Renaissance. This is not entirely correct: there was a continuous Latin Platonist tradition in the Middle Ages, and Plato and his ideas were not simply 'lost'. Nevertheless, there was a resurgence of interest in the Platonist variety of philosophy in this period, and this went together with an increasing sympathy for paganism. The status of Plato only really began to rise in earnest when Greek studies were established in northern Italy in the 1390s by Manuel Chrysoloras—a pupil of Plethon—and his own pupils. An important point to note in this context is that Plethon not only influenced western Europe in the sense that his ideas and associates migrated there: in his old age, he personally made a journey to the west. Ironically enough, he was acting as a representative of the Orthodox Christian faith at the time. He participated in the Council of Ferrara–Florence in 1438–39, an assembly of clerics which was intended to bring about a reunion of the Catholic and Orthodox communions.[56] By this point, the Byzantine Empire had been reduced to a shadow of its former greatness, and the Byzantines needed western help to defend what remained of their territory against the Ottomans. Plethon opposed the union of the churches, even though this meant rejecting much-needed aid for the struggling Byzantine state. His motives for taking this stance are a matter of speculation. One possibility is that he regarded the Muslim invaders as less of a threat to his religious project than a reunited Catholic-Orthodox Christendom.

While he was in Florence, Plethon wrote a tract promoting Platonist philosophy entitled *On the Differences Between Plato and Aristotle*. This turned out to be the opening salvo in a polemic between partisans of the two Greek philosophers. Prominent among the supporters of Aristotle was George of Trebizond, a Greek émigré of deranged and fanatical views. George's response to Plethon, *Comparison of the Philosophers Plato and Aristotle*, was published in 1458. It has been said that this work 'has an excellent claim to rank among the most remarkable mixtures of learning and lunacy ever penned'.[57] It condemned Plato as an idolater and demon-worshipper; and it affirmed that his successors were Mohammed, Plethon and (probably) Cardinal Bessarion. Bessarion, a protégé of Plethon, was one of the Greek intellectuals who had migrated to Italy; he was also an associate of members of the Roman Academy. The *Comparison* was eccentric; but George was neither the first nor the last person to embrace the idea that Platonism and paganism could be blurred together to form a dangerous rival to Christianity. Bessarion replied to George in his *Against the Calumniator of Plato*, a text influenced by Plethon which was first published in 1466.[58]

At this point in the story, we come to the greatest Platonist of the Renaissance: the Florentine philosopher Marsilio Ficino (1433–1499).[59] The son of a physician, Ficino was fortunate enough to be patronized (to varying degrees) by the powerful Medici family, starting in 1462 with the founder of the dynasty, Cosimo. It has traditionally been thought that Cosimo's project was to re-found the Academy of Plato in Florence, with Ficino as the leading figure in it; but this idea is probably fanciful.[60] The conventionally Christian Cosimo was far from being an enthusiast for Platonism. Nevertheless, he assigned Ficino to translate the works of Plato into Latin from a Greek manuscript which he had obtained from Plethon. He then quickly derailed this project by reassigning Ficino to translate another manuscript, this time one which had been brought to Florence from Macedonia by an agent of his, a monk called Leonardo da Pistoia. This was the *Corpus Hermeticum*, which we met in Chapter 1 as a collection of the sacred writings of the Egyptian Hermeticists. Ficino finished translating this important text from the classical pagan esoteric tradition in 1463, and the translation was published in 1471 (he subsequently published his translation of Plato in 1484, choosing this year because it featured an astrological conjunction between Jupiter and Saturn). The texts of the *Corpus Hermeticum* are relatively late productions; they were composed after the time of Christ and are influenced by Platonist philosophy. But this was not known in the Renaissance: the texts in the collection were regarded as containing pure primeval wisdom from the ancient land of Egypt. Not until 1614 did the classical scholar Isaac Casaubon show how late the *Corpus* was.[61]

Ficino is generally regarded as a Christian Platonist rather than a pagan; indeed, he was a Catholic priest. But there have always been doubts about where his loyalties lay. His own writings were not necessarily consistent over time, and some have suggested that he simply got more conservative as he got older. His early biographer Giovanni Corsi wrote in 1507 that his priestly ordination in 1473 meant that 'from being a pagan, he was made a soldier of Christ'.[62] Yet this does not entirely fit with the record. In 1473–74, during the period immediately after his ordination, Ficino wrote both the relatively orthodox *De Christiana religione* (published 1476) and the *Theologia Platonica* (published 1482), which was a more adventurous combination of Christianity and Neoplatonism.

Scholars have had difficulty catching Ficino out saying something unambiguously pagan. Perhaps the best-known example of him professing what appears today to be paganism is his belief in a form of magic involving planetary spirits such as the spirits of Mercury and Venus. At first sight, this seems to come dangerously close to the worship of pagan deities. But in fact there was a long tradition of respectable Christian writers accepting that the planets were divine beings who existed under the supreme God; as well as more contentious attempts to invoke them in magic rituals.[63] We do not, then, have proof here of Ficino's paganism. Yet he remains a somewhat ambivalent character. By his own admission, he decided not to publish certain translations of pagan texts 'in case I should seem to be calling my readers back to the ancient worship of gods and demons [*deorum daemonumque*] which has for so long been deservedly condemned'.[64] (Even in this protestation there is ambiguity: as we indicated previously, *daemones* were not necessarily demons.) Ficino was committed to the revelations of Moses and Christ; and yet he also accepted Plethon's *prisca theologia* theory of a succession of pagan sages who included Zoroaster, Hermes Trismegistus, Orpheus, Pythagoras and Plato. How far these beliefs were contradictory has been a matter of scholarly debate.[65]

Ficino was not an isolated figure: rather, he may be seen as the founder of a tradition of philo-pagan Christian Platonism. His most famous follower was the young aristocrat and polymath Giovanni Pico della Mirandola (1463–1494). Pico was one of the most precocious figures of the Italian Renaissance, as well as one of the most erratic. At one point, he nearly got himself killed when he ran off with—or abducted—a young woman named Margherita who had married into the Medici dynasty. He ended up settling in Ficino's Florence, where he died at the age of thirty-one. His distinctive contribution to the Platonist scholarship of the day was to enrich it with material which he had found in the Jewish mystical tradition known as the Kabbalah. As with Ficino, it is debated how far Pico was a true-believing Catholic. He openly rehabilitated the practice of magic; and he famously fell foul of Pope Innocent VIII over his

*900 Theses* (1486). These were philosophical propositions which Pico planned to debate publicly in Rome against all comers: they bore witness to influences from Neoplatonism, the *Chaldaean Oracles*, Hermeticism and the Kabbalah. The *Theses* exemplify the way in which Pico sought to reconcile Christianity with ancient pagan systems of thought: an endeavour which seems to modern eyes to have come remarkably close to advocating the worship of pagan gods. In Chapter 1, we encountered the *Orphic Hymns*, a collection of hymns to polytheistic deities which were used by ancient esotericists. These texts were also used by Ficino and Pico, and in his *Theses* Pico had this to say about them:

> Nothing in the field of natural magic is more effective than the hymns of Orpheus, if they are accompanied by the right kind of music, a proper mental intention and the other circumstances which are known to the wise.
>
> The names of the gods whom Orpheus sings of are not names of deceitful demons who are the source of evil rather than good. On the contrary, they are the names of natural and divine virtues which have been bestowed by the true god on the world for the greatest advantage of human beings, if they know how to make use of them.[66]

This seems to be about as far as a Christian could go without explicitly embracing polytheism. Yet, as with Ficino, there is less here than meets the eye. These statements are bound up with the longstanding Christian ideas about the pagan planetary deities that we referred to above: Pico's ideas were part of that tradition and do not mark him out as a pagan.[67] Ultimately, he was an unorthodox Catholic: his philosophical approach has been described as 'Christosyncretism'.[68]

Looking beyond Florence, the influence of Ficino and his circle spread widely in western and eastern Europe. The impact of their ideas was felt most immediately in the Italian states. Worthy of particular mention here because of his quasi-pagan ideas is the Dominican philosopher Tommaso Campanella (1568–1639). In the final part of his utopian work *The City of the Sun* (1602), Campanella describes a fictional religion which comprises an unusual mixture of trinitarian monotheism and veneration of the sun and other celestial bodies. We may also note that, as an exponent of the tradition of Christian planetary magic, Campanella performed a magical ceremony for Pope Urban VIII in which he invoked the planets Venus and Jupiter.[69] Further afield, Ficino's school worked its influence in France, Germany, and as far away as Poland and

Hungary. In England, the prominent churchman John Colet (1467–1519) stood as an intellectual heir of Ficino, Pico and the Neoplatonists. It is a mark of how threatening Renaissance humanism could be to some that, in 1516–17, Colet complained that a bishop had called his St Paul's School a 'house of idolatry' (*domum idolatriae*) because it taught pagan poets.[70] Colet's friend Sir Thomas More (1478–1535), who is remembered as a zealous religious conservative, was also influenced by Florentine thought, and by Pico in particular: he translated the latter's Latin biography into English in 1510. More is an important reminder that humanist interests were not necessarily a mark of deviation from the Christian path, or even of tolerance for heterodoxy.

Our survey of paganizing elements in the Renaissance is almost complete; we may close by mentioning two odd episodes which occurred in the later years of the period. Both of them involved alleged attempts to carry out animal sacrifice. The first episode took place in Rome in 1522, during a time of plague. It appears that a Greek by the name of Demetrius the Spartan sought to ward off the plague by slaughtering a bull in the Colosseum. This was interpreted by some as an act of pagan worship; but it remains unclear whether we really do have an instance here of an offering to a polytheistic deity, or whether the ritual would more accurately be characterized as an act of Christian folk magic, deriving from Italian or Greek traditions.[71] As we have seen, the 'sacrifice' of bulls to saints remains part of some modern Greek festivals; similarly, Scottish Presbyterian ministers travelling in the Western Isles in the seventeenth century reported islanders sacrificing bulls to St Columba.[72] The second episode took place in France in 1553. It involved a group of people associated with the *Pléiade*, a name conventionally given to certain contemporary poets who were influenced by classical, pagan and esoteric ideas (as well as by the philo-pagan poet Michael Marullus). One of the poets, Étienne Jodelle, had recently staged two plays composed in the classical style, and the group decided to carry out a ceremony in order to celebrate this revival of classical drama. The ceremony—which is known as the *pompe du bouc*—took place in the forest of Arcueil, not far from Paris. It may have involved the sacrifice of a goat to Bacchus, although the poets later denied this and we may never know for certain what happened. Prior to the *pompe*, the poets had been criticized for their paganizing tendencies, and it seems that the incident was intended as a provocation to conservative Christian opinion—one which met with considerable success.[73]

By the time that the Renaissance played out, a religious movement was in train that was far more threatening to the established order of things than the experiments with paganism that we have been looking at. Pico's *900 Theses* made very little difference to anything, but the *95 Theses* of Martin Luther changed Europe forever when they were made public in 1517. The coming of the Protestant Reformation deserves some attention here because it permanently shifted the way in which paganism, as a word and concept, was treated in the Protestant world.

In short, Protestant polemicists adopted the practice of claiming that Catholicism was a form of paganism. This was an example of a tendency that we remarked on in the Introduction: when Christians have wanted to find a word with which to place their enemies beyond the pale, they have consistently reached for 'pagan'. In the minds of Protestants, however, calling Catholicism pagan was more than just a rhetorical tactic: it was a justified factual description. To educated writers who had a knowledge of classical culture, the Roman church's priestly rituals and panoply of saints and angels looked disconcertingly familiar. One eighteenth-century Irish priest who converted to Anglicanism wrote that he had been 'startled to find a perfect affinity and resemblance of habits, rites, ceremonies, &c.' between ancient paganism and Catholicism.[74]

Oddly enough, the idea that Catholicism had resemblances to ancient pagan religion pre-dated the coming of the Reformation: it had originally emerged from Renaissance art and scholarship.[75] But it came into its own once the Reformation had turned the Catholic system of worship into a target for polemic. The first concerted attempt to prove that Catholicism was a residue of paganism seems to have been made in 1539 by the leading Swiss Protestant reformer Heinrich Bullinger; the theory was subsequently pursued by no less a figure than John Calvin.[76] This interpretation of Catholicism had significant consequences; amongst other things, it meant that Catholics were pagans in need of *de novo* evangelization, and Catholic lands were mission territories. The mission of the early church needed to be enacted again in the present.

The idea that Catholicism was a form of paganism had a long life. Indeed, it became something of a cliché.[77] A publication of major importance in this regard was Conyers Middleton's widely read *Letter from Rome* (1729). Middleton set out to show that the integrity of Catholicism as an expression of the faith of Christ was fatally compromised by its contamination with paganism, whether this had come about through the corruption of the clerical establishment or the superstition of the common people. To a Protestant reader, his argument must have seemed intuitively persuasive. Where else had Catholics got their incense, holy water, miraculous images, orders of priesthood, and the like? Did not the suspicious names of saints like St Mercury and St Bacchus disguise surviving pagan gods? Yet Protestant readers might not have realized what Middleton's agenda was. Middleton was nominally an Anglican clergyman, but in reality he was a freethinker and his covert target was not Catholicism but Christianity as a whole. Interestingly, it would not be long before another, far more influential Enlightenment sceptic, Voltaire, would seek to defend ancient pagans from the charge of idolatry by arguing that most of them, like their Renaissance successors, in fact venerated abstract virtues under the symbolic forms of the gods.[78] Voltaire's defence of paganism was especially pointed when set alongside his routine attacks on the absurdity of Catholic Christianity; Voltaire was claiming, in effect, that Catholics were more idolatrous than pagans.

Protestants were still asserting that Catholicism was pagan well into the nineteenth century. Conyers Middleton's work was still being republished in the Victorian period; and another treatise worth mentioning in this regard is Alexander Hislop's *The Two Babylons* (1853). Unlike Middleton, Hislop was a true believer, a minister of a strict Scottish Presbyterian sect. He linked both the doctrines and the rituals of Catholicism to ancient Babylonian paganism, making use of the advances in scholarship that had taken place since Middleton's time. Hislop's work was repeatedly reissued, and it is still sometimes found in modern fundamentalist Protestant circles. While Catholics usually attempted to rebut attacks of this kind, occasionally they adopted a bolder strategy. In 1836 Nicholas Wiseman, the future Cardinal Archbishop of Westminster, replied to the accusations of a Mr Poynder that popery was 'in alliance with heathenism' by admitting the premises of Poynder's argument. The ancient Hebrews, Wiseman maintained, had borrowed their rites from pagan Egypt, and therefore we should not be surprised if the Catholic church had rites derived from the pagan worship of Greece and Rome: 'The institution of such rites', Wiseman argued, 'instead of leading to idolatry, is the best preservative against it'.[79] Attempts to turn the Reformation critique on its head were rare, however, and comparisons of Catholicism with paganism remained a feature of British and Irish Protestant polemic until the 1850s, after which they fell away somewhat as other concerns asserted themselves in contemporary society.[80] We are now running ahead of ourselves, however. Before we look more closely at conceptions of paganism in the nineteenth century, we must take some time to examine the period that preceded it, and the ways in which paganism persisted into revival even in the Age of Reason itself.

# CHAPTER FOUR

# Paganism in the Enlightenment

The eighteenth century was a pivotal period in European religious history. For the first time since the days of the Roman Empire, the Christian monopoly had been broken. The established churches were discredited by decades of bloody persecution and war. The Western worldview had been changed for ever by the ideas of Newton and Descartes. Mechanistic philosophy and the scientific revolution were aggressively challenging received assumptions about how the world worked—in particular, theories rooted in the realm of the supernatural. Christianity was evolving and retreating in the face of the intellectual and social revolution which is conventionally known as the Enlightenment. So far, so familiar. What is less well known is that these developments were accompanied by the first stirrings of what was to become the modern pagan revival.

Pagan experimentation had essentially been dormant since the deluges of the Reformation and the Counter-Reformation had washed over Europe. In the sixteenth and seventeenth centuries, the religious politics of the continent were thrown into turmoil as Christians devoted their intellectual energies to working out who was following the wrong version of Christianity and their physical energies to killing them. It was difficult in this environment for revivals of paganism to win support. In 1593, Cardinal Robert Bellarmine felt able to argue with confidence against ecclesiastical censorship of ancient Graeco-Roman texts: 'For there are none today who would not laugh at the doctrines of the Pagans; and we never hear of Christians being perverted by the books of the Pagans and defecting to Paganism in the way that they are defecting to the heretics every day.'[1] Accordingly, early modern experiments in religious unorthodoxy before the onset of the Enlightenment tended to take the form of Christian heresies and brands of Christian-adjacent esotericism such as Rosicrucianism, alchemy and Christianized Kabbalah. Yet—and this goes directly to the overarching theme of this book—paganism was still there, covered perhaps by thicker ice than usual or in the form of seeds which were drier than usual, but nevertheless still there and still waiting to be revived as a religious system.

One sign that European paganism remained a relevant issue in the sixteenth and seventeenth centuries was the extent of Christian anxiety about paganism's continued existence at the fringes of Europe. At the height of the Reformation, regions such as rural Samogitia in the Baltic and Sápmi in northern Scandinavia were still only cosmetically Christianized, and the scandal of the survival of pagan cults in Christian Europe became a stick with which to beat religious opponents. In the Baltic region, Catholics attributed the failure to properly convert the Lithuanians to the Calvinist Radziwiłł family's introduction of Protestantism and the resulting religious confusion. Lutherans and Calvinists, meanwhile, accused the Catholics of failing to introduce the peasantry to proper Christianity, and of neglecting their pastoral duties, while writing off Lithuania's Orthodox Christians as little better than pagans anyway.[2]

In seventeenth-century Sweden, which had risen to become one of the great military powers of Europe, the anxieties took a rather different form. In 1671, rumours that Sweden's military success was down to the Swedes employing Sámi sorcerers in their army prompted Magnus Gabriel de la Gardie, the country's lord high chancellor, to commission a thorough ethnographic study of the Sámi that would dispel this and other false rumours.[3] The task was taken up by the antiquary Johannes Schefferus, who never actually visited Sápmi but treated Sámi religion and 'sorcery' in detail in a resulting book, *Lapponia* (1673).[4] Schefferus simultaneously portrayed Sámi religion as a surviving curiosity and a thing of the past, soon to be extinguished by Christianity, while identifying other Sámi practices as 'sorcery'—which denied them even the meagre dignity of being considered pagan, and opened up the possibility of *noiadis* (Sámi shamans) being prosecuted for witchcraft.[5] However, not all Sámi people lived within the sphere of influence of Lutheran Sweden and Denmark. Sámi living under Russian rule in the Kola Peninsula in the late seventeenth century came under the jurisdiction of the Russian Orthodox Archbishop Afanasii of Kholmogory (c.1641–1702), who was untroubled by Sámi and Nenets people who remained loyal to their ancestral beliefs. Afanasii reserved punitive measures for insincere converts who reverted to ancestor-worship, introduced syncretistic practices into Orthodoxy or—worst of all—became Old Believers (an Orthodox sect which rejected the seventeenth-century liturgical reforms of Patriarch Nikon).[6]

While the anxieties of the sixteenth and seventeenth centuries were rooted in Christian sectarianism and concern for religious purity, the principal religious dynamic of the Enlightenment was the decline of Christianity in the face of the advance of sceptical rationalism. A leading French churchman wrote:

> Even women began to free themselves from prejudices. The spirit
> of unbelief travelled through the whole world, together with liber-
> tinism … The corruption became almost universal. People flaunted
> their materialism, Deism and scepticism; the Faith was degraded
> among the people, the middle class and the communities; it was no
> longer fashionable to believe in the Gospel.[7]

This created something of an opportunity for paganism. It has been argued that
modern pagan thought has particular affinities with Enlightenment thought:
for example, in the value that it places on 'natural' religion and in its anti-
authoritarian orientation.[8] We should not exaggerate, however. In general, the
Enlightenment did not provide an especially promising context for revivals of
paganism. It was, fundamentally, a secularizing movement which was characterized by an optimistic view of the powers of human reason. It did not sit
well with priests, sacrifices, mysticism or magic. Some contemporary thinkers
gravitated towards pantheism or atheism, while others preferred Deism or
liberal forms of Christianity. On the whole, Enlightenment religion tended not
to rise above the level of a rather bloodless intellectual monotheism coupled
with a commonsensical moral code.

The Enlightenment was definitely 'pagan' in one sense: that is, in the generic
sense of being broadly non-Christian or anti-Christian. Consistent with its
historical function as an othering term, the word 'pagan' came to be used by
Christians to describe the godless or barely religious version of modernity
that emerged from Enlightenment thought and practice.[9] In fact, calling
Enlightenment philosophers 'pagans' was not entirely a case of gratuitous
Christian polemic: the *philosophes* did draw on the writings of classical pagan
antiquity for resources to support the fight against Christianity, albeit those
resources tended to be rationalistic rather than religiously pagan. In this vein,
Peter Gay described the intellectuals of the age as being 'wrapped in the
toga of Cicero or Lucretius' as they looked to the great classical writers as
'signposts to secularism'.[10] (It is significant that Gay gave his landmark work
*The Enlightenment* the subtitle *The Rise of Modern Paganism*.) It is worth noting
that some eighteenth-century thinkers took up the anti-Christian apologetic
writings of ancient religiously pagan intellectuals like the Emperor Julian.
Voltaire was the best known of these; another was Thomas Taylor, a Platonist
philosopher and pagan revivalist whom we will soon meet.

Once we have offered the appropriate caveats as to the fundamentally
rationalist nature of the Enlightenment, we have to recognize something else:
something which by this point in this book should be wholly unsurprising. Once

the Christian monopoly over European religion had been broken, it was *all but certain* that a sustained pagan revival would get under way. The persistence of paganism in European public culture—in particular, the prominence of the Graeco-Roman classics in education, art and literature—made this practically inevitable. In the absence of Christian doctrinal restraints and physical repression, it was only a matter of time before people began to reanimate aspects of classical pagan religion: just as had happened in Byzantium and at the Renaissance, but in a more enduring way. This obviously did not mean that Enlightenment-era classicism equated directly to paganism, any more than had been the case with classicism in previous centuries. We have just noted that Graeco-Roman thought provided resources for secularist philosophy; and from the other side, one strand of Christian thought saw the ancient classics as offering an apologetic for Christianity. It was argued that a study of ancient pagan religion would reveal some confused remnants of the original true faith which had been revealed to the patriarchs of Genesis.[11] Nevertheless, by the mid-eighteenth century there was a sense in some circles that classicism had got out of hand. One English writer put the matter like this:

> If a pond is dug, Neptune ... emerges from the bason, and presides in the middle; or if a vista is cut through a grove, it must be terminated by a Flora, or an Apollo ... Temples are erected to all the train of deities mentioned in Homer or Ovid, which edifices, as well as their several statues, are adorned with Latin or Greek inscriptions ... These persons of taste may be considered as a sort of learned idolators, since they may be almost said to adore these graven images, and are quite enthusiastic in their veneration of them.[12]

Meanwhile, in a London coffee house, a 'sneering papist' was said to have remarked that Catholics were accused of worshipping statues; but was it not the case that 'the protestants of the Church of England worship the images of heathens?'[13] In similar vein, a conservative Anglican cleric, William Jones of Nayland, wrote in 1776 that he was 'told once by a school-boy, that one of his companions asked him very seriously, which was the uppermost, Jupiter or God Almighty?'[14]—a comment reflecting a longstanding concern that the almost exclusive diet of pagan classical literature taught to children at grammar schools might make them pagans. The Irish-French Catholic scholar Luke Joseph Hooke went so far as to write a refutation of ancient pagan religion in his 1752 work *Religionis Naturalis et Revelatae Principia*.[15] This was an unusual move: an academic exercise rather than a reaction to contemporary interest in paganism.[16]

Nevertheless, a work of this kind served to legitimize paganism as a potential rival to Christianity: a thinkable alternative. The same sense of paganism as a thinkable option may also be seen in David Hume's playful suggestion that classical polytheism must still exist in some unknown part of the universe:

> Where is the difficulty of conceiving that the same powers or principles, whatever they were, which formed this visible world, men and animals, produced also a species of intelligent creatures, of more refined substance and greater authority than the rest? That these creatures may be capricious, revengeful, passionate, voluptuous, is easily conceived ... [T]he whole mythological system is so natural, that in the vast variety of planets and worlds, contained in this universe, it seems more than probable that, somewhere or other, it is really carried into execution.[17]

The classics aside, there was another reason why the Enlightenment period saw an increasing interest in pagan religions. The processes of exploration and colonialism had introduced Europeans to unfamiliar religious systems in other parts of the world. When European writers wanted to describe the traditional beliefs and practices of Indigenous peoples, one of the words that they instinctively reached for was 'pagan'.[18] During the seventeenth and eighteenth centuries, writings on these beliefs and practices evolved from Christian polemic into the modern discipline of comparative religion.[19] It is noteworthy that the main British pioneer in this area, Lord Herbert of Cherbury, had a relatively generous approach to pagans.[20] Increasing knowledge of religions in different cultures had the potential to encourage a benevolent tolerance of religious difference, even if in practice there was a tendency for it to end up in anti-Christian partisanship. More importantly for our purposes, it also helped some people in the Christian West to go the further step beyond studying non-Christian religions to *practising* them.

One non-European influence on Enlightenment thought which can be described as pagan came from China. In Christian eyes, Confucianism was a pagan religion, and its rites were famously condemned as such by the Vatican despite the appeals of Jesuit missionaries. Yet the religion of Confucius was admired by Enlightenment intellectuals: advanced thinkers of the period such as Leibniz and Voltaire thought highly of the teachings of the Chinese sage. For Voltaire, he was 'the philosopher who had found a substitute for revealed religion, the ideal Deist'; and Confucian religion was 'a tolerant deism, without dogma and without priesthood'.[21] The influence of Confucianism on European

Enlightenment thought may be illustrated by a story from 1730. An English gentleman sent his son to the Temple, a centre of the legal profession in London, and his son was talked into becoming a Deist by the barristers there. It is a grim tale, which ends with the son's repentance and early death. The father records his son's confession of infidelity to him in these words:

> Father, I must to my Confusion own, that I have been a Deist since ever I came here: I stood it out for a Month; but my Companions … argued, That Christian Religion was no more but a Comment of the Fathers, who at best were but a Pack of Enthusiasts, Persecutors, immoral, ignorant and sanguinary Vilains; and that Pythagoras, Thales, Anaxagoras, &c. and above all, Confucius the Chinese Philosopher, had more Religion and Morality, than all the Fathers put together.[22]

Confucius here is put on an exalted level with—or above—the Presocratic Greek philosophers as a teacher of religion and morals. This is not revived paganism, exactly, but the tendency to look to the ancient classics and to non-European religious thought for a worldview superior to that of Christianity is not a million miles from it.

The 1790s saw the nearest thing that the Enlightenment produced to an organized attempt to revive pagan religiosity, when the French revolutionaries experimented with new religions to replace Catholicism. The French revolutionary cults were the product of rather mixed influences, but among these there was a decidedly pagan component. The Cult of Reason, for example, which existed briefly in 1793–94, had atheistic associations, but its atheism had definite limits. The most notorious episode in the short-lived history of the Cult came when the Festival of Reason (*Fête de la Raison*) was celebrated in Paris on 10 November 1793. Models of a temple and altar were placed inside the cathedral of Notre Dame; and, in answer to a musical prayer, the female figure of Liberty—in reality, Sophie Momoro, a politician's wife—made a dramatic appearance. Similar celebrations were held all over France, with varying details, in which local women played the roles of goddess-like figures.[23] Here is a contemporary account of the spectacle in Notre Dame:

> In the middle of this church was erected a mount, and on it a very plain temple, the facade of which bore the following inscription: 'A la Philosophie.' Before the gate of this temple were placed the busts of the most celebrated philosophers. The torch of truth was

in the summit of the mount upon the altar of Reason, spreading light ...

Two rows of young girls, dressed in white, each wearing a crown of oak leaves, crossed before the altar of reason, at the sound of republican music; each of the girls inclined before the torch, and ascended the summit of the mountain. Liberty then came out of the Temple of Philosophy towards a throne made of grass, to receive the homage of the Republicans of both sexes, who sung an hymn in her praise, extending their arms at the same time towards her. Liberty descended afterwards to return to the Temple, and on re-entering it, she turned about, casting a look of benevolence on her friends. When she got in, every one expressed with enthusiasm the sensations which the goddess excited in them by songs of joy, and they swore never to cease to be faithful to her.[24]

This was not the only revolutionary experiment with something that looks like paganism. In 1794, there was Robespierre's short-lived Cult of the Supreme Being, which had Deistic overtones but retained some of the liturgical features of the Cult of Reason. One could go on. There was talk of creating 'priestesses' for the purpose of '*at least* directing festivals and weddings'.[25] Pagan figures appeared in illustrations of key revolutionary texts, as shown by J. F. Lefèvre's *Calendrier national* and Jean Jacques Lagrenée's *Declaration des droits de l'homme et du citoyen*; and note may be taken of the role of the Egyptian goddess Isis in contemporary iconography.[26] It is always possible to say that the revolutionaries' paganizing tendencies were confined to aesthetics: a colourful but thin veneer laid on top of Enlightenment rationalism. One might alternatively dismiss them as a repackaged version of traditional Catholicism: for example, the central symbolic role given to female figures may initially look surprising and 'pagan', but it might equally be seen as a concession to centuries-old Marian piety. Yet revolutionary philo-paganism cannot simply be explained away. There was something new stirring here: an attempted revival of pagan forms as a popular alternative to Christianity for the first time since the end of the Roman Empire.[27] The attempt failed; but there was nothing inevitable about that.

There were also other experiments with paganism in France in this period, as a matter of private enterprise rather than state policy.[28] The 1780s saw the development of a quasi-Masonic group of occultists known as the 'Illuminés d'Avignon'. These were Catholics, of a sort, but they showed distinct tendencies towards pagan goddess-worship: they regarded the Virgin Mary as divine, attributed to her 'the attributes of Diana, Hecate and the Sybil of the Syrians', and had a female high priest known as the 'Great Mother'.[29] A more straight-forwardly pagan figure was Xavier Godefroy d'Yzarn de Freissinet de Valady, the marquis de Freissinet. He adopted the Pythagorean philosophy, professed polytheistic beliefs and admired the Emperor Julian.[30] He did not have much chance to propagate his religious views, however, as he fell foul of the revolutionary authorities and went to the guillotine in 1793 at the age of 27. Then there was Gabriel André Aucler (1751–1814), a lawyer who adopted the Roman name Quintus Nautius Aucler and believed that he was of ancient priestly lineage. Aucler condemned monotheism and thought that the Emperor Julian had not gone far enough. Influenced by the ancient esoteric-Platonic tradition, he posited the existence of numberless gods and spirits between humankind and the ultimate supreme being. He also advocated practical paganism: he favoured the restoration of the Roman festival calendar, and he and his family celebrated pagan rites. By the end of his life, he had apparently repented of his ideas, although some people were apparently still practising them into the 1820s.[31]

It is impossible to write a history of pagan revivals without making reference to a certain well-known institution which came to a position of prominence in European culture in the age of the Enlightenment: the men's fraternal movement known as Freemasonry. Freemasonry tends to be thought of as either a conservative quasi-Christian movement (in English-speaking countries) or an anticlerical, secularist one (in Continental Europe and Latin America). Yet these stereotypes do not do justice to the reality. Freemasonry was a more interesting phenomenon than one might suppose, one which had links to esoteric currents and played a significant role in the development of modern paganism.

As is well known, the Masonic movement originated among working stone-masons in the Middle Ages. In the early modern period, however, it turned into something quite different: an organization that had increasingly little to do with the construction industry and which harboured some unorthodox religious perspectives. Freemasonry came into being in its modern form in Scotland from the end of the sixteenth century onwards, and it took on board ideas deriving from Renaissance esotericism that happened to be fashionable at the time.[32] Another influence on the development of the order was Rosicrucianism, a Christian esoteric movement inspired by three pamphlets published in Germany between 1614 and 1616. These pamphlets told of a 'Fraternity of the Rosy Cross' which had been founded by one Christian Rosenkreuz, who had supposedly lived between 1378 and 1484. Everyone today agrees that the pamphlets were a hoax; they fall to be interpreted against the background of the religious politics of the time when they were published.[33] But the Rosicrucian legend captured the imagination of some Freemasons, just as it continues to capture the imagination of some esotericists today.

From its home in Scotland, the Masonic movement went on to attract adherents south of the border—a Grand Lodge was founded in London in 1717—and it spread extensively in continental Europe, notably in France. There is a colourful and intricate history here of male sociability and boyish fantasy. In the latter part of the eighteenth century, there was a growth in exotic Masonic titles and degrees, as well as in quasi-Masonic and schismatic Masonic bodies. This led to growing suspicion about the behaviour and intentions of the movement's members, and Freemasonry came to be the subject of conspiracy theories which blamed it for bringing about the French and other revolutions.[34]

Generally speaking, these anti-Masonic conspiracy theories were paranoid nonsense. To a large extent, Freemasonry in the age of the Enlightenment appears to have been more or less what it is today—a club for bored and affluent men of conventional religious views. In 1738, the order was condemned by the Catholic Church, in Pope Clement XII's bull *In eminenti*, but the condemnation was widely ignored. Nevertheless, eighteenth-century Freemasons were by no means all conservative Christians. Freemasonry did not insist on the dogmatic strictures of the established churches, and this created space for a very real element of religious dissent among the brethren. As Margaret Jacob has written:

> [F]reemasonry endorsed a minimalist creed which could be anything from theism to pantheism and atheism. Not surprisingly, the lodges in England had a high representation of pro-1688–89 Whigs and scientists, while in Paris by the 1740s the philosopher and freemason, Claude Helvétius, was a materialist. The leader of Amsterdam freemasonry, Rousset de Missy, was a pantheist. Montesquieu, also a freemason, was probably some kind of deist. In both London and Amsterdam Jewish names can be found in the lodge records ... Rarely do lodge ceremonies, even in Catholic countries, contain overtly Christian language. Many of the religious positions we associate with the Radical Enlightenment appeared conspicuously in some lodges.[35]

This leads us on to an interesting question: how far did religious dissent among Freemasons shade into esoteric and pagan ideas? There was historical precedent for Masons dabbling in this area. For example, one of the oldest Masonic texts—the Matthew Cooke Manuscript, which dates back to the time of working stonemasons in the fifteenth century—happily mixes Biblical legend with material from Graeco-Roman paganism. Here the text describes how the Masons' forebears ensured that their technical knowledge survived the Biblical flood, to be recovered by the esoteric masters Pythagoras and Hermes Trismegistus:

> [T]hey wrote their science[s] in the 2 pillars of stone ... And so it was that God sent vengeance so that there came such a flood that all the world was drowned, and all men were dead therein, save 8 persons, And that was Noah, and his wife, and his three sons, and their wives ... And after this flood many years ... these 2 pillars were found, and ... a great clerk that [was] called Pythagoras found that one, and Hermes, the philosopher, found that other, and they taught forth the sciences that they found therein written.[36]

This link with the pagan and esoteric past recurred through later Masonic history. In the Enlightenment period, one figure who brought together Masonic and paganizing tendencies was the Irish radical and freethinker John Toland (1670–1722). Toland wrote an unusual pamphlet entitled *Pantheisticon, Sive Formula Celebrandae Sodalitatis Socraticae* ('Pantheisticon, or Order of Service of the Socratic Society'). This work, which was published in 1720, purported to describe the activities of pantheistic groups ('Socratic Societies') which existed in England and other European countries. These groups supposedly celebrated a formal liturgy, which included material from Cicero, Horace and other classical writers. With its classicism and pantheism, the text has a broadly pagan air; and Toland compares the members of the Socratic Societies to Pythagoreans, mystery-priests and Druids. The pantheistic theology contained in the pamphlet appears to be influenced by the philo-pagan philosopher Giordano Bruno, and it fits with elements of both ancient and revived paganism.[37] The Socratic liturgy even came close to incorporating some explicit polytheism: the publisher and journalist Prosper Marchand wrote a prayer to Bacchus for inclusion in it, although this ended up not being published:

> All-powerful, eternal Bacchus, who hast established human society especially in drinking, grant, being propitious, that the heads of these men, who are heavy from yesterday's drinking, be lightened by today's, and that this be done, through cups of cups. Amen.[38]

It has to be recognized that the *Pantheisticon* is not really a pagan text. The classical sources which it quotes include rationalistic and anticlerical sentiments, and it sits more comfortably in the freethinking mainstream of the Enlightenment. All the same, it is an ambivalent piece of work, one which perhaps reflects a deeper ambivalence on the part of its author: scholars have noted that there were 'two Tolands: one, the ... firebrand of the deists, volatile spokesman for a natural religion based solely on reason; the other ... proponent of esoteric, pantheistic philosophy'.[39] It also has to be recognized that the *Pantheisticon* is a fantasy: the Socratic Societies never existed. But it was a fantasy that imitated life. There *were* organized groups in the Masonic orbit which catered to people with unorthodox religious views. A reasonably well-known example is a group of religious dissidents in The Hague called the 'Knights of Jubilation', evidence for which survives among Toland's papers.[40] Such circles formed part of the soil from which eighteenth-century Freemasonry grew. From this perspective, we begin to see how natural it was to find men with esoteric and philo-pagan affiliations in the Masonic milieu.

There is nothing very surprising about this. The colourful, ritualistic, occultic aspects of the Masonic lodges both attracted and repelled many contemporaries precisely because they looked remarkably like a rival religion to Christianity. This was a reflection of Freemasonry's pre-Enlightenment roots: as David Stevenson wrote in this context, 'at heart the movement was not an Enlightenment but a Renaissance phenomenon'.[41] So it was that, in the eighteenth and nineteenth centuries, Freemasonry was repeatedly linked with ancient pagan religion both by its friends and by its enemies. A founding text of the anti-Masonic movement claimed that Masonry 'adopts, without revulsion, all the dreams of paganism'.[42] For some writers, the craft was comparable to the ancient esoteric solar cult known as Mithraism.[43] The popular revolutionary pamphleteer Tom Paine thought that it was descended from Druidic sun-worship;[44] and this theory found its way into the mainstream of Masonic literature through Richard Carlile's *Manual of Freemasonry*.[45] A number of nineteenth-century writers looked to the Latin writer Apuleius, a Platonist philosopher who was an initiate of several mystery cults, as a kind of ancient Freemason.[46] From a rather different perspective, Pope Leo XIII condemned the order in 1884 as an attempt 'to bring back after a lapse of eighteen centuries the manners and customs of the pagans'.[47]

In this context, it seems quite unsurprising that pagan revivalists would draw on Freemasonry as a source once the modern pagan movement got under way. The most influential philo-pagan organization of the nineteenth century, the Hermetic Order of the Golden Dawn, was founded by high-degree

Freemasons and incorporated Masonic materials into the core of its rituals. In the twentieth century, Masonic influences—including a secret lodge-type structure and certain items of ritual and vocabulary—came to be adopted into the pagan witch religion known as Wicca. We will come back to these movements in the following chapters. For the time being, it is sufficient to note that modern paganism would look quite different if it had not taken on the influence of the collection of unorthodox religious symbology, ideas and ritual behaviour that we know as Freemasonry.

At this point in the story, we may address one of the central historical problems of pagan studies: who was the first modern pagan? Or, in more precise language: who was the first European through whom the persisting pagan heritage broke out into revival in the Enlightenment era? The answer is perhaps surprising, and deserves more attention than it has so far received. The first person in modern times who can be shown to have embraced paganism as a revived religious system was not a Robespierrean revolutionary or a high-degree Freemason. It was a teacher called John Fransham (1730–1810), who spent most of his life living in the city of Norwich in England.[48]

Fransham was a genuine English eccentric. The surviving evidence paints a picture of a strange man, given to unusual behaviour and morbid fears, and neglectful of his appearance and cleanliness. He disliked slavery, imperialism and democracy. He had difficulties with women, and he never married. He seems to have spoken freely about polytheistic gods in daily conversation, and he does not appear to have made a secret of his antipathy towards Christianity, a religion which he scorned for practising homophobia and tolerating cruelty to animals. He left a significant body of writings behind him, but only a small quantity of these were published during his lifetime: in 1760, for example, he published an anonymous *Essay on the Oestrum or Enthusiasm of Orpheus*, which gave indications of his pagan and Platonist leanings.[49] Most of his works, however, remained unpublished at his death. This includes in particular his most explicitly pagan text, a set of hymns to the classical gods entitled *Antiqua Religio*.

Fransham had a great attachment to the Graeco-Roman classics—Latin and Greek were among the subjects that he taught to his pupils, along with mathematics and French—but of course this in itself was not unusual and does not explain his paganism. In some ways, his religious views comported with Enlightenment norms. He lived in an orderly, harmonious universe which existed under a single supreme being: 'that universal genius, nature, cause, ground, substratum, or necessary law, which unites and sustains the universal system'.[50] Also typical for the period was his sceptical cast of mind. One of his biographers recalled:

> [S]carcely a sentence could be uttered in his presence, or any infor-
> mation communicated to him, without his rejoining with 'Are you
> sure that is true? On what do you ground your belief?—You should
> be very cautious of the evidence of testimony. A Mathematician
> believes nothing without proof.' &c. &c.[51]

We may ask how and why Fransham made his intellectual journey from these fairly conventional eighteenth-century attitudes to the novelties of pagan polytheism. The 'why' is not difficult to answer. Like many other modern pagan revivalists, it is apparent that he was looking for an alternative both to the rigours of orthodox Christianity and to the spiritual emptiness of secular rationalism. The 'how' is a little less straightforward. Fransham arrived at Paganism by essentially two routes. First, he used classical deities as personifi-cations of philosophical concepts. For example, his *Antiqua Religio* begins with a set of hymns to three deities, a kind of pagan holy trinity: Jupiter, the supreme divine being; Minerva, who personifies truth and the laws of the universe; and Venus, the power of generation and unity. It is noteworthy that the hymn to Jupiter seems to profess a vaguely Platonist panentheism:

> He is the nature absolute, supreme,
> Original to all: the common spring
> Whence all beside perpetually flow
> In close dependence: the uniting power
> Which makes of all one comprehensive whole:
> Most vital principle, of beings inmost;
> Soul of all souls, and of the universe,
> Whose right and prosperous and happy state
> By him consisteth and supported is.
> To all his presence is most intimate:
> All things are full of Jove, in him subsist:
> Pervading all, he constitutes the bounds,
> Connexions and relations of all worlds.[52]

The second route that took Fransham to polytheism was the theory that the individual parts of the universe, both large and small, are each overseen by presiding spirits or divinities. This theory could be applied to the major gods of the pantheon, as well as to the governing spirits of winds, locations, families, nations, and so on. In the following passage, Fransham salutes the sun god Phoebus Apollo; the dawn goddess Aurora; the moon goddess, known as Phoebe, Diana and Hecate; and Pluto, the god of the night and the underworld, together with his consort Proserpina:

> Let us not then unmindful be of thee,
> Bright Phoebus, of the Sun immediate Lord ...
> Hail, roseate goddess of the morn! benign
> Regard thy votaries, O Aurora fair ...
> Hail, Phoebe, gently bright, with lustre mild,
> Regent of night, guide of the moon-light-dance ...
> Thou art Diana call'd & Hecate:
> For in thy ample & incessant course,
> Thou dost suggest, that pure & calm delights
> Fade not with age: that light may fresh emerge
> Even in the midst of Pluto's gloomy reign.
> Hail, king of night & all the vast unknown!
> Thy realm is dark to those who live without.
> But still the great majorities, ev'n there,
> May their felicities & solace find,
> With kind Proserpina in peaceful shadow.[53]

If John Fransham was the first modern pagan, why has no-one today heard of him? He was not an entirely obscure figure in his own time. He had contacts both within local Norwich society—the city was a relatively major intellectual centre—and at national level. But it seems likely that his personal eccentricities held him back. A more gregarious, charismatic and strategic individual might have got further. As it is, Fransham's experimentation with ancient polytheism amounts to a kind of road not travelled; an opportunity missed. It is interesting to speculate what would have happened if a pagan revival movement inspired by Fransham had taken secure root in Georgian society.

Fransham was not the only pagan Englishman of his time. Another, better-known figure who trod the same path was the writer and philosopher Thomas Taylor (1758–1835). As with Fransham, Taylor embraced paganism under the influence of classical scholarship, although beyond that the two men's intellectual positions largely diverged. Taylor was profoundly influenced by Platonist philosophy. Fransham's writings appear to show some Platonic influences; but the younger man was a full-blown, true-believing Platonist. What is more, he was a radical, pagan Platonist who rejected figures like Marsilio Ficino and Giovanni Pico della Mirandola for partially Christianizing the great sage. Taylor, like Fransham, was anti-Christian.[54]

Taylor was brought up as a Presbyterian and was originally destined for the ministry; in his youth, he developed interests in mathematics and philosophy. The great turning-point of his life was his pagan 'conversion', which seems to have taken place in his twenties. He retained his pagan convictions for the rest of his life. Fortunately from the perspective of his career, he was able to find wealthy patrons, most notably the businessman William Meredith and his brother George. Like his beloved Plato (and also like John Fransham), he was a political authoritarian: he stood as an opponent of the embryonic Western movements for liberalism, democracy and feminism.

Taylor's devotion to the Platonist philosophical tradition was remarkable. 'Not even Ficino had read the late Neoplatonists ... with such zeal and empathy.'[55] A less sympathetic commentator wrote: 'while studying Plato [he] accidentally met with Plotinus, whose writings he accepted as a kind of revelation ... From Plotinus he went to Proclus, and read him through three times, a feat probably performed by no other mortal since the Renaissance.'[56] Starting in the 1780s, Taylor published a series of translations of Platonist texts, together with some scholarship of his own. His translations included versions of works by Plotinus, Porphyry, Iamblichus and Proclus, as well as the Emperor Julian; he produced an edition of the *Chaldaean Oracles*; and he republished the ancient Platonist philosophers' criticisms of Christianity. Most impressively of all, he translated the entirety of Plato's and Aristotle's works into English—the first person ever to do so.[57] Nevertheless, his output had its limitations. He was not a great Greek scholar, and he had an unorthodox approach to translation: his English renditions of texts were skewed to his preferred philosophical ideas.[58]

It was said that Taylor engaged in devotional worship of the gods, although the evidence on this is not as clear or strong as one would wish.[59] Other modern pagan revivalists subsequently drew on his work in their own ritual worship: specifically, his translation of the *Orphic Hymns*, which he published in 1787, came to be quite widely employed for this purpose, although it has recently fallen out of fashion.[60] In fact, Taylor's version of the *Hymns* illustrates some of the weaknesses of his translation methods. His rendition of the hymn to the goddess Athena may serve as an example here. Here is an extract from his translation:

Gymnastic virgin of terrific mind,
Dire Gorgon[']s bane, unmarried, blessed, kind:
Mother of arts, imperious; understood,
Rage to the wicked, wisdom to the good:
Female and male, the arts of war are thine,
Fanatic, much-form'd dragoness, divine:
O'er the Phlegrean giants rous'd to ire,
Thy coursers driving, with destruction dire ...[61]

Here is our own rendition, which aims to be closer to the Greek:

O athletic maiden, your bold spirit makes us tremble;
You slew the Gorgon; you flee from the marriage-bed; you are
    rich in blessings.
You inspire us, bestowing wild frenzy on the wicked and good
    sense on the virtuous.
You are male and female by nature; you are the bringer of war;
    you are wisdom.
You are resplendent in honours, O dragon of changing form; you
    possess us with your spirit.
You destroyed the Phlegraian giants, O driver of horses ...

As a pagan revivalist, Taylor did not quite realize his promise. This is more surprising than in the case of John Fransham, as Taylor was *famous* in a way that Fransham was not. His particular form of paganism did not survive him, and it has few adherents today outside certain Platonist circles. His influence on the persistence of paganism into the modern revival was real; but it was indirect. He did not leave behind a school of disciples or successors who promoted his teachings among subsequent generations. Instead, he was read for inspiration by people who ended up taking the pagan revival in a very different direction from his own philosophical approach. Taylor was, so to speak, the last pagan of the Enlightenment. He was a product of the age of the *lumières*—albeit, like Fransham, an eccentric one who rejected certain Enlightenment principles like philosophical materialism and democratic politics. He came to paganism as a cerebral intellectual, not as a poet or prophet: he *thought* his way to believing in the old gods. He was a practitioner of scholarship and philosophy; a man who, like many of his contemporaries, made use of the expanding free-thinking of the age to promote unorthodox ideas about religion which he had found in classical texts. To that extent, he was engaged in the same project as figures like Voltaire and John Toland.

But Taylor was also a transitional figure. Mixed in with the legacy of the Enlightenment, there is something else detectable in his work—something which points not backwards to the genteel salons of eighteenth-century philosophers, but rather forwards to the counter-cultural pagan revivalists of the nineteenth and twentieth centuries. Consider this passage from his translation of the *Orphic Hymns*:

> [W]e may justly conclude, that the age of true philosophy is no more. In consequence of very extended natural discoveries, trade and commerce have increased; while abstract investigations, have necessarily declined: so that modern enquiries, never rise above sense; and every thing is despised, which does not in some respect or other, contribute to the accumulation of wealth; the gratification of childish admiration; or the refinements of corporeal delight. The author of the following translation, therefore, cannot reasonably expect, that his labours will meet with the approbation of the many: since these Hymns are too ancient, and too full of the Greek philosophy, to please the ignorant, and the sordid. However, he hopes they will be acceptable to the few, who have drawn wisdom from its source.[62]

There are several interesting themes here. The idealization of ancient Greece as the source of pure wisdom; the flight from modernity and the rejection of contemporary majoritarian culture; the contempt for materialism and commerce. One gets a whiff here of something quite distinctive, something which would profoundly influence the form in which paganism would be revived in modern times. That something is Romanticism.

Romanticism was a complex and variegated phenomenon. In very broad terms, it departed from the ordered, intellectual world of the Enlightenment in the direction of irrationalism and transgression. It celebrated the emotional, the marginal, the old, the wild and the taboo. But—contrary to popular perceptions—it was not *merely* a reaction against the Enlightenment. It also drew on much older sources of ideas and aesthetics, including Neoplatonist philosophy and other elements of the esoteric tradition. Neoplatonist conceptions of a transcendent divine power underlying the material world found a ready audience among poets and artists who sensed that nature was intrinsically sacred. The Romantic movement brought together intellectual panentheism with poetic intuition.

The early British Romantics were plugged into the developing tradition of modern paganism, as represented by Thomas Taylor. As will be clear, Taylor himself cannot be described as a member of the Romantic movement; but he was read by the Romantics, including key figures such as Shelley, Byron and Coleridge. Not all Romantics, of course, were philo-pagans; and indeed Romanticism did not lead to any one particular religious destination. Some figures who were influenced by Romanticism, such as John Henry Newman and the Anglo-Catholics, embraced conservative and authoritarian forms of Christianity. Martin Bernal wrote in this regard of 'the division within the Romantic movement between the "progressive" lovers of Greece and Germany, and the "reactionary" passion for Christian ritual and the Middle Ages that could lead the unwary to Rome'.[63] We are plainly concerned here with the first of these tendencies, although it bears keeping in mind that Romantic paganism had reactionary iterations too.

The origin of the Romantic pagan current amounts to an interesting question in itself. Did it first start with British poets reading Taylor? It seems not. The roots of the movement appear to lie elsewhere. In his magisterial study *The Triumph of the Moon*, Ronald Hutton took the story back to late eighteenth-century Germany, and specifically to Friedrich Schiller—author of the philo-pagan poem *Die Götter Griechenlandes* ('The Gods of Greece', 1788)—and his fellow literary giants Goethe and Hölderlin.[64] One might also make mention here of Friedrich Schlegel and his novel *Lucinde* (1799), with its motifs of sexuality and goddess-worship. Hutton's argument was that Romantic paganism migrated from these sources to Shelley, Keats and other early nineteenth-century British writers. And this argument appears to be essentially correct. The line can convincingly be traced back to the Germans of Schiller's era. Indeed, Goethe closed his masterpiece *Faust* with some lines which, addressed to the Virgin Mary amidst a mixture of pagan and Christian motifs, form almost a manifesto for modern pagan attitudes to the divine feminine:

DOCTOR MARIANUS
Let every finer sense
be offered willingly to your service;
Virgin, Mother, Queen,
Goddess—have mercy!

CHORUS MYSTICUS
Everything that is transient
is only a parable.
Here, what is deficient
becomes true reality.
> Here, what is indescribable
> comes to pass.
> The Eternal-Feminine
> draws us onwards.

Nevertheless, the thesis that the Romantic pagan revival began in Germany is incomplete. The origins of the movement lie at least partly in Britain, albeit in a somewhat earlier period than that of Shelley and his contemporaries.

One seemingly promising source of early Romantic paganism comes readily to mind: the Druid revival, which got under way in earnest in the late eighteenth century. If one mentions modern paganism to the average British person, they are as likely as not to think of Druids celebrating the summer solstice at Stonehenge. Yet, when one looks more closely, Druid revivalism proves to be a less promising source of Romantic paganism than one might expect. One of the more surprising features of the Druid revival movement is that for most of its history it has tended *not* to be pagan. Neo-Druid theology has generally turned out to be monotheistic, Christianizing or universalist. The Stonehenge solstice celebrations are one example of this. They originated in 1912 with a socialist activist by the name of George Watson MacGregor Reid. Reid's influences were eclectic—they included the Kabbalah, Islam, Zoroastrianism and Buddhism—but he cannot be called a pagan, and in part his ideas were explicitly Christian.[65]

The problematic and ambivalent relationship between revived Druidry and revived paganism began early: as early, in fact, as the main precursor of the Druid revival, the notorious William Stukeley (1687–1765). Stukeley was an eccentric scholar with esoteric interests whose influences included Pythagoras and Neoplatonism. He was happy to call himself a Druid, and he referred to his friends and acquaintances as Druids and Druidesses. He even built in his garden a 'temple of the Druids', and a 'chapel' containing a Roman altar. Yet calling him a Druid revivalist claims too much for his idiosyncratic endeavours; and calling him a pagan gives insufficient weight to the monotheistic tendency of his ideas. He ended up finding his vocation as an Anglican priest.[66]

When the Druid revival got going more seriously later in the eighteenth century, it took a number of different forms. Some Druidic clubs—the Druidical Society founded in Anglesey in 1772, the Ancient Order of Druids founded in London in 1781—were social, cultural or philanthropic bodies which had no pagan religious associations.[67] The first Druid revivalist who had proto-Romantic pagan tendencies was William Jones (1746–1794), who went on to become famous as a colonial judge and linguistic scholar in India. In around 1779–81, Jones seems to have run a group of amateur poets called the 'Druids of Cardigan', whom he regaled with his verses on wine, women, pagan mythology and goddess-worship. He wrote the following lines in protest at the anti-Catholic 'Gordon riots' of 1780, proclaiming that followers of different religions were really worshippers of the same universal goddess:

> What means all this frensy, what mad men are they
>       Who broil and are broil'd for a shade in religion?
> Since all sage inspirers one doctrine convey
>       From Numa's wild nymph to sly Mohamed's pigeon.[68]
>             Then Druids arise,
>             Teach the world to be wise,
> And the grape's rosy blood for your sacrifice pour,
>             Th' immortals invoke,
>             And under this oak
> Kneel, kneel to the Goddess whom all men adore.

> By various high titles this Goddess is nam'd,
>       At Ephesus Dian, in Syria Astarte,
> In New Rome 'tis Mary, Heaven's Regent proclaim'd,
>       In Old Rome 'twas Venus, the buxom and hearty.
>             But crown'd and enthron'd
>             Her Godhead is own'd
> In desert, in valley, on mountain, on shore,
>             Then join our gay crew,
>             Turk, Roman and Jew,
> And kneel to the Goddess, whom all men adore.[69]

This is a remarkable text, and it undoubtedly has a place in the lineage of Romantic paganism; but we should not press it too far. Jones was not really a pagan: indeed, another verse of his poem criticizes ancient Greek polytheism. He seems to have been a kind of nonsectarian monotheist, albeit one who took the important and daring step of turning God into a Goddess.

We cannot close our examination of the early Druid revival without making mention of the best-known and most influential Druid revivalist of all, Iolo

Morganwg (1747–1826). Morganwg was a colourful character who posed as an initiate of the ancient Druidic tradition. From the 1790s, he convened *gorseddau* or bardic meetings and initiated others into his movement: this was the origin of Gorsedd Cymru, which continues to be a major cultural organization in Wales. But Morganwg was not a pagan: he was an unorthodox Christian. As with William Stukeley, his vision of Druidry was monotheistic; and he developed a great admiration for Unitarianism.[70] If Morganwg had had the data and the inclination to pursue a revival of genuine ancient Celtic polytheism, the course of the Druid revival would have run differently, with consequent wider knock-on effects for Welsh and British culture. But he did not and it did not.

If the Druids have little to offer us, where else in eighteenth-century Britain might we look for traces of Romantic proto-paganism? A more promising line of inquiry is provided by the activities of the politician Francis Dashwood (1708–1781), also known as Baron Le Despencer. Dashwood founded a curious society which was meeting by the early 1750s at Medmenham Abbey, a former Cistercian religious house in Buckinghamshire. Known by several names— including the 'Order of the Friars of St Francis of Wycombe' and the 'Monks of Medmenham'—this was one of the notorious eighteenth-century hellfire clubs. A group of hedonistic upper-class men, including several Members of Parliament, assembled together in a mock-religious atmosphere amidst statues of pagan deities and Latin inscriptions. Dashwood also had the phrase *Fay ce que vouldras* ('Do what you will') inscribed over the entrance to his Abbey, a quotation from Rabelais which was later made famous by Aleister Crowley.[71] The intellectual and politician Horace Walpole visited Medmenham in 1763, although as an outsider to the order he was not permitted to enter the chapel, which was allegedly furnished with obscene images. He later wrote of the property:

> Thither at stated seasons they adjourned; had each their cell, a proper habit, a monastic name, and a refectory in common— besides a chapel, the decorations of which may well be supposed to have contained the quintessence of their mysteries, since it was impenetrable to any but the initiated. Whatever their doctrines were, their practice was rigorously pagan: Bacchus and Venus were the deities to whom they almost publicly sacrificed.[72]

It is apparent that the Monks' paganism had more to do with classical aesthetics and with alcoholic and sexual libertinism than with the literal worship of ancient deities. They did not subscribe to pagan religious beliefs—in real life, so to speak, Dashwood had Unitarian sympathies—but they were pagans in the general Christian othering sense of being transgressors against the orthodox faith and its moral strictures. Their project was one of recreational blasphemy, for which ancient paganism was a symbolic language that came readily to hand. So did Roman Catholicism, although here there is an ambiguity: were the Monks *mocking* Catholic symbolism or defiantly *adopting* it as a means of rejecting the established Protestantism of their culture?

The Monks ceased to function in the 1760s, but the demise of the group did not stop Francis Dashwood from continuing to dabble in his distinctive brand of paganism as transgressive entertainment. In 1771, he had a portico on his estate, which was modelled on the Temple of Bacchus at Teos, dedicated to the Greek god with the help of his wealthy friends:

> [A] Bacchanalian procession was formed, consisting of Bacchanals, Priests, Priestess, Pan, Fawns, Satyrs, Silenus, &c. all adorned in proper habits, and skins wreathed with vine leaves, ivy, oak, &c. in the most picturesque manner imaginable. This procession arriving in the portico, the High Priest addressed the statue in an invocation, which was succeeded by several hymns and other pieces of music, both vocal and instrumental ... At the close of the evening, the procession, which consisted of Ladies and Gentlemen, returned to the temple, and finished the ceremony with a congratulatory ode to the Deity of the place.[73]

The Monks' former secretary, Paul Whitehead, died in 1774, and Dashwood had his heart ritually interred in 'a procession after the mode of the Heathen funeral rites'.[74] So much for Dashwood, the Monks and the evidence which they have left of the paganizing revelries of the English Georgian upper classes. Another Englishman worth mentioning in this context is the Gloucestershire landowner Benjamin Hyett (1708–1762). Sometime around the 1740s, Hyett constructed a summer house called 'Pan's Lodge', and organized processions in honour of the god. It has been suspected that Hyett's activities were in the same mould as Dashwood's; but this case remains somewhat obscure, and more research on it would be beneficial.[75]

No survey of British proto-Romantic flirtations with paganism is complete without mentioning Richard Payne Knight (1750–1824). Knight was a prolific writer and numismatist, but he is remembered today for one reason and one reason only—a scandalous work entitled *An Account of the Remains of the Worship of Priapus*, which he published in 1786 in a limited edition.[76] In this book, he set forth a theory that religion had originated in the worship of creative energy, as symbolized by the sexual organs. He was influenced in this line of scholarship by a report that the cult of Priapus had survived until the recent past in the town of Isernia in central Italy, with wax phalluses being employed as offerings at a Catholic festival.[77] Knight's work—which drew on the ancient esoteric tradition as well as modern discoveries from India and elsewhere—has an interesting place in the history of ideas. His scholarship can be seen as standing in the tradition of Protestant polemicists who sought to prove that Catholic practices amounted to survivals of paganism. But, more pertinently for our present purposes, Knight can be seen as having some claim to be considered a forerunner of the Romantic pagans. There is his obvious interest in eroticism; and his own personal religion appears to have been a Platonic-type pantheism which was quite at home in the Romantic milieu. He would later be read by important figures in the twentieth-century pagan revival, including Aleister Crowley and Gerald Gardner.

Having surveyed the evidence, we may conclude that there were certain manifestations of proto-Romantic paganism in eighteenth-century Britain; and that these, together with the current of German Romantic paganism and the writings of Thomas Taylor, fed into the work of the British Romantic writers and poets of the early nineteenth century. It is to these writers and poets that we now return. We are concerned here with a circle of figures who were active in the 1810s and '20s, and who knew each other personally: they included Percy and Mary Shelley, John Keats, Thomas Love Peacock, Thomas Jefferson Hogg, Leigh Hunt and Edward Trelawny. There grew up among these people a highly influential form of Romantic paganism, which for convenience we may call 'Shelleyism'.[78] It is important to emphasize that we are not dealing here with eccentric Christian heretics in the mould of Iolo Morganwg. The attachment of the people in question to ancient pagan deities and what they took to be ancient pagan attitudes was open and explicit, and they referred to themselves using the terms 'pagan', 'Bacchic' and 'Athenian' (the conservative Poet Laureate, Robert Southey, preferred to call them the 'Satanic school'). Their pagan inclinations were apparent in their writings, public and private, and sometimes even in their behaviour. Percy Shelley, for example, not only wrote poems to classical deities—translations, emulations and original compositions—he also kept busts of Apollo and Venus in his study and built altars to Pan.[79] When he was drowned in 1822 at the age of 29, his friends performed pagan funeral rites for him and one of his companions involving incense, salt, wine and oil (Byron asked to keep Shelley's skull, but he was told no because it was suspected that he might use it as a drinking cup).[80]

The substantive content of Shelleyism was characteristically Romantic: it was a religion of joy, sensuality and freedom. It is immediately recognizable as the direct ancestor of mainstream modern pagan spirituality and practice, as promoted by figures from Aleister Crowley to Vivianne Crowley and from Starhawk to Silver RavenWolf. This is the form in which revived pagan religion has asserted itself most strongly and for longest; and it comes straight from the literary circle of Shelley, Keats and their associates. Their style of religiosity could have an affective, devotional dimension, as in Keats' address to the moon as the inspirer of poets in 'I stood tip-toe upon a little hill' (1817):

> O Maker of sweet poets, dear delight
> Of this fair world, and all its gentle livers;
> Spangler of clouds, halo of crystal rivers,
> Mingler with leaves, and dew and tumbling streams,
> Closer of lovely eyes to lovely dreams,
> Lover of loneliness, and wandering,
> Of upcast eye, and tender pondering!
> Thee must I praise above all other glories
> That smile us on to tell delightful stories.
> For what has made the sage or poet write
> But the fair paradise of Nature's light?

It could also have a more radical, political edge. Leigh Hunt wrote the following to Thomas Jefferson Hogg in 1818, fantasizing about a popular pagan revival and having a dig at Nicholas Vansittart, the Tory Chancellor of the Exchequer:

> I hope you paid your devotions as usual to the *Religio Loci* [spirit of the place], and hung up an evergreen. If you all go on so, there will be a hope some day that old Vansittart & others will be struck with a Panic Terror, and that a voice will be heard along the water saying 'The great God Pan is alive again,'—upon which the villagers will leave off starving, and singing profane hymns, and fall to dancing again.[81]

This is Shelleyism as an expression of counter-cultural liberation. Paganism in this mode was a spiritual and moral antidote to the repressions of the nineteenth-century Church of England and Tory Government, fashioned from the materials of the Greek and Roman classics that had been drilled into its practitioners. Quite how far it amounted to a full-fledged system of belief and practice is open to question, but that perhaps misses the point. It was a cultural and ethical orientation which exercised a significant pull over its adherents, and to dismiss it as superficial or unserious smacks of Protestant censoriousness. As Ronald Hutton has written in this context: 'It is impossible to tell how serious all this was; but even if it was largely in play, that is in itself ... a hallmark of "genuine" modern paganism.'[82]

Shelleyism was not, for better or for worse, a long-lasting phenomenon. It petered out in the 1820s. It is sometimes said that a pagan group was active at Cambridge University in the early decades of the nineteenth century, and it has been claimed that the group used texts drawn both from pagan antiquity and from Shelley and Keats. This, however, seems to be a false report based on a rumour started by the sensationalist writer Montague Summers in the 1920s.[83] For several decades in the early- to mid-nineteenth century, the pagan revival stalled. Shelleyism began to look like a false start. But the pagan cause was not dead—it never is. Paganism continued to persist, and it was not long before it began to break out into revival again.

# CHAPTER FIVE

# Poets and Priests: The Victorian Era

The nineteenth century was a crucial period for the revival of pagan beliefs and practices, and nowhere more so than in England. To enter Victorian England is to step into a place of profound religious change and disturbance. Traditional Christian culture was under siege as never before, facing intellectual challenges from the outside in the form of science and scepticism and from the inside in the form of liberalizing theology from Germany. In public life, the once formidable legal privileges of the Anglican church were reduced and diminishing. Meanwhile, throughout the country, the social upheavals of industrialization broke the organic links between people, place and parish that had been fundamental to the English religious experience for centuries. Given this ferment of social and religious change, and given that resources from ancient paganism continued to persist in contemporary culture, it was unsurprising that some people would seek to reactivate those resources in order to help with thinking about and living in the emerging modern world—or in order to avoid doing so.

The religious history of the Victorian age is sometimes told as a flat, monochrome narrative of progress: a pious evangelical form of Christianity retreating in the face of Charles Darwin. And to a certain extent this was true. Evangelical Protestantism did reach its peak and enter decline in this period, and scientistic secularism did take hold in public culture. This was the 'Sea of Faith' retreating, as described in Matthew Arnold's 'Dover Beach'; or the *Victorian Crisis of Faith*, to use the title of a well-known book.[1] Yet other creedal options were available beyond orthodox Protestantism and orthodox naturalism. The Victorian era saw continuing outbreaks of the non-rational, Romantic ways of thinking that we met in the last chapter, both in the field of religion and elsewhere. As James Webb wrote:

> Just when the Age of Reason seemed to be bearing fruit in the 19th century, there was an unexpected reaction against the very method which had brought success, a wild return to archaic forms of belief,

and among the intelligentsia a sinister concentration on superstitions which had been thought buried.[2]

The historian and intellectual G. M. Young likewise wrote (in rather racist
vein) of a 'a flight of perplexed unstable minds into the [Catholic] Confessional,
into Spiritualism, into strange Eastern Cults'.[3]

It was perhaps unsurprising that a flight from secular industrial modernity
could take the form of a renewed commitment to religious observances.
Revelatory texts, mystical symbols and sacramental rituals served well to inject
beauty and transcendence into the ugliness of British urban life. *Which* religion
should be chosen was a secondary point, and open to debate. This takes us back
to our observation in Chapter 4 that Romantic religiosity had both progressive
and reactionary forms: 'left' and 'right' wings, so to speak. Which kind one
chose depended on whether one thought that the antidote to Victorian factories
and stock exchanges was a return to an idyllic traditional feudal order or a social
revolution which would ring in a new age of freedom. Ironically, the existence
of the choice itself was a symptom of a rapidly modernizing society which was
developing a capitalist consumer culture. Among the choices available on the
shelves of the contemporary spiritual supermarket—along with G. M. Young's
reactionary brands of Christianity, talking to the dead and religious systems
from Britain's Asian colonies—was a familiar product which found a ready
constituency in this age just as it had in others: revived classical polytheism.
As we have noted, this religious current tended to fall on the 'left' wing of
the Romantic response to modernity; but it had adherents on the obscurantist
'right' as well.

There was also another driving force of pagan revival in the nineteenth
century that was much more important outside Great Britain: that other
wayward child of the Romantic movement, nationalism. European nationalisms
exploded from the 'Year of Revolutions' of 1848, proclaiming the idea that
nations were constituted not by historically conditioned dynastic rights or the
consent of aristocratic elites but by the shared culture, language and heritage
of a people. From Ireland to Ukraine, intellectuals began the long project
of forging awareness of nationhood in territories long dominated by colonial
powers, and revivals of folk culture—folklore, folk music, folk dance, folk art
and so on—were to the fore of such efforts. For the early nationalists, national
particularity was everything—and it was thus inevitable, perhaps, that this
particularity would be extended eventually into the sphere of religion through
the revival (or invention) of 'native faiths'. This development of nationalism
lay in the future, for now; the vast majority of nineteenth-century European

nationalists were mainstream Christians or secular agnostics, but their ethno-graphic work provided the evidential basis for later movements of native faith, and their elevation of the distinctive 'national character' of peoples sometimes came close to a religion. While nationalism in the sense we are talking about here was absent from Victorian Britain—Britain was, after all, a colonial power seeking to subjugate other nations rather than a nation seeking to define itself under a colonial yoke—the concept of 'national character' was equally important to its inhabitants.

We may briefly touch on a terminological point here. In line with the historical tendencies that we have noted in the Introduction and previous chapters of this book, the word 'pagan' was frequently used in the Victorian period as a general othering term. It could be used in a relatively precise sense to describe living non-Abrahamic religions, like G. M. Young's 'strange Eastern Cults'. It also often had a broader, pejorative sense of 'bad and not Protestant'. Sometimes, consistently with what was said in Chapter 4, it was used to mean godless secularity; on other occasions, as indicated in Chapter 3, it was used as a polemical description of Roman Catholicism. These usages of the word were predictable and unremarkable. But the term 'paganism' also began to appear in public discourse to describe distinctive cultural trends which challenged conventional Protestantism by deploying the language and symbols of pre-Christian antiquity.[4]

We saw in Chapter 4 how figures in the Romantic movement in the arts experimented with paganism in the earlier part of the nineteenth century, and we saw that these figures included giants like Shelley and Keats. We also noted that this phenomenon of 'Shelleyism' did not last beyond the 1820s, although it then became dormant rather than defunct. Pagan revivalism began to feature again in British culture after the middle of the century. A key date in this regard was Monday 24 July 1854, when it appears that the first attested pagan magical rite of modern times was performed in London by the magus Éliphas Lévi (1810–1875). Lévi, whose birth name was Alphonse Louis Constant, was the leading figure in the revival of occultic magic in France: a social radical and a former cleric who saw no contradiction between his Catholicism and esoteric paganism. As to the events of 1854, Lévi claimed that a mysterious wealthy elderly lady contacted him at his hotel while he was on a visit to England, and subsequently met him outside Westminster Abbey. He went on to conduct a ritual at her behest: this purported to summon the spirit of the ancient Pythagorean holy man Apollonius of Tyana. By Lévi's account, the rite was explicitly pagan. It drew on the ancient Greek esoteric tradition, as well as the Egyptian and Zoroastrian religious currents:

In our own evocation of Apollonius, we used the magical philosophy
of Patricius for the ritual, containing the doctrines of Zoroaster and
the writings of Hermes Trismegistus. We recited the Nuctemeron
of Apollonius in Greek with a loud voice, and added the following
conjuration:

> Vouchsafe to be present, Father of All, and thou Thrice Mighty
> Hermes, Conductor of the Dead. Asclepius, son of Hephaistus,
> Patron of the Healing Art: and thou Osiris, Lord of strength
> and vigour, do thou thyself be present too. Arnebascenis,
> Patron of Philosophy, and yet again Asclepius, son of Imuthe,
> who presidest over poetry ...

> Apollonius, Apollonius, Apollonius! Thou teachest the Magic
> of Zoroaster, son of Oromasdes; and this is the worship of the
> Gods.[5]

It should be said that we have only Lévi's word that any of this took place,
and some elements of his account are distinctly suspicious. But the truth of
Lévi's life was sometimes stranger than fiction, and it is likely that he really
did perform a pagan ritual in collaboration with one or more English occultists
during his 1854 visit to London (and subsequently performed at least two
further such rituals in the city).[6]

If this is so, what Lévi did was rather exceptional for the period. It was
another generation before occultists in England began practising in earnest
anything which might be regarded as a ritual form of pagan religion. Modern
paganism was not primarily created by followers of the esoteric tradition like
Éliphas Lévi. This may initially seem surprising, as esotericism has come to
be central to modern pagan belief and practice. This is true even at the level
of popular stereotypes: the Wiccan with her tarot cards; the robed Crowley
follower summoning up spirits. But matters were different in the nineteenth
century. The English pagan revival was indebted, at its inception in the early
decades of the century, to Shelleyist artistic rebels. This continued to be
the case in the mid-to-late Victorian period: revived paganism came to be
a presence in mainstream culture largely through the work of writers and
artists. Like Lévi and other occultists, these people were influenced by the
colourful, transgressive thought-world of Romanticism. But they did not, for
the most part, engage in incense-filled rituals or perform invocations to pagan
gods. Their interests were not fundamentally *supernatural*. They did tend to
have an attachment to ancient polytheistic mythology and to what they took

to be ancient pagan worldviews; but their 'paganism' amounted as much to a commitment to identifiably modern forms of political, social and sexual radicalism as it did to any adherence to archaic religion.[7]

This brand of radical artistic paganism occupied a fairly distinctive niche in Victorian British society. As we have intimated, it essentially amounted to a resumption of Shelleyism. But it is also the case that its immediate antecedents lay outside Britain. Just as the forerunner of Victorian esoteric paganism was Éliphas Lévi, so Victorian literary paganism seems to have been, at least in part, an import from France. Romantic philo-pagan sentiments were apparent in French literature from the 1830s, and were expressed by figures including Alfred de Vigny, Charles Augustin Sainte-Beuve, Gérard de Nerval, Théophile Gautier and Leconte de Lisle.[8] In 1842, for example, the young Théodore de Banville could write in his poem 'Érato':

> O Gods—what shall I say?—mighty, bright and beautiful,
> victors adorned with bloody spoils,
> carrying bows, tridents, thyrsoi, torches,
> lyres, drums and shining arms ...
> No, you are not dead! In vain the envious man
> says that Erebos has closed your radiant mouths:
> I still love you—I know that your voice still
> speaks, and I see you, far from the befuddled crowd![9]

On the British side of the Channel, the linkage between the arts and pagan revivalism began with the Pre-Raphaelites, an artistic movement founded in 1848 which emphasized the natural, the sensual and the archaic.[10] The link was subsequently strengthened as Pre-Raphaelitism evolved into Aestheticism in the 1870s. The Aesthetic movement promoted the idea of aesthetics as a good in itself—art for art's sake—rather than as a vehicle for moral improvement. After Aestheticism came Decadence, a more cynical and counter-cultural tendency, which reached its zenith in the 1890s. The writers and artists who worked within these currents saw themselves, and were seen by their contemporaries, as participating in a revival of ancient paganism.

The key figure in the rebirth of Romantic artistic paganism in Britain was the poet Algernon Charles Swinburne (1837–1909), whom we briefly met in Chapter 1. Swinburne was influenced by the Pre-Raphaelites, and he in turn influenced the Aesthetic and Decadent movements. As Marion Gibson has put it: 'In verses of hallucinogenic beauty, his Proserpine and Aphrodite reeked of opiates and disaffection.'[11] Swinburne's greatest contribution to the growing canon of philo-pagan poetry began with the seminal First Series of his *Poems and Ballads* (1866). This work caused a sensation when it was published, with its radical leftwing politics and its preference for paganism over Christianity, although its underlying stance is closer to atheism than to religious paganism. This points to a tension in Swinburne's life and writings. He has sometimes been identified as a pagan—in the 1860s, he was immediately recognized as a paganizing successor to the earlier Romantic poets[12]—but he never embraced any particular religious affiliation. His poetry, which can be challenging and less than transparent, combined pagan, Christian, anti-Christian and humanist elements. It has been observed that '[t]here is finally no neat proposition which will sum up Swinburne's religious broodings'.[13]

A good example of Swinburne's output is his 'Litany of Nations' from *Songs Before Sunrise* (1871). This is a litany to a mysterious Great Goddess linked with the earth, who is identified with the Egyptian deity Isis:

> If with voice of words or prayers thy sons may reach thee,
>> We thy latter sons, the men thine after-birth,
>> We the children of thy grey-grown age, O Earth,
> O our mother everlasting, we beseech thee ...
> Isis, thou that knowest of God what worlds are worth.
>> Thou the ghost of God, the mother uncreated.
>> Soul for whom the floating forceless ages waited
> As our forceless fancies wait on thee, O Earth;
> Thou the body and soul, the father-God and mother.
>> If at all it move thee, knowing of all things done
>> Here where evil things and good things are not one.
> But their faces are as fire against each other ...
> By the golden-growing eastern stream of sea;
>> By the sounds of sunrise moving in the mountains;
>> By the forces of the floods and unsealed fountains;
> Thou that badest man be born, bid man be free.[14]

The prayer goes on to appeal for freedom and social justice, drawing on Swinburne's radical politics. Swinburne may not have been a pagan, exactly; but when one reads verses like these, one starts to realize why he deserves his place in the lineage of the pagan revival. It is no surprise that he was subsequently read by several important pagan revivalists whom we will meet in the next chapter: Aleister Crowley, Dion Fortune and Gerald Gardner.

Swinburne was the best-known paganizing British writer of the Victorian age, but he was not the first. He was preceded by George Meredith (1828–1909), a poet and novelist linked with the Pre-Raphaelite circle who (not coincidentally) lived with Swinburne for a time. Meredith rejected conventional Christianity, and he has often been seen as having pagan leanings: he manifested a characteristically Romantic and pagan concern about mankind's separation from nature. In his 'Ode to the Spirit of the Earth in Autumn' (1862), he wrote of a 'Mother Nature' or 'Mother Earth':

> Oh, mother Nature! teach me, like thee,
> To kiss the season, and shun regrets.
> And am I more than the mother who bore,
> Mock me not with thy harmony!
>     Teach me to blot regrets,
>     Great mother! me inspire
>         With faith that forward sets
>         But feeds the living fire.
>         Faith that never frets
>         For vagueness in the form.
>         In life, O keep me warm!
>         For, what is human grief?
>         And what do men desire?
>     Teach me to feel myself the tree,
>         And not the wither'd leaf.
> Fix'd am I and await the dark to-be!
>         And O, green bounteous Earth!
>     Bacchante Mother! stern to those
>     Who live not in thy heart of mirth;
>     Death shall I shrink from, loving thee?
>     Into the breast that gives the rose,
>         Shall I with shuddering fall?[15]

Something very important is going on in the last two poems that we have quoted, and that is their focus on a Great Goddess associated with the earth. This divine figure came to be of central importance to the modern pagan revival, and Swinburne and Meredith were far from being the only nineteenth-century intellectuals to write about her. The rise to prominence of a Mother Nature figure linked with the earth (and the moon) was a major development in the contemporary artistic and scholarly climate, and one that was already

apparent in Shelley and Keats.[16] In part, the growth of interest in a Great
Goddess is attributable to a Romantic attachment to the divine feminine:
'The Eternal-Feminine / draws us onwards', as Goethe proclaimed in the
words quoted in Chapter 4. But it was also, in part, a genuine recovery of
one aspect of ancient paganism, albeit an atypical one: a belief in a universal
goddess identified with Isis. This belief was transmitted to modern times most
notably through Apuleius' *Golden Ass*, which was read by Keats, Shelley, and
later Aesthetic and Decadent writers.[17] It took firm root among modern pagans.
The worship of a Great Goddess, of whom the individual goddesses of ancient
pantheons may be seen as manifestations, has become a characteristic feature
of revived paganism (notably, but not exclusively, in the Wicca movement).

Alongside the Great Goddess or Mother Nature, pagan-minded Victorians
also had a particular interest in a male god—the ancient Greek deity Pan.
Pan's home was in rural Arcadia in central-southern Greece, and the Greeks
had represented him in part-human, part-goat form. The unruly figure of Pan
appears again and again in the work of nineteenth- and twentieth-century
philo-pagan writers, including Algernon Swinburne.[18] As Somerset Maugham
remarked: 'In a hundred novels his cloven hoof left its imprint on the sward;
poets saw him lurking in the twilight on London commons, and literary ladies
in Surrey and New England, nymphs of an industrial age, mysteriously surren-
dered their virginity to his rough embrace.'[19] By way of example, we may quote
here the arch-Decadent Oscar Wilde, who both chose to adopt the language
of classical paganism and had it pressed on him by his enemies.[20] He wrote the
following lines in his poem 'Pan':

> O Goat-foot God of Arcady!
>     This modern world is grey and old,
> Ah what remains to us of Thee? ...
>
> Then blow some Trumpet loud and free,
>     And give thy oaten pipe away,
> Ah leave the hills of Arcady!
> This modern world hath need of Thee![21]

In summoning Pan from ancient Greece to Victorian London, Wilde was not
doing anything very unusual. Pan was a remarkably popular god. One reason
for this was the fact that he could be depicted in several different ways: as a
pastoral figure from a world of flocks and shepherds; as a transcendent cosmic
deity of everything (*pan* in Greek); and as an untamed source of pan-ic and

terror. He had figured in the pagan experiments of the circle around Shelley in the early nineteenth century, and all the major Romantic poets of that period had written about him. Interestingly, they had been more concerned with Pan as a transcendent god of nature than as a pastoral deity: they were influenced in this regard by Thomas Taylor's translation of the 'Hymn to Pan' in his version of the *Orphic Hymns*. The 'Cult of Pan' which subsequently arose in Victorian and Edwardian times tended to be less focused on mystical transcendence. The best-known expression of the Cult was perhaps Arthur Machen's Decadent horror story *The Great God Pan*, which was illustrated with a frontispiece by the Decadent artist Aubrey Beardsley.[22] This highlights the point that Pan was also a subject for visual artists in this period. The painter Edward Calvert, who appears to have had pagan beliefs, even had an altar to Pan in his garden.[23]

One of the paganizing figures of the age who participated in the Cult of Pan was the Scottish writer Kenneth Grahame (1859–1932)—the prime example of this coming in his children's classic *The Wind in the Willows*.[24] Grahame hated the vulgarity and boredom of modern industrial urban life, as represented in his case by his job as a senior official at the Bank of England in London. We have noted that anti-modernism was the principal mode through which the persisting pagan heritage broke out into revival in Victorian Britain, and so it was perhaps inevitable that a man of that outlook, at that time, would end up embracing a pagan view of the world. Grahame's writings exhibit a sense of the continuing immanence of the old pagan gods amidst the trappings of contemporary civilization. Some of them were collected in 1893 in a book entitled *Pagan Papers*—which, like Machen's *The Great God Pan*, had a frontispiece depicting Pan created by Aubrey Beardsley. At one point in *Pagan Papers*, Grahame writes of the Greek hunter Orion manifesting through an English stockbroker:

> Who could have thought that the Hunter lay hid in him? Yet, after many weeks, they found him in a wild nook of Hampshire. Ragged, sun-burnt, the nocturnal haystack calling aloud from his frayed and weather-stained duds, his trousers tucked, he was tickling trout with godless native urchins; and when they would have won him to himself with honied whispers of American Rails, he answered but with babble of green fields. He is back in his wonted corner now: quite cured, apparently, and tractable. And yet—let the sun shine too wantonly in Throgmorton Street, let an errant zephyr, quick with the warm south, fan but his cheek too wooingly on his way to the station; and will he not once more snap his chain and away? Ay, truly: and next time he will not be caught.[25]

A final figure worth mentioning in the context of late Victorian literary paganism is another Scotsman, William Sharp (1855–1905). Otherwise known by the pen-name Fiona Macleod, Sharp was a writer of the Celtic Revival who was influenced by the Aesthetic and Decadent movements.[26] He was an explicit, self-described pagan. For our purposes, he is particularly noteworthy because he made the one and only attempt of the period to start a regular pagan publication. It has to be said that Sharp's attempt at pagan journalism is mostly significant for demonstrating the limitations of the market for this sort of material: his journal, *The Pagan Review*, lasted for only one issue, dating to August 1892. For Sharp, paganism seems to have connoted a mixture of this-worldliness and individualism, combined with interests in sexuality and women's emancipation. He may have settled on the word 'pagan' as a description for his outlook while staying in Paris and mixing in Decadent circles; and his magazine certainly fits within the Decadent current.[27] The writings which he put into the magazine (he wrote every article in it) drew on both ancient and Indigenous paganisms; but his interest in religious pagan practice seems to have been limited. Nevertheless, the great Irish poet and esotericist W. B. Yeats consulted him when forming his plans for a pagan-influenced mystical order—an intriguing proposition which never came to fruition.[28]

These developments did not go unnoticed by wider society. The transgressive 'paganism' of the Bohemian artist or writer seems to have been a recognized phenomenon in Victorian Britain—a small but significant feature of the shifting cultural and religious landscape. It was significant enough, indeed, to have attracted contemporary criticism. It seems to have become almost a cliché for opponents of this form of paganism to say that it was inauthentic because the Romantic, artistic figures who embraced it had overlooked the essentially conservative nature of actual pagan culture. This is the origin of the 'hermeneutic of concoction' which we referred to in the Introduction. The earliest example of this trope seems to come from 1879, when the *Leamington Spa Courier* criticized paganizing writers of the Aesthetic school for peddling a false representation of the ancient world: 'a spurious, debased, and grotesque idea of what the genius of Athens and Rome was'. A few years later, in 1892, a review of William Sharp's *Pagan Review* suggested that '[r]eal paganism to the modern neo-Pagan would have seemed Tory in politics, bald in art, and unadventurous in morals'. Later in the 1890s, the classical scholar and clergyman Lewis Campbell brought up the theme in his Gifford Lectures. The idea finally received its fullest expression in the early years of the twentieth century in the work of the Christian popular writer G. K. Chesterton.[29] Yet criticism of this sort had little impact on those who promoted Romantic revived paganism. This was perhaps predictable. Figures like Algernon Swinburne and Kenneth Grahame knew enough about the Graeco-Roman classics to realize that Pericles and Julius Caesar had not been Shelleyists; but they were untroubled by this. They were not antiquarians but creative reinterpreters.

We have been focusing on countercultural Romantic paganism as a literary and artistic phenomenon, but it was not confined to those circles. At this point, we may return to the Druid revival. In spite of its monotheistic roots, neo-Druidry produced some figures in this period who can be regarded to some extent as Romantic pagans. One such figure was Myfyr Morganwg (1801–1888), otherwise known as 'the Archdruid'. Morganwg—no relation to the earlier Druid revivalist Iolo Morganwg—was a clockmaker by profession, but he is better known to Welsh history as a writer, poet and musician. His religious outlook combined Druid and Hindu theological ideas; and his conducting of religious ceremonies and veneration of pagan deities led to opposition from Christians of a more conventional persuasion. Nevertheless, he was well enough regarded by his contemporaries to be introduced at the 1883 National Eisteddfod, a Welsh national cultural festival, as 'the Archdruid of Wales'.[30]

The best-known Druid revivalist of the Victorian period is Dr William Price (1800–1893), a physician from Monmouthshire and a very unusual character. Price was a political and social radical, and he extended this radicalism to matters of religion. He claimed to be a Druid by hereditary succession and did not hesitate to dress the part. There seems to have been an element of provocation in his conduct, and at times he faced public anger and ridicule. But there was also a fundamental sincerity, even if his personality quirks—and indeed mental health problems—seem to have prevented him from attracting a lasting community of followers. When his first son died in infancy in 1884, he famously attempted to cremate the body. Cremation has traditionally been taboo among Christians because it has been taken as a rejection of the doctrine of the resurrection of the dead. As a result of this transgressive ceremony, Price was arrested and tried; but he was acquitted after the judge ruled that burning a corpse was not against the law.[31] It should be said that Price, in common with other Druid revivalists, did not break altogether with Christianity: he had declared the unfortunate child to be the Messiah, giving him the Welsh name 'Iesu Grist Price', and he chanted praise to Jesus while burning his body. Nevertheless, the pagan overtones of the cremation are unmistakable. When interviewed shortly afterwards, Myfyr Morganwg acknowledged that Price was a 'very strange man'; but he noted that cremation had been practised in the (pagan) cultures of Homeric Greece and ancient Britain, and argued that it was consistent with the Druidic belief in reincarnation.[32]

Price's cremation of his child was regarded as idiosyncratic and scandalous at the time; but we may briefly make mention of an odd transatlantic precedent. The first person to be cremated in America was reputedly the Baron de Palm, a Bavarian aristocrat and an eccentric supporter of the Theosophical Society. The Theosophical Society was the famous esoteric group which was founded in 1875 and followed the ideas of the Ukrainian mystic Helena Petrovna Blavatsky. It was associated with promoting South Asian forms of spirituality—as seen through the eyes of the colonial West—and its ethos was not so much paganizing as syncretic and universalist ('There is no religion higher than truth', as its slogan went). Nevertheless, when the Baron died in 1876, he received what was described as a 'pagan funeral' in Washington, Pennsylvania. The event included eclectic religious symbolism, black triangular admission tickets and palm twigs to ward off evil spirits.[33]

So much for the radical, counter-cultural brand of Victorian paganism. Alongside the colourful rebelliousness of revivalists who followed the Shelleyist and Druid traditions, the period also saw moves to reanimate the persisting pagan heritage in another, more sober form. Jennifer Hallett has referred to this tendency as 'responsible paganism'. Like the rebellious variety that we have been looking at, it was indebted to Romanticism and a desire to find a spiritually richer alternative to industrial modernity; but it drew on the idealistic strand of Romanticism rather than the transgressive strand. 'Responsible' pagans looked to ancient Greece as a youthful society characterized by beauty, physical health and moral simplicity. Their paganism was free-living, but also clean-living: joyous and innocent. We might make special mention here of two scholars, John Addington Symonds (1840–1893) and G. Lowes Dickinson (1862–1932), along with the mystical socialist and poet Edward Carpenter (1844–1929). None of these men seems to have had specific personal religious commitments; but they looked into their Greek books and decided that they admired the broadly pantheistic worldview that they saw there. Hallett comments that they 'were not robust pagans, but were instead feeling their way towards religious ideas they felt they could accept'.[34]

This enterprise could shade into something like religious prophecy. Edward Carpenter's pen-portrait of the future of humankind was positively purple:

> The meaning of the old religions will come back to him. On the high tops once more gathering he will celebrate with naked dances the glory of the human form and the great processions of the stars, or greet the bright horn of the young moon which now after a hundred centuries comes back laden with such wondrous associations—all

the yearnings and the dreams and the wonderment of the generations of mankind—the worship of Astarte and of Diana, of Isis or
the Virgin Mary; once more in sacred groves will he reunite the
passion and the delight of human love with his deepest feelings
of the sanctity and beauty of Nature; or in the open, standing
uncovered to the Sun, will adore the emblem of the everlasting
splendour which shines within.[35]

Carpenter was also an influential member of an organization that stood in
broadly the same tradition of 'responsible paganism': the Fellowship of the
New Life. Founded in 1883, the Fellowship was a socialist group which drew
inspiration from 'the Pythagorean, the Socratic or Platonic, and the Epicurean
brotherhoods' of the ancient world, although it also had Christian connections.[36] We have here a distinctive iteration of modern paganism which was
both similar to and distinct from the Shelleyist version.

There is one further fact about the three men mentioned above—Symonds,
Dickinson and Carpenter—which is worth drawing attention to. All of them
were gay. Several of the other figures whom we have met in this chapter are
also believed to have been gay or bisexual: Algernon Swinburne, Kenneth
Grahame and Oscar Wilde. It has not escaped the attention of scholars that
paganism was linked with homosexuality in this period.[37] So, interestingly, was
the Catholic variety of Christianity, which we have seen had long been stigmatized as 'pagan' and which was making inroads into the Church of England
thanks to the Anglo-Catholic movement (an important manifestation of the
right wing of Romanticism).[38] This link was in part the result of stereotyping
by hostile outsiders: the highest place in the hierarchy of Victorian society went
to the masculine, muscular Protestant Christian man, while a lower place was
assigned to his effeminate twin who was unhealthily addicted to the pagan
idolatry and rituals of classical antiquity or papal Rome. The effeminacy was
as important in this context as the idolatry: it should be clear by now that
paganism was a term and concept that connoted dissidence from conventional
moral norms as well as from orthodox religiosity. It was also the case, however,
that the link resulted in part from free choices made by gay and bisexual men
to embrace pagan worldviews: such worldviews being associated with classical
cultures which had seemingly not shared the homophobia of nineteenth-century
Britain. Paganism was also linked with lesbianism in this period, although
less closely: it has been argued that Katharine Bradley and Edith Cooper, the
same-sex couple who wrote poetry under the name Michael Field, 'managed
to rationalise their desires ... with the help of pagan ritual'.[39]

We now move on to the final subculture of Victorian society that we will
be looking at in this chapter, one which was distinct both from rebellious
Shelleyists and from responsible socialists. We are back in the world of Éliphas
Lévi: the world of esoteric paganism, a realm of mysticism, clairvoyance and
magic. The latter part of the nineteenth century saw a definite increase of
interest in the occult. This interest could manifest itself in different styles of
engagement with the subject, styles which we might loosely and metaphorically
term 'Protestant' and 'Catholic'. In the Protestant camp was, most notably,
the democratic mass movement of Spiritualism, which in many ways could
be regarded as an exoteric rather than an esoteric current.[40] By contrast, the
'Catholic' wing of occultism—hieratic and ritualistic—consisted of private
societies and lodges in which lawyers, engineers and minor clergymen sought to
unravel the secrets of the universe. Lévi was a key influence on this movement,
although he died a little too early, in 1875, to fully participate in it. The occult
revival had no particular religious allegiance—and some of its manifestations
were explicitly Christian—but parts of it were heavily indebted to ancient
pagan ideas and symbols. It is here that we start to find the first examples of
what look like attempts to revive paganism as a system of cultic practice.

The best-known and most influential private group of the occult revival was
the organization known as the Hermetic Order of the Golden Dawn. This was
founded in London in 1888 by William Wynn Westcott and William Robert
Woodman, who were both doctors, and Samuel Liddell MacGregor Mathers,
who was Westcott's protégé and a kind of professional eccentric. It was no
accident that all three men were high-grade members of that older 'Catholic'
esoteric movement, Freemasonry. The Golden Dawn was the first modern
British magical order to get anywhere. It followed a Masonic model in which
the member passed through a succession of grades and rituals on their path to
spiritual enlightenment. The order broke up in confusion from around 1900,
and its successor groups were mostly moribund by the outbreak of World
War Two. Nevertheless, it had a profound influence on the development of
modern esotericism and paganism. As its full name suggests, the Golden Dawn
was a Hermetic organization: its claimed doctrinal ancestry went back to the
Hermetic movement of pagan Graeco-Egyptian antiquity. It was also professedly
a Rosicrucian organization, and its founders had been members of an English
Rosicrucian group by the name of the Societas Rosicruciana in Anglia (SRIA).

The origin story of the Golden Dawn is well known to scholars of occultism.
By 1887, Dr Westcott had come into possession of some papers written in a
cipher derived from the *Polygraphiae* (1561) of the German churchman and
esotericist Johannes Trithemius. Different variants of the story recount that the

document was found in different locations in Victorian London: according to the most Romantic version, it was found in an anonymous bookshop on Farringdon Road. Within the pages of the manuscript was a paper on which was written the address of a German Rosicrucian by the name of 'Fräulein Sprengel' (her full name was later said to be 'Anna Sprengel'). Sprengel was a fictional character, but Westcott nevertheless managed to enter into an exchange of letters with her in which she authorized him to found a Rosicrucian group in England. These letters were almost certainly forged by or at the behest of Westcott.[41]

The origin of Westcott's cipher manuscript has never been conclusively established. Internal evidence shows that it cannot have been written long before Westcott is said to have found it, and it has plausibly been suggested that it was originally composed by a recently deceased occultist by the name of Kenneth Mackenzie for a forerunner group of the Golden Dawn known as the 'Society of Eight'.[42] In any event, it contained only an outline of ritual and doctrine. It was fleshed out considerably by the Golden Dawn founders, and in particular by the idiosyncratic Samuel Mathers. Mathers' methodology was essentially to go to the British Museum's Reading Room and read as much of the institution's stock of esoteric literature as he could get his hands on.

The result of Mathers' eclectic reading was that the Golden Dawn's rites brought together a mixture of material drawn from sources including Rosicrucianism, Kabbalah, Indian religion, Freemasonry, Christian magic, and the ancient pagan systems of Greece, Egypt and Mesopotamia. How much Mathers and his fellow magicians knew about the ultimate provenance of these materials is not always certain: in at least some cases, they were mediated through more recent sources, including Éliphas Lévi.[43] In any event, the result was a complex and rather confusing system. One of the best-known initiates of the Golden Dawn was the writer Arthur Machen, whom we have already met in connection with his novel *The Great God Pan*. Machen later criticized what he saw as the incoherence at the heart of the order (which he called the 'Twilight Star'):

> Any critical mind, with a tinge of occult reading, should easily have concluded that here was no ancient order ... For ancient rituals, whether orthodox or heterodox, are founded on one *mythos* and on one *mythos* only. They are grouped about some fact, actual or symbolic, as the ritual of Freemasonry is said to have as its centre certain events connected with the building of King Solomon's Temple, and they keep within their limits. But the Twilight Star embraced all mythologies and all mysteries of all races and all ages, and 'referred' or 'attributed' them to each other and proved that

they all came to much the same thing; and that was enough! That
was not the ancient frame of mind; it was not even the 1809 frame
of mind. But it was very much the eighteen-eighty and later frame
of mind.[44]

In fact, as is evident from what was said in Chapter 4, Machen underesti-
mated how old interest in comparative religion and mythography was. But he
was not wrong about the 1880s. These subjects formed an especially important
part of the intellectual climate of the years in which the Golden Dawn was
created and began to function. At the time when the order came into existence,
the great comparative scholar of language and mythology F. Max Müller
was about to begin his influential Gifford Lectures (1888–92); and the first
edition of James Frazer's anthropological classic *The Golden Bough* (1890) was
shortly to appear.[45] The Golden Dawn cannot properly be understood outside
this context. Another important part of the context from which the order
sprang was—yet again—the aesthetic and moral atmosphere of Romanticism.
The Golden Dawn was identifiably a product of the era of Mahler, Baudelaire
and Gauguin: and, of course, the pagan and pagan-adjacent writers and artists
whom we have met in this chapter, including Machen himself. We ought to
evaluate Samuel Mathers' texts and rituals not as a monument of scholarship
but as a work of late Romantic performance art.

The significance of the Golden Dawn for our purposes is that it was the
first successful attempt at creating something like a modern pagan religion
in the sense of a fully developed system of ritual, symbolism and belief. The
qualification 'something like' is necessary because the Golden Dawn both was
and was not a pagan order: there was always an ambiguity to it. This was made
clear enough to new initiates. The Golden Dawn's pledge form stated:

> Belief in a Supreme Being, or Beings, is indispensable. In addition,
> the Candidate, if not a Christian, should be at least prepared to take
> an interest in Christian symbolism.[46]

As a Rosicrucian body, the Golden Dawn drew explicitly on the Christian
tradition. Yet its rites also made explicit reference to pre-Christian pagan
deities such as Isis, Osiris and Horus; and they employed cross symbolism and
the concepts of death and resurrection in a way that elided Osiris with Jesus
Christ.[47] The order's theology also included a quasi-monotheistic conception
of the goddess Isis which was influenced by Apuleius; and, outside the realm
of formal rituals, two initiates of the order claimed to have received a vision of

a figure who identified herself as 'the mighty Mother Isis' and spoke to them about Jesus.[48]

We should guard against the temptation to resolve the ambiguities here and to place the Golden Dawn and related esoteric orders into 'Christian' and 'pagan' categories. For example, some writers have tried to frame A. E. Waite's Fellowship of the Rosy Cross, a Golden Dawn successor order, as Christian, in contrast to the occultic, pagan Golden Dawn.[49] Such distinctions, however, seem tendentious; an attempt to impose categories on the source material which it does not comfortably fit.[50] It is important to note that the ambiguity of the Golden Dawn—the mixing of Osiris with Christ and the Kabbalah—was not gratuitous. Egil Asprem has noted that the order's style of esoteric eclecticism was characterized by a 'search for a universal, *perennial* truth underlying the particular phenomena'.[51] This process involved a quest for a fundamental nucleus of truth or *sophia perennis* which discerned in the diversity of the world's religious and spiritual systems a deeper unity. The adepts of the Golden Dawn—like Éliphas Lévi and Madame Blavatsky's Theosophists—sincerely believed in a common denominator of spirituality which applied across different cultures. In addition, the inconclusive nature of the order's doctrine and symbolism served a practical purpose. The constituencies from which the order recruited ranged from Anglican clergymen to the likes of Aleister Crowley (whom we will meet in the next chapter). Its not-quite-pagan, not-quite-Christian character meant that it could attract radical experimenters without frightening away more conventionally minded recruits.

The pagan experiments of the Golden Dawn milieu survived the break-up of the order. Around the turn of the twentieth century, while living in Paris, Samuel Mathers and his wife Moina attempted to practise the worship of Isis both publicly and privately, seemingly in conjunction with the French esoteric writer and journalist Jules Bois. Their endeavours included dramatic rites in the Théâtre La Bodinière.[52] Mathers' theology at this time was that 'each force of the universe is regulated by a god. Gods are, therefore, innumerable and infinite'.[53] This is oddly reminiscent of John Fransham, although there is no reason to believe that Mathers knew of Fransham's ideas.

What of forms of modern paganism elsewhere in Europe? We have noted that paganism was a significant influence on French literature in the mid-nineteenth century. To some extent, this continued into later years. In 1870, the 15-year-old Arthur Rimbaud could write the following lines in his poem 'Sun and Flesh':

>            – O Venus, O Goddess!
> I mourn for the times of ancient youth,
> of lusting satyrs, of animal fauns—
> lovestruck gods who bit the bark of the tree-boughs,
> and kissed the blonde nymph amidst the water-lilies!
> I mourn for the times when the sap of the world,
> the water of the river, the pink blood of the green trees
> filled the veins of Pan with a whole universe! …
>
> I mourn for the times of great Cybele,
> gigantically lovely, who used to ride, so they said,
> in a great bronze chariot through the wonderous cities;
> through the great vastnesses, her two breasts poured out
> the pure stream of endless life,
> and man sucked in happiness at her blessed nipple,
> like a small child, playing on her knees[54]

This should all seem quite familiar by now: a piece of creative writing that laments the demise of the (sexualized) world of classical paganism and reveres a Great Goddess figure. Rimbaud originally wrote it as a creed for poets under the title 'Credo in unam', a feminized version of the opening of the Christian creed, 'Credo in unum Deum', 'I believe in one [male] God'. It is unsurprising that Rimbaud was a writer in the Symbolist current, which was related to the British tendencies of Aestheticism and Decadence.

Nevertheless, it appears that Shelleyist literary paganism was not a major force in France in the later nineteenth century. Jules Bois investigated the subject in the 1890s; he interviewed the writer Louis Ménard, who said that he thought that he might be the last pagan in existence. As with the British literary pagans, Ménard's paganism did not involve cult acts: he seems to have regarded the classical gods as personifications of the natural world, Artemis being the moon, Apollo the sun, and so on. Bois also interviewed another contemporary writer, Gilbert Augustin-Thierry, who revered the goddess Isis. Among other manifestations of French paganism, Bois mentioned having encountered a group of young men wearing panther skins who were set on worshipping the nymphs in the Bois de Boulogne; and he suggested that the radical politician Louis Pauliat venerated an image of Athena.[55] Religious expressions of paganism in France in this period were relatively unusual, however, not least because, as Ronald Hutton has commented, 'French radicals were at once more anticlerical than their English equivalents and much less enamoured of the countryside'.[56]

When French people of this period were looking for religiously heterodox resources to furnish an alternative to Catholicism and rationalism, they tended to find them in the worlds of non-pagan occultism, blasphemy and Satanism.

Meanwhile, to the south in Italy, evidence came to light attesting that a whole ancient pagan religion had survived into the modern age among peasants in rural Tuscany. The evidence in question was published by an American folklorist, Charles Godfrey Leland, in his 1899 book *Aradia or the Gospel of the Witches*.[57] *Aradia* was a short book which made some big claims. It contained the supposed *Vangelo* or Gospel of a surviving religion of witches, together with other Italian folkloric material. The *Vangelo* told of a messianic figure called Aradia, who was the daughter of the goddess Diana and her brother Lucifer. Its ethics were sexually radical and politically subversive: it supported the killing of feudal lords who treated the common people like slaves. If one took *Aradia* at face value, the conclusion was that Leland had discovered an authentic grassroots version of the sort of religion that the likes of Shelley and Swinburne had tried to recreate from their classical schooling. It would be a genuine pagan survival, not merely an example of paganism persisting into revivalism.

The theory that ancient paganism had survived into the Christian era in the form of what was labelled witchcraft was not a new one. In origin it went back to the 1820s, when a German jurist, Karl Ernst Jarcke, had concluded that witchcraft was 'originally a tradition from pagan Germanic times, a pagan nature-philosophy and nature-religion which lived on among the people, and which had its own ... ceremonies and sacraments'.[58] Jarcke believed that over time this pagan religion had degenerated into devil-worship. The idea of witchcraft as surviving paganism was taken up by other writers, notably Jules Michelet, who published a more sympathetic version of it in *La Sorcière* (1862). By the time that Leland was writing in the 1890s, it was far from being a novel proposition.

Seen in that context, the *Vangelo* seemed to confirm a contemporary theory quite neatly—too neatly, perhaps. Where did the text come from? Leland's version of events was that he had received it in 1897 from an Italian informant called Maddalena. This is very probably correct. We know that Maddalena was a real person; and it is noteworthy that Leland did not make his own revisions to the *Vangelo* before it was published as he did with other material. Maddalena herself seems to have obtained the text, at least in part, from an Italian contact or contacts: the contents of the *Vangelo* show signs of having been transcribed from an oral source.[59]

We can, however, be quite sure that the *Vangelo* is not what it claims to be, namely the sacred text of a surviving revolutionary pagan witch religion.

In the years since it was published, nothing else like it has been found in any part of Italy. It probably incorporates genuine popular traditions; but it seems to owe something to Maddalena too. As to its contents, Aradia was a genuine figure from Italian and other European folklore. From the Middle Ages onwards, we find stories of a female divinity who goes on travels during the night accompanied by a retinue of spirits and human souls (we alluded to this idea in Chapter 2 in connection with Heinrich Institoris). This super-natural female figure was called by a number of names, and these included Diana and Herodias (Aradia). The church condemned these beliefs but did not regard them as a manifestation of a pagan religion; and it is likewise difficult for a modern scholar to show that they amounted to a survival of ancient paganism.[60] They came to be incorporated into the theories of early modern witch-hunters, and this appears to be the origin of the material in the *Vangelo*. The *Vangelo* is therefore not the scripture of a surviving nineteenth-century sect of witches, but rather something quite different: 'a fantasy [of witchcraft] developed by northern Italian witch-hunters in the early sixteenth century, with the sympathies reversed to favour its practitioners'.[61]

Further afield, folklore collectors motivated by Romantic nationalism eagerly sought evidence of pre-Christian religion still present in folktales and folksongs. The Latvian *dainas* (traditional song cycles) are particularly well known in this regard, and the idea that the *dainas* contained information about pre-Christian Latvian religion can be traced to the Lutheran pastor Gotthard Friedrich Stender (1714–1796), the author of a grammar of the Latvian language. Whether or not Stender was right to interpret the *dainas* in this way, one recorder of Baltic folklore, Theodor Narbutt (1784–1864) went further and openly invented new mythology and new deities for Lithuania, such as the 'goddess of love' Milda and the sea-nymph Jūratė. Narbutt's invented folktales were not forgeries, however; nor were they presented as fiction. Rather, Narbutt believed that it was a patriot's duty to channel 'the soul of the nation' to make up what was lacking in the national mythology—rather as J. R. R. Tolkien set out in the twentieth century to supply an imagined mythology for England.[62]

Lithuania, however, was better off than some of the new nations awakening their national consciousnesses in East Central Europe, since it had previously existed as a polity with a literary tradition (albeit in Latin and Polish) for hundreds of years. Mythographers in Latvia and Estonia acted even more boldly than Narbutt and stitched together fragments of folklore into new vernacular epics, in the belief that every nation ought to have a national epic. Friedrich Reinhold Kreutzwald completed the Estonian national epic, about the giant Kalev (the *Kalevipoeg*) in 1853, while in Latvia Andrejs Pumpurs's epic of the bear-slaying warrior *Lāčplēsis* was published in 1888.[63] While none of this nation-building activity through literature represented a pagan revival in and of itself, figures like Narbutt and Pumpurs laid the conceptual groundwork for later pagan revivals which will be examined in Chapter 6. After all, if it is possible to revive (or reinvent) an entire national mythology, it is a fairly short step from that to reinventing a national religion.

It is clear that sympathetic commitment to paganism was a growing reality in nineteenth-century Europe, and in Britain in particular. A growing number of people who were looking for an alternative to the moral oppressiveness of Christianity and the spiritual deadness of secular modernity were coming to find it in the persisting patrimony of ancient pagan traditions, which they duly set to work reanimating. Some of these people composed poems and other works of art in which they sought to restore the vitality of ancient religion, while others performed rituals in which they invoked pagan gods. Some perceived themselves as having an affinity with Greeks or Druids, while others sought to blend paganism with Christian faith in a deliberately ambiguous mixture. In any event, a pagan revival was proceeding with increasing strength and confidence. For the first time in centuries, paganism had come close to reaching the point of being reinvented as a mass movement—but it was not quite there yet. That development was to take place in the twentieth century.

# CHAPTER SIX

# The Emergence of Modern Paganism

In the last years of peace before the Great War came crashing through everything, dissatisfied refugees from modernity continued to experiment with pagan ideas and images which had persisted from the ancient past. As in the Victorian period, Britain had a central place in these developments. In many ways, they amounted to an extension of the trends that we have already seen: in particular, the Romantic literary form of paganism that came ultimately from Percy Shelley's circle and ended up finding a place in the works of figures like Algernon Swinburne and Arthur Machen. This version of modern paganism had reached its zenith between the 1870s and the 1890s—the high days of the Aesthetic and Decadent movements—but it continued to be a cultural presence in the early years of the new century. As we turn to look at pagan revivalism in the Edwardian period, the first people who present themselves to view are the poet Rupert Brooke and his circle of friends—one of whom, Virginia Woolf, famously referred to the group as 'the neo-pagans'.[1] This term was not unjustified.

Brooke is mostly remembered today as a handsome young chap—'A young Apollo, golden-haired'[2]—who wrote the jingoistic poem 'The Soldier' (1914) and died of disease at the age of 27 on his way to certain death at Gallipoli. But he was a more interesting character than his popular reputation would suggest. Born in 1887, he imbibed influences from the Decadents while still at school, and he shared their struggles with conventional sexuality. He was no stranger to classical pagan imagery; and he and his friends 'talked ... of the urgency of some kind of ritual, mystery, initiation, symbolism and ... planned a great litany of the four elements'.[3] This is a fascinating glimpse of a potential experiment in modern paganism—but it was an experiment that faltered. One of Brooke's biographers has suggested that the group evolved 'towards a mystical nature cult';[4] but it seems that they never quite got there. Nevertheless, Brooke's pagan sympathies can be discerned in his poetry. His well-known piece 'The Old Vicarage, Grantchester' (1912) is generally remembered for its mawkish final line about honey for tea, but there is more to it than that. It depicts pre-war Cambridge as a landscape inhabited by pagan Greek divinities:

> would I were
> In Grantchester, in Grantchester!—
> Some, it may be, can get in touch
> With Nature there, or Earth, or such.
> And clever modern men have seen
> A Faun a-peeping through the green,
> And felt the Classics were not dead,
> To glimpse a Naiad's reedy head,
> Or hear the Goat-foot piping low[5]

The previous year, Brooke's correspondence reveals that he had become involved in paganesque activities in Germany. On 1 March 1911, he wrote to his mother from Munich:

> I went to the 'Bacchus-Fest' in Greek dress. That was a very beautiful business, because all the dresses harmonized in kind, and all were good. People look so much better in Greek than in modern dress! There were a few English there and I talked broken German to German young ladies. I strolled home in my incongruous dress … a little before seven in the morning … The ball hadn't ended, however! It went on to about 8.30![6]

It is amusing to compare this to the more revealing account that he told to another member of the 'neo-pagans', the painter Jacques Raverat:

> I took off my clothes and went to a Bacchus-Fest, where all was roses and the apparel second century A.D. The young lay round in couples, huggin' and kissin' … I found a round damp young sculptress … We curled passionate limbs round each other in a perfunctory manner and lay in a corner … I felt that I wasn't really quite the perfect Greek—that, you know, one wants, if one's Grown-Up, something more than the undraped half of the damp outer expanses of no-one-in-particular, kissing isn't enough, one wants to kiss $X$ or $Y$ … I suddenly realized of her—and she of me—that she was in exactly the same state, that she, too, was trying Greece, was quite a conscious, sensible intellectual, real, modern person.[7]

This was evidently not a pagan observance in the religious sense. But the mixture of themes on show here—the Bacchic terminology, the dramaturgy of 'trying Greece', the young adult sexuality—sits more or less within the tradition of Romantic paganism. We will come back to Germany shortly.

Other examples of paganism among Brooke's contemporaries are not difficult to find. The writer Edward Thomas, who rated himself as nine-tenths pagan, wanted to see a statue of Demeter in the English countryside and regarded reciting passages of Shelley in the forest as a religious experience.[8] The well-known novelist H. Rider Haggard combined Christian with pagan sympathies, and wrote in his autobiography: 'I have a respect for Thor and Odin, I venerate Isis, and always feel inclined to bow to the moon!'[9] The poet Eleanor Farjeon wrote of an episode from 1912–13 in which she slept out in the open in Berkshire with the suffragette Olive Hockin. The next morning, while bathing in a lake, the two women found 'a flat stone ... like a little altar' on which was placed a 'crown of wild parsley'. Hockin immediately knew what it was: 'Godwin', she said, 'has been sacrificing to the deity'—referring to their friend Helton Godwin Baynes, a doctor and future Jungian psychologist. There followed an encounter with a pack of hunting hounds, which led Farjeon to imagine that she had taken part in the Greek myth of Artemis and Actaeon.[10] Farjeon was not new to such paganizing sentiments. Several years previously she had published some pagan verse in *Pan-Worship and Other Poems* (1908).

Experiments with paganism in this period were not confined to Shelleyist writers and poets. Paganism began to reach something like a mass audience by another route: a route which was largely distinct from the phenomenon of pagan persistence which forms the subject of this book. What we have here is not primarily a revival of paganism as a result of enduring cultural themes which have persistently tempted people to reanimate ancient European beliefs and practices; but rather an effort to transplant living Indigenous religious traditions into majority-white Euro-American culture. Whether these endeavours should be regarded as imperialist attempts at cultural appropri-ation, or as attempts to challenge imperialist assumptions by upholding the value of Native traditions, remains a matter of debate.

What we are dealing with here is the woodcraft movement: the early twentieth-century movement for the formation of children (particularly boys) through practical experience of outdoor life.[11] Woodcraft was founded in America in 1902 by the British-Canadian naturalist Ernest Thompson Seton, and it came to Britain in 1907 when Robert Baden-Powell founded the Boy Scouts. The Scouts may be described as broadly Christian, or at least monothe-istic, but other woodcraft organizations were more spiritually adventurous.

As we have intimated, the movement took inspiration from the beliefs and practices of non-European Indigenous peoples (or colonial perceptions of them): Seton's original organization, the Woodcraft Indians, drew on his ideas about Native American cultures.

On the other side of the Atlantic, the Order of Woodcraft Chivalry was formed in 1916 by a breakaway from the Scouts under the leadership of a lapsed Quaker by the name of Ernest Westlake (Seton was made honorary 'Grand Chieftain'). Interestingly, elements of ancient European paganism managed to find their way into the Order. Westlake was influenced by Edward Carpenter and revered a holy trinity of Pan, Artemis and Dionysus along with Aphrodite.[12] Another leading member of the Order, Harry Byngham, was a more robust pagan. He was influenced not only by Carpenter and John Addington Symonds but also by theories about phallus-worship and the ideas of Aleister Crowley. His veneration for Dionysus ran so deep that he changed his name to 'Dion'. In 1928, some members of the Order held a 'dionysian' camp in the New Forest which involved 'ritual games' of some sort.[13]

Woodcraft was not confined to children. At least one group, the Kindred of the Kibbo Kift, admitted members of all ages. Led by John Hargarve, a difficult man with some unpleasant views, the Kibbo Kift was perhaps the most exotic woodcraft group of all. Like Westlake and Byngham, Hargrave was influenced by Edward Carpenter, and he seems to have been a kind of pantheist or panentheist, viewing the individual as part of divinity. The religious side of the Kibbo Kift was somewhat eclectic, including not only Native American culture but also ancient Egyptian paganism, Freemasonry and (again) Aleister Crowley. The organization included an exclusive inner order, the 'Ndembo', which drew on the Golden Dawn and Hargrave's interpretation of Congolese religion.[14]

In hindsight, from the point of view of the pagan revival, the rise of the woodcraft movement looks like a missed opportunity. Here was a chance for ideas and practices deriving from Indigenous traditions which were 'pagan' in the broad sense, and to a certain extent from persisting ancient pagan traditions, to break through to a mass audience. The conservative Scouts, who came to dominate the movement, were largely not disposed to go down this path. But could not other woodcraft organizations have taken up the challenge? Probably not, it has to be said. Their constituency was fundamentally too Christian to allow religiously adventurous ideas to make much headway. Controversy resulted when people were taken out of their comfort zone: to one critic, for instance, the Order of Woodcraft Chivalry was the 'Order of Witchcraft Devilry'.[15] Christian sympathies lingered on not only among woodcraft members and their parents but also among leaders, including notably Ernest

Westlake. In the final analysis, moreover, woodcraft religion was arguably characterized not so much by anything akin to a committed paganism as by a deliberately vague universalism: an attempt to elide the painful religious distinctions between colonizers and colonized through formulations such as 'the Great Spirit'.

We now move on to the most famous twentieth-century pagan of them all: Edward Alexander Crowley (1875–1947), better known by his adopted name of Aleister Crowley. Crowley tends to be remembered in the popular imagination today as an exceptional figure, an addict of drugs, sex and devil-worship— 'the wickedest man in the world', as the popular press dubbed him. But in fact there was less to Crowley than meets the eye. He was a man of his time: a recognizable product of the cultural currents that we examined in the previous chapter. After rejecting a fundamentalist Christian upbringing, he began his career as an aspiring Decadent poet, with the lifestyle to match; he admired Apuleius and Swinburne; he passed through the Golden Dawn; and he thought that he was a reincarnation of Éliphas Lévi.[16] In his 'autohagiography', which was published in 1929, there is a well-known passage in which he speaks of his claimed memories of past lives:

> Shortly before the time of Mohammed, I was present at a Council of Masters. The critical question was the policy to be adopted in order to help humanity … My own task was to bring oriental wisdom to Europe and to restore paganism in a purer form.[17]

The supposedly purified form of paganism which Crowley restored was his religion of Thelema, the foundational text of which, *The Book of the Law*, was written in 1904 and published in 1909. The book begins with the following striking lines:

> Had! The manifestation of Nuit.
> The unveiling of the company of heaven.
> Every man and every woman is a star.
> Every number is infinite; there is no difference

Crowley liked to play with religious symbolism from Christianity (notably the Great Beast and the Whore of Babylon from the Book of Revelation); but his religious system can reasonably be described as pagan. It certainly drew on ancient pagan traditions: in particular, the religion of pharaonic Egypt, from which the deities of Had and Nuit mentioned above were drawn.[18] Crowley's ideas in this regard were creative and outran Egyptological scholarship. (A popular guide to Egyptian religion states: 'Notions on Egyptian deities in anything written by Aleister Crowley can be totally disregarded.')[19] The fact is that Crowley fetishized Egypt in a similar way to the Golden Dawn and previous generations of occultists;[20] indeed, as we saw in Chapter 1, the link between Egypt and occult wisdom is as old as the Western esoteric tradition itself. The god Pan also featured in Crowley's religious vision: his best-known poetic work is probably his 'Hymn to Pan', which ended up being read at his funeral.[21] All of this points to the essentially pagan nature of his outlook. Similarly, Crowley's transgressive ethics were shocking to mainstream opinion, but they were entirely consistent with the counter-cultural aspect of Shelleyist Romantic paganism. Crowley *could* have served as the founding figure of an Edwardian mass pagan movement. His personality and reputation, however, did not equip him to be an effective salesman for his product. Crowley is a fairly familiar figure in pop culture today—most educated people have heard of the man, his lifestyle and his religious deviance—and Thelema continues to exist as a significant religious movement. But the modest success that Crowley's ideas continue to experience is largely the result of a later revival of interest which began in the 1960s, a generation after the man himself went to meet his gods.

The catastrophe of World War One did not halt the course of the pagan revival, and the interwar years saw further efforts at recreating pagan religion. Crowley's sulphurous career continued on its course: it was in this period that he attempted to found a Thelemic commune in Sicily, an endeavour which ended up with him being deported by Mussolini's government. Another significant contemporary figure was a friend of Crowley's, the psychotherapist and mystic Dion Fortune (born Violet Mary Firth).[22] Fortune was the author of a series of magically themed books, both fiction and non-fiction: the former included her esoteric masterpiece *The Mystical Qabalah*, while among her novels *The Sea Priestess* and the posthumous *Moon Magic* are especially significant. Fortune's books are still read by pagans today, although the group that she founded, the Fraternity of the Inner Light, is an explicitly Christian organization. It has been said that Fortune's 'magic became more or less Christian according to the phases of her life and seems to have ended up as a hybrid of religions'.[23] For our purposes, it is noteworthy that she went through something of a pagan period in the latter part of the 1930s. Consistently with what we have seen of other modern pagan revivalists, she had a particular interest in the deities Pan and

Isis.[24] During her pagan period, she celebrated a Rite of Isis, and perhaps a Rite of Pan, in a converted church in Belgravia, London.[25]

Most significantly, it is in the interwar period that we find the first evidence of people attempting to recreate witchcraft as a revived pagan religion. The midwife of the modern pagan witch movement was Dr Margaret Murray. Murray was an Egyptologist at London University, but her lasting contribution to the history of ideas lay some distance outside the field of Egyptological research. In 1921, she published *The Witch-Cult in Western Europe*, a curious book in which she argued that the records of early modern witch trials bore witness to the existence of a living pagan religion which had survived the apparent triumph of Christianity.[26] Academics were mixed in their reactions to the book, but it was appreciated by lay readers, including those with unusual religious interests.[27] The publication of *The Witch-Cult* set in motion a train of events that eventually led to the breakthrough of modern paganism into popular culture in the form of the pagan witch religion Wicca.

As we saw in the last chapter, the idea that early modern witchcraft was a survival of ancient pagan religion was not a new one. Charles Leland's *Aradia* had appeared in the relatively recent past, with its claim that a pagan witch sect still survived in modern Italy. There is no evidence that Murray had read *Aradia*, but she may have come across the theory of witchcraft as a pagan survival through the folklorist Sir George Laurence Gomme or the mathematician Karl Pearson, who was one of her colleagues at University College London.[28] In any event, Murray played a key role in popularizing the idea that witches were pagan rebels among English-speaking readers. Following *The Witch-Cult*, she published a further book on the same theme, *The God of the Witches*,[29] as well as an influential article for the *Encyclopaedia Britannica*. As the years passed, Murray's views became increasingly eccentric. By 1950, she was claiming that 'many' murders in modern Britain were human sacrifices carried out by witches.[30] In her last book on the subject in 1954, she attempted to apply her theory to argue that mediaeval figures such as Edward II and Thomas Becket had likewise been killed as witch sacrifices.[31]

It has long been suspected that some readers drew on Murray's work to recreate their own witch covens.[32] There is some doubt, however, as to when this would first have happened. The earliest clear evidence of a revived witch ceremony influenced by Murray comes from a group of Oxford students in early 1929, although the ceremony was not explicitly pagan.[33] The main other candidate for an early Murrayite coven is the so-called New Forest Coven which appears to have influenced Gerald Gardner in the creation of Wicca. Gardner claimed that, while living in retirement in Highcliffe on the south coast of England in the late 1930s, he stumbled on a coven of witches through an esoteric society called the Rosicrucian Order Crotona Fellowship. Gardner's biographer Philip Heselton accepts the story of this coven as basically correct and has attempted to track down the other members of it. These seem to have included a local resident by the name of Katherine Oldmeadow, who wrote a series of children's books and a book on herbalism. Her writings included suggestive references to subjects such as pagan deities, divination, numerology, initiatory societies and witchcraft; she even claimed that 'white witch[es]' still exist. Her attitude towards witches seems to have become much more favourable around 1925–26. This could mean that she and her associates became involved in Murrayite activities at around this time.[34] Equally, it could mean nothing of the sort.

A few other contemporary candidates for practising a revived witch religion in this period can be touched on more briefly. Alexander Keiller, a businessman and archaeologist, had an interest in witchcraft, although he was not an adherent of Murray's theories. His secretary reported that, on Hallowe'en during the 1930s, he carried out a pagan ritual in the garden of the manor house at Avebury, a well-known prehistoric sacred site: 'He carried before him a phallic symbol, and bowing three times before the Statue of Pan, he chanted "witchlike" incantations.'[35] There are also claims that the Wiccan activist Gavin Frost (1930–2016) was involved with a coven which was connected with a Murrayite group that had been active at Cambridge University in the 1930s.[36] This group was supposedly called the 'Pentangle Society', the 'Pentangle Club' or the 'Pentacle Club'. A Pentacle Club does exist at Cambridge: it is a society for stage magicians. Whether some of its members in the interwar period dabbled in esoteric activities remains to be proven. Finally, there is evidence that a Murrayite witch coven was in existence in East Anglia by at least 1953; the members worshipped a god and a goddess, and they observed the four 'great sabbats' that Murray had written about.[37]

Staying for the moment in Britain, the remaining evidence of modern paganism before World War Two is somewhat scanty. In 1934, there appeared a curious book entitled *Strange Cults and Secret Societies of Modern London*. The author was Elliott O'Donnell, a prolific writer who had an interest in super-natural subjects. O'Donnell reported that there existed in London a movement of tree worshippers, some of whom were consciously 'attempting to revive the Cult of Tree Worship as it is alleged to have been practised by the ancient Romans, Greeks and Druids'; although the movement also allegedly had Asian origins.[38] In addition, he told his readers about the Gorgons, 'a secret society of women, who love open-air life and cocktails but have no liking for men'. They were led by a high priestess known by the name of the Greek mythological character Medusa, and they engaged in nature-worship: 'The sun, the moon, the stars, river, woods and pools, all are deified objects.'[39] If O'Donnell is to be believed, we have here further contemporary evidence of groups which embraced pagan ideas and practices. But O'Donnell was not necessarily an honest man, and *Strange Cults* does not come across as a reliable book. It has unattractive elements of sensationalism and racism—not to mention sexism, in the case of the Gorgons—and it is impossible to say how much of its contents are true.

The eve of World War Two saw the foundation of a much better-documented pagan religious body: the Church of Aphrodite.[40] The Church was established in the USA by one Gleb Botkin, a Russian émigré whose father had been court physician to the Tsar. Botkin was a former novice monk who had become disillusioned with both monarchism and Orthodox Christianity. He legally incorporated the Church in New York in 1939: the judge who dealt with the application apparently commented sardonically that it was better than Mary Baker Eddy's Christian Science sect.

In spite of its name, there is room to question how far the Church of Aphrodite was really pagan. The religious system that Botkin promoted was explicitly monotheistic—as well as creedal and hierarchical—and his goddess-based theology was related only relatively loosely to the Hellenic figure of Aphrodite. Botkin's organization would no doubt have looked more familiar to a modern Russian Orthodox cleric than to an ancient Greek priest of the goddess. Nevertheless, the Church may be seen as drawing on the tradition of Romantic modern pagan belief in a Great Goddess; Botkin preached a universal female divinity whom he identified with 'the Star of Love of the ancient Semites, the Astarte of the Phoenicians, the Eastre of the Anglo-Saxons, the Aphrodite of the Greeks, the Kwanon of the Japanese'. One of the prayers that he composed gives an idea of his spiritual outlook:

> For the light and warmth of our sun, for the radiance of our moon, for the brilliance of our stars, we thank Thee, O Aphrodite. For the loveliness of our sky, for the sweetness of our air, for the magnificence of our seas, we thank Thee, O Aphrodite. For the fertility of our valleys, for the grandeur of our mountains, for the beauty of our forests, we thank Thee, O Aphrodite.
>
> For, Thou art the Universal Cause, and everything that breathes in Heaven, on earth and in the deep of the sea, is Thy Creation.[41]

This is entirely typical of the Goddess-worshipping strand of modern paganism. Interestingly, there is reason to believe that Botkin's religious vision, while distinctively personal in some ways, was a product of its time and environment. It has been claimed that '[b]y the end of the 1930s several neo-Pagan groups attempting to recreate Hellenic Paganism had come to dominate the New York spiritualist and occult scene'.[42] Botkin's endeavour appears to have been the most successful of these: the Church of Aphrodite seems to have attracted dozens if not hundreds of adherents. It faded away only after his death in 1969, by which time history had moved on and the pagan revival had passed into the hands of a new generation of devotees.

It is time for another comment on the changing meanings of the word 'pagan'. To people in the interwar years, the term—if it meant anything—would probably not have meant worshippers of the Great Goddess. The rhetoric of 'modern paganism' or 'neo-paganism' was more widely used in this period to describe the rising political ideologies of Nazism and Communism.[43] These movements were decidedly this-worldly in their concerns—they were not so much religions as rivals to religion—but the word 'pagan' evidently felt appropriate to describe them, as it retained much of its force as an othering label for things that were perceived as being bad and non-Christian. Sometimes this usage of the term could descend into bathos. In southern England, a Christian cleric wrote to his local newspaper at the start of World War Two:

> There are many people in this country who honestly believe that the present European conflict is the inevitable result of two pagan ideologies, which in Nazi Germany and Soviet Russia have subordinated every right of God and man to the interests of a deified State. This renascent paganism cannot be defeated simply by military conquest, and no durable peace can be envisaged without a universal acceptance of the divine and natural law in the government of nations.
>
> Religion can best achieve this result. Whatever, therefore, hinders the Church in its salutary mission of weaning the masses from religious indifference, and even paganism itself, is all the more deplorable in present circumstances. It must have surprised many religious and God-fearing people in Tewkesbury, that Sunday morning should be chosen for a public demonstration by the

Tewkesbury Auxiliary Fire Service and that this should be promi-
nently announced in your paper.[44]

The parochial nature of this clergyman's concerns should not blind us to the
fact that his sentiments were widely shared. At the other end of the clerical
hierarchy, Pope Pius XI had warned of the 'pagan state-worship' (*statolatria
pagana*) of Italian Fascism and the 'new heathenry' (*Neuheidentum*) of the Nazis.[45]

Communism was clearly not a pagan ideology in any religious sense. Nazism
was somewhat different. While references to the Nazis as 'pagan' amounted
largely to rhetorical othering, Nazi ideology did contain some limited but
significant pagan religious elements. The importance of these elements must
not be exaggerated. One sometimes finds speculation in sensationalist popular
literature about the influence of pagan and occult ideas on the Nazis; and such
speculation is mostly idle. Nevertheless, in spite of the broadly areligious
character of Nazism, there was always a sense in which it exploited the
persisting heritage of paganism. Ideas corresponding to Margaret Murray's
theory of witchcraft as a pagan survival were circulating in Germany and were
endorsed by no less a figure than Heinrich Himmler.[46] Himmler's SS experimented with paganesque liturgies, including the following wedding ceremony:

> On the table lay a yellow sun disc made of flowers on a blue
> background; to the left and right stood torchbearers and behind
> the table a bowl, containing fire ... The choir opened the ceremony
> with a chorus from *Lohengrin*. A representative of the new usage,
> SS Comrade Elling, gave the dedication—an address based on
> the song from the Edda Helga and Sigrun ... Then the bridal pair
> were offered bread (representing the germinating force of earth)
> and salt (the symbol of purity) on silver vessels. Finally, the pair
> thus married according to German custom received their wedding
> rings.[47]

Another Nazi pagan entrepreneur in the same vein was Jakob Wilhelm Hauer:
by 1933, he had developed the 'German Faith Movement' which he hoped (in
vain, as it turned out) the Nazis would adopt as Germany's official religion.[48]

These ideas did not come out of nowhere. If we seek to track down where
the occult interests of (some) Nazis came from, the trail takes us into the
dark world of pre-1914 German nationalism. One component of this world
was the curious phenomenon of Ariosophy: a form of racist esotericism which
emerged from the Theosophical movement. It was associated with two figures

in particular, Guido von List (1848–1919) and Jörg Lanz von Liebenfels (1874–1954). One of the ingredients of Ariosophy was a liking for pre-Christian Teutonic paganism. In List's theories, this became 'Wotanism', named after the supreme god Wotan; although List's ideas were also indebted to other sources, including Freemasonry and the Kabbalah. Another pagan revivalist from the same racial-nationalist milieu was Ludwig Fahrenkrog (1867–1952). In 1912, Fahrenkrog and his associates founded the *Germanisch-deutsche Religions-Gemeinschaft* and consecrated the first public pagan altar in Germany since the advent of Christianity. After World War One, this soup of ideas reached the fledgling Nazi Party via an occult group called the Thule Society; the Thule Society was in turn connected with the *Germanenorden*, a quasi-Masonic order founded in 1912 which mingled pagan and Christian influences with a very contemporary racism.[49] It is only fair to note that paganizing ideas in Germany were not confined to the far right. In 1880, the atheist socialist Eugen Dühring wrote in praise of Nordic paganism as a superior alternative to the allegedly egotistical and servile creed of Judaism.[50]

The fantasies of pagan Ariosophy—to repeat—were nothing like central to Nazism. Hitler himself personally disliked this sort of thing: 'We must not', he told his followers, 'tolerate the infiltration into the movement of mystically inclined, occultic researchers into the supernatural world.'[51] But fascism and modern paganism are both children, in their own way, of the Romantic movement; and so it is wholly unsurprising that the irrationalist Romantic nationalism which *was* central to Nazism had a pagan religious fringe. A line, albeit not an entirely straight one, can be drawn between the 'Wotanism' of List and the Wagner-loving art school dropout Hitler. Interestingly, there was also a market, albeit a more limited one, for this sort of mystical-racist Germanic paganism outside Germany. We might give particular mention here to Alexander Rud Mills (1885–1964), an Australian lawyer who embraced Germanic paganism and at one stage claimed to have up to 120 followers in Melbourne, of all places.[52] Perhaps the high point of his career was his publication, in 1936, of a fascist pastiche of the Anglican *Book of Common Prayer*.[53]

As we saw in Chapter 5, from the mid-nineteenth century onwards nationalist movements in Continental Europe reappraised—and in some cases reinvented—cultures for those nations whose identities were emerging from the crumbling Austrian, Ottoman, and Russian empires, especially in Central and Eastern Europe. That process of cultural reappraisal extended to the sphere of religion primarily in conventional and expected ways. Thus countries in south-eastern Europe such as Serbia, Bulgaria and Romania asserted their Orthodox Christian identity as an expression of anti-Ottoman nationalism, while further to the north Poland and Lithuania asserted a Catholic identity as an expression of anti-Russian resistance. Germany and Austria-Hungary's defeat in World War One, combined with the Russian Revolution and subsequent civil war, greatly diminished Germany, Austria and Russia (for a time, at least) as dominant powers in East-Central Europe and opened up a geopolitical space in which the dreams of nineteenth-century nationalists were able to take on real political form, supported by the Treaty of Versailles's doctrine of 'self-determination' for nations. A minority were eager to take nationalism to a level beyond linguistic and cultural revival to explore the possibility of revivals of 'native faith'.

One interesting example of this time of ferment was a pagan revival that was underway inside the Russian Empire. In the 1870s the Finnic Mari people of the north bank of the Volga (sometimes known in older writings as the 'Cheremis Tatars'), who were superficially converted to Orthodox Christianity under Muscovite expansion in sixteenth century, initiated a revived pagan religion known as the Kugu Sorta ('Big Candle'). Kugu Sorta represented a fusion of Mari animism and Russian Orthodox popular religion and combined a kind of monotheism with the veneration of Mari ancestral spirits. Remarkably, leaders of the Kugu Sorta even presented the newly constituted faith at the Kazan Scientific and Industrial exhibition of 1890, along with a codification of a statement of faith (of sorts). In a petition to the Tsar of 1892 the Mari neo-animists declared that their ancestors had been baptised by force or deceit, and requested the freedom to practise their religion without the interference of Orthodox clergy.[54] Although many members of the Kugu Sorta were exiled to Siberia in 1893, the Mari religious revival of the nineteenth century had significant long-term consequences, and Mari traditional faith is one of three major recognized religions in today's Mari El Republic in the Russian Federation alongside Orthodox Christianity and Islam. Mari El's pagans periodically receive attention as 'Europe's last pagans',[55] although it would be more accurate to consider them the children of Europe's first successful national pagan revival.

While Mari religion was forced, along with all other expressions of religiosity in the Soviet Union, to retreat into obscurity for much of the twentieth century, the short-lived independence of the new Baltic republics in the period 1918–1940 opened up the possibility of pagan revivals in a region noted for its strong pagan traditions and late adoption of Christianity. In predominantly Catholic Lithuania, this period was characterized by intense cultural and linguistic revival and the widespread adoption of 'pagan' forenames, as well as the hero-worship of pagan figures of Lithuania's history such as Grand Duke Gediminas. However, Lithuania's cultural revival did not result in an actual pagan movement, and 'pagan' imagery was instead adopted by Lithuanian Catholic organizations—such as the figure of the *vaidilutė* (the virgin priestess responsible for maintaining the sacred fire) who was promoted as an exemplar by Catholic youth organizations for Lithuanian young women seeking to keeping alive the flame of the nation's culture.[56] It was not until the late 1960s, under Soviet occupation, that Lithuania's pagan Romuva movement developed.[57]

The absence of a pagan revivalist movement in Interwar Lithuania can perhaps be attributed to the potent significance of a Catholic religious identity for most Lithuanians and the Catholic church's intimate involvement in resistance to the Russian Empire's efforts to eliminate Lithuanian cultural distinctiveness. In neighbouring Latvia, by contrast, the dominant Lutheran church had opposed revolution in 1905 and was perceived by many Latvians as an institution imposed on their nation in the past by German colonists. Accordingly, in 1925 Ernests Brastiņš (1892–1942) and Kārlis Marovskis-Bregžis (1885–1958) launched a revived Latvian pagan religion known as Dievturi, even providing the new religion with a catechism (modelled, ironically, on Martin Luther's) in 1931.[58] In the same year (1925) an Estonian pagan revivalist movement, Taarausk ('the Creed of Taara'), was also launched, proposing a revival of the cult of the Estonian thunder god Taara.[59] However, whereas right-wing nationalist movements in Lithuania and Estonia remained largely religiously indifferent, revived paganism in Latvia became highly politi-cized and associated with far-right nationalist and xenophobic sentiment in the *Pērkonkrusts* ('Thundercross') movement.[60]

In both Estonia and Latvia, countries that came into being as states for the first time after World War One, the development of pagan revivals in the 1920s can be attributed to a certain degree of disaffection with Christianity as a colonial imposition. The Republic of Lithuania, by contrast, considered itself a revival of an ancient state—the Grand Duchy of Lithuania—which had been Catholic for the last four centuries of its existence. There was thus no political motivation for Lithuanians to adopt or confect a revived native faith. However, the politicization of paganism in Latvia, in contrast to Estonia, is harder to explain. Agita Misāne attributed it to the antisemitic, xenophobic and conspir-acist ideology of the Pērkonkrusts movement (which made it akin to some of the esoteric German nationalist movements from which Nazism emerged) in contrast to the more conventional nationalism of the Estonian right.[61] However, like the Mari pagan revival of the 1870s, the Latvian pagan revival of the 1920s had a genuine impact on the nation. Dievturi revived after the end of the Soviet occupation in the 1990s, and it is a mark of the cultural acceptability of revived paganism in contemporary Latvia that Raimonds Vējonis, who was president of Latvia between 2015 and 2019, openly described his religious affiliation as 'pagan',[62] and one 2018 study reported that around twenty percent of Latvians identified with 'Latvian faith'.[63]

Neither Mari native faith nor Latvian Dievturi have become majority religions in their respective regions. However, they have been successful pagan revivals in the sense that outsiders have come to identify the Mari El Republic with paganism, and a large number of Latvians are content with a pagan identity and with the presence of avowed pagans in positions of authority in their society. By contrast, pagan revivalist movements in Poland, Estonia and Lithuania, even if many people in those countries may see them as harmless or even positive, remain the special interest of a small minority. Like Lithuanian Romuva, the Russian Slavic native faith movement known as Rodnoverie (which has also developed in a distinctive form in Ukraine) is a late arrival, developing in its full-fledged form only in the 1990s after the fall of Communism.[64] Rodnoverie is reportedly popular in sections of Russia's armed forces, but the immense cultural, political and ideological significance of the Russian Orthodox Church to contemporary Russia makes it unlikely that a statistically significant number of people will ever articulate their Russianness through a revived native faith.

It is worth observing, at this point, that something which set Gerald Gardner's religion of Wicca apart among the various forms of paganism revived in the first half of the twentieth century—and which might go some way towards explaining its appeal and success—was the fact that Wicca was *not* one of Europe's native faith movements. In other words, Gardner did not attempt to revive a historically attested (or supposedly historically attested) form of pagan religion that had a distinctively English or British identity. This was in part down to the influence of Margaret Murray. Murray's witch-cult was, by definition, a hidden religion and thus only visible 'between the lines' of the historical record, rather than openly described. Furthermore, the very title of *The Witch-Cult in Western Europe* proclaimed that the religion was not nationally specific; and Murray's insistence on the extreme antiquity of the witch-cult had the effect of distancing Wicca from any historically attested forms of paganism (such as, for example, Anglo-Saxon polytheism). Murray, in common with Sir James Frazer, adhered to the notion that the earliest stages of human religiosity were best understood as universal impulses rather than as geographically particular traditions. The effect of all this—admittedly by accident, rather than by design—was to lend the nascent religion of Wicca a more universal character than the native faith movements with their roots in nationalism. A comparison of Wicca with those movements thus reveals two very different streams of pagan revival, the one based on reviving a supposed secret religion practised across cultures and borders and the other focused on one specific national and ethnic tradition.

This is not to say, of course, that scholars and practitioners of Wicca are free from anxieties that the religion is too Eurocentric and too culturally white, or that modern pagan traditions derived from the nationalist revivals of the early twentieth century are always politically nativist or racist in their contemporary expressions. However, by their very nature native faith movements are limited in scope to those who belong to or identify with a regionally particular tradition. Wicca is not subject to such limitations, as its global popularity attests. However, it is important not to lump together the native faith movements, since significant differences exist between them. In particular, 'antiquarian' revivals such as Wotanism and Dievturi, which arose from the recovery of national folk cultures and were pioneered by small groups of educated intellectuals, were very different from 'bottom up' revivals which sought to reanimate what may well have been genuine vestiges of traditional pagan religion, such as in Mari El or Sápmi. There were no pagans in Latvia before 1925. It is rather less clear if we can say with certainty that no pagans existed in Mari El before the Kugu Sorta revival of 1877, or that traditional Sámi animism had been wiped out before 1978, when protests against the damming of the Alta Kautokeino River precipitated a revival of Sámi culture and religion.[65] In part this is down to the very nature of animism itself, and whether it can even be considered 'religion' in the same sense as polytheism—a complex question that lies beyond the scope of this book.

We are nearly at the end of our story, which concludes with the emergence of paganism as an international mass movement. This development had several different sources, including the 1960s revival of interest in Aleister Crowley that we mentioned earlier. But its main impetus came from the growth of Wicca, the pagan witch religion that Gerald Gardner released into the placidly conservative world of 1950s England. Gardner was an interesting—indeed, unique—figure. Born into an upper-middle-class family near Liverpool, he spent much of his life in South and South-East Asia working in business and as part of the British imperial administration. His religious and esoteric interests were eclectic, ranging from Spiritualism and Freemasonry to Buddhism, Islam and Indigenous traditions. For most of his life, he had no particular religious affiliation. He is sometimes seen as an idiosyncratic character whose personal foibles—from his asthma to his alleged sexual proclivities—ended up becoming embedded in the religion which he founded. But Wicca was fundamentally nothing new. It was no more—or less—than the most recent product of the persistence of paganism in Christian European culture: the latest watering of the seeds, the latest defrosting of the ice, or whatever other metaphor one wishes to use. It is no coincidence that the books that Gardner seems to have had in his own library included a series of works by people whom we have already met in this book, including Apuleius, Aleister Crowley, Samuel Mathers, Dion Fortune, Algernon Swinburne, William Sharp, Kenneth Grahame, and even the Catholicism-is-pagan polemicist Alexander Hislop.[66] Gardner's historical role was to reanimate the same pagan materials as his predecessors as part of the same tradition of pagan persistence, not to create something new.[67]

As we have noted, Gardner claimed to have encountered a group of pagan witches—the 'New Forest Coven'—during his retirement in the 1930s. That encounter may have ultimately led to his decision to start promoting Wicca in the 50s. Even if this is so, however, Gardner continued to dabble with various other possibilities in the intervening period, including Druid revivalism, Christian esotericism and Thelema.[68] Importantly, he also read *The White Goddess*, the wildly eccentric theory of poetry published in 1948 by the writer Robert Graves.[69] Graves had a set of ideas about Goddess-worship and female supremacy which were transparently products of the Romantic tradition, and it is to a large extent through him and Gardner that such ideas have reached twenty-first century paganism. It bears noting that Graves' notions on such matters were filtered through his own masochistic psychology. His fears and desires are barely beneath the surface when he expounds his theories about the Great Goddess and the human matriarchs of prehistoric antiquity:

> Ancient Europe had no gods. The Great Goddess was regarded as immortal, changeless, and omnipotent; and the concept of fatherhood had not been introduced into religious thought. She took lovers, but for pleasure, not to provide her children with a father. Men feared, adored and obeyed the matriarch; the hearth which she tended in a cave or hut being their earliest social centre, and motherhood their prime mystery.[70]

Such was the mixture of influences that were swirling around in Gardner's mind as he composed the basic texts for what became Wicca. He started initiating his first converts in 1949–50, and he made his religion public from 1951. These developments were bound up with a trio of books that he published in the period 1949–59: a novel entitled *High Magic's Aid*, which was indebted to Margaret Murray and Charles Leland; and two purportedly non-fictional works, *Witchcraft Today* and *The Meaning of Witchcraft*.[71] The foreword to *Witchcraft Today* was written by Murray herself (Gardner appears to have known her through the Folklore Society). In the latter two books, Gardner claimed to be writing not as a witch but as an anthropologist: one who had had the good fortune to discover a secret pagan witch-cult that had survived from Neolithic times into postwar England. The witches—or 'Wica'—whom he had uncovered worshipped a mother goddess and a horned god, and practised magic and clairvoyance. He suggested that their religion had been influenced by the Celts, the Egyptians and the Graeco-Roman mystery cults, and that it had in turn influenced Freemasonry.

Gardner's religion appeared at just the right time. In Britain, the 1950s saw something of a recession for alternative and esoteric religious practices. Older forms of unorthodoxy, such as Spiritualism and Theosophy, were in decline. What remained of the Golden Dawn tradition was moribund, and the great prewar esoteric leaders Aleister Crowley and Dion Fortune were both dead. This left a gap in the market. The Christian churches had had a good war, and they were enjoying their last period of real cultural power; but they were losing their grip, and the sixties counterculture was just around the corner. A lot of Britons wanted to be told that a pre-Christian magical fertility cult still existed in their land. Gardner spoke to this audience with a distinctively Romantic sense of rebellion against convention. He quoted a witch as saying:

> Ours is a religion of love, pleasure and excitement. Frail human nature needs a little warmth and comfort, to relieve us from the hardness and misery of life and from the cold austerity of the Church's preaching.[72]

Elsewhere, he linked his religion with 'a spirit of romance, a love of the spice of life, and a dislike of smug respectability'.[73]

Gardner's colourful claims were never taken seriously in academic circles, and in due course they were forensically refuted, probably first in 1962 in Elliot Rose's *A Razor for a Goat*.[74] But by then a critical mass of people had come to believe in them. Moreover, even if Gardner's history was false in a literal sense, Wicca was nothing novel. He was right to claim that his newly publicized religion was a genuine expression of a persisting pagan theme in European history—one which, to labour the point once again, had repeatedly generated pagan revivals across the centuries just like his. The ingredients of Wicca go back to pagan antiquity and the ancient esoteric tradition. The best-known Wiccan liturgical text, the Charge of the Goddess, derives ultimately from Apuleius;[75] and Gardner seems to have known of and endorsed the ancient Neoplatonist writer Sallustius.[76] From Renaissance and Enlightenment esotericism, Wicca took on Masonic influences.[77] In Wiccan theology, the horned God may be seen as a Romantic refashioning of Pan;[78] while the Goddess represents the divine feminine, as reanimated from classical mythology by a line of poets ending in Robert Graves. This comes through from Gardner's own description of her:

> The goddess of the witch cult is obviously the Great Mother, the giver of life, incarnate love. She rules spring pleasure, feasting and all the delights at a later time with other goddesses and has a special affinity with the moon.[79]

The point is clear. Gerald Gardner stood at the end of a centuries-long tradition of pagan revivalism going back to antiquity. His new religion was simply the latest of many projects which emerged in European Christian culture with the aim of breathing life again into the persisting materials of ancient pagan religion. In one, and only one, respect did Gardner break new ground, and that is that Wicca—unlike the ideas and endeavours of Plethon, Marsilio Ficino, Thomas Taylor, Percy Shelley, Heinrich Himmler and the other figures whom we have met—turned into an enduring global movement.

# Epilogue: Pagan Pasts, Pagan Futures?

This book has set out to challenge naïve historiographical understandings of the survival, continuity and re-creation of paganism as a religious tradition, while recognizing that 'paganism' is a largely subjective designation and a word that is best used as a 'conceptual placeholder' rather than as a reified reality. In rejecting a 'survivalist' account of pagan continuity, it has done nothing new; as we have seen, such paradigms have long been challenged, and Ronald Hutton famously challenged the historical credibility of claims of 'inherited' traditions of pagan witchcraft by practitioners in his book *The Triumph of the Moon* as long ago as 1999. On the other hand, the rival account of revived paganism as a modern concoction remains influential in both scholarly and popular circles, and is often deployed to belittle contemporary pagans. In any event, in the same way as it is incumbent on the historian who critiques conventionally used terms to provide more meaningful alternatives, so it is not enough for the historian approaching the *longue durée* of Europe's pagan traditions to offer only sceptical critique. In *The Triumph of the Moon*, Hutton pointed the way forward to a renewed self-understanding for contemporary pagans as the creators of their own religion—an impressive achievement—as an alternative to ahistorical myths of hereditary witchcraft.

In much the same way, it is the aim of this book to point the way forward to an alternative historiography of pagan persistence to replace the models of pagan survivalism and modern concoction. While it is fairly easy to point out the absence of historical continuity between different expressions of avowedly pagan religiosity throughout Europe's post-classical history, it is harder to account for the very fact that paganism kept springing up afresh at different times *in the absence of* any kind of institutional or personal continuity. It is important to bear in mind that the privileged position assigned to institutional continuity in the historiography of religious movements reflects the importance of such continuity in Christian self-understanding; there is no prima facie reason why a kind of verifiable 'apostolic succession' should matter in religions very unlike Christianity. Yet paganism did not simply return throughout history as a cultural theme, but frequently as a living reality—even if, as we have shown, some revivals were short-lived and supported only by a tiny minority—or even just a single individual. These people did not *have* to revive paganism: they could have invented new Christian heresies or totally novel forms of religion. So why paganism? The answer is because, in European culture and its colonial derivatives, paganism is always close at hand. It is the spectre haunting Europe; the ghost at the Christian (and secular) feast.

Paganism is thus more than just a cultural trope, and hence the metaphors we have reached for in this book: the re-germinating seeds, the organism thawing from the ice, and so on. These metaphors are not intended to reify paganism as a reality that somehow carries on existing between its various revivals—which would be a strange metaphysical claim indeed. Rather, they are an attempt to account for what Ludo Milis called the 'permanent functional meaning' of paganism;[1] the apparent human tendency to return to a pagan mode of religiosity, when circumstances make it possible to do so. It is perhaps beyond the scope of the historian or the scholar of religious studies to speculate about the deeper human tendencies that bring about pagan revivals—it is, rather, properly the domain of the anthropologist. But as Ramsay MacMullen recognized, if the historian is to get past a reliance on prescriptive, elite accounts of religious behaviour and understand how ordinary people actually practise religion on the ground, some degree of rapprochement with anthro-pology may be necessary.[2]

The observation that the twenty-first century is a post-secular age, at least for Europe, is made so frequently that it is almost a cliché. It is an idea that gives hope to adherents of the mainstream monotheistic faiths—hope that the age of doubt is over, and that the faithful will return. But just because people have had enough of secularism, we cannot assume that they will return to the embrace of those faiths that the secular thinkers of the Enlightenment and the nineteenth century rejected. Furthermore, one key reason why the present century is a post-secular age is surely that many people have passed beyond *rejecting* the monotheistic faiths and into simply forgetting them. Today's spiritual searching is motivated not by the desire to find a replacement for Christianity in one's life; it is, rather, a much more open-ended search for ultimate meaning which does not take any of the monotheistic traditions as a given. There is no 'Christianity-shaped hole' that spiritual seekers in Europe are seeking to fill.

The numbers of people identifying as pagans in contemporary Europe are growing, but they remain small. It seems unlikely that a pagan 'mass conversion' of the kind imagined by George Gemistos Plethon (see Chapter 3) or Thomas

Jefferson Hogg (see Chapter 4) will ever happen. But paganism never was a confession; in one sense, for a pagan to clearly define their religious identity is a contradiction in terms, and the imposition of a Christian mode of religiosity-as-confession on something quite alien. Hutton has noted that, within the pagan community itself, people formally initiated to various traditions often perform 'open' rituals at festivals for the benefit of a much larger group of people who identify as pagans but whose religious practice is more haphazard.[3] But just as a minority of initiated pagans are only a tiny proportion of the pagan community, so self-identifying pagans are only a fraction of those people in twenty-first-century Europe who have something approaching a recognizably pagan outlook, even if they would never think of calling themselves 'pagans'. For example, the insistence of many people in twenty-first-century Britain that they are 'spiritual but not religious' comes closer to the spirit of pre-Christian paganism than an earnest confessional pagan identity. Similarly, a willingness to draw spiritual beliefs and practices from multiple traditions across cultures into a personal spiritual path might have been recognizable to a learned pagan in the late Roman Empire. After all, 'not religious' usually means that someone is not an adherent of a monotheistic creed, or is unwilling to sign up to doctrines and dogmas. It need not mean that someone will be hostile to an entirely different mode of religiosity such as paganism offers.

The cult of the Green Man in contemporary Britain is perhaps the perfect example of the cultural influence revived paganism can wield, quite apart from the numbers of its self-conscious adherents. As Hutton has well documented,[4] the Green Man has the distinction of being a pagan god entirely created in the twentieth century—proof, if any were needed, of the vitality of modern paganism and its capacity for development. But unlike other deities of modern paganism, the Green Man is not only immediately recognizable to virtually everyone in Britain, but he is also associated specifically with the idea of paganism. And in spite of that association, the image of the Green Man remains widely popular, including among people who would never consider themselves to be pagans. Most gardeners who put up Green Man plaques in their gardens are no more self-defining pagans than many of those who wear a cross as jewellery are self-defining Christians; the point is that the Green Man, like the cross, has entered the cultural mainstream while also maintaining a status as a religious image. The diffusion of the image has normalized the idea that there are pagans in modern British society, and that being a pagan is a legitimate religious identity.

If a simultaneously post-Christian and post-secular future awaits Europe, then the character of paganism will undoubtedly change too. Just as native faith movements forged in the ferment of nineteenth- and twentieth-century nationalisms may not always be meaningful or appealing to young people with a more inclusive and internationalist outlook, so forms of paganism revived in reaction to a perception of Christianity as culturally and morally repressive will start to seem baffling to generations unfamiliar with a Christian moral hegemony. Likewise, ideas of pagan identity modelled on the mystery religions and based on secrecy and group initiation may have little appeal in an online world where the instant availability of information is an expectation, and online networks are much easier to establish than real-world groups. The paganism of the future may be more eclectic, more individual, less community focused, and more online; a kind of 'Chaos Paganism' mirroring the eclecticism of 'Chaos Magick' in the occult world.

As we have seen, especially in the later chapters of this book, 'pagan' is a word that has had a number of different meanings, only some of which have referred to the active practice of pagan cults involving things like sacrifice and the worship of polytheistic gods. As Europe advances into its post-Christian and post-secular future, the human religious impulse will surely continue to assert itself. For a significant proportion of people, secularism will not be enough. If people remain 'spiritual but not religious', selecting practices from the world's religions in which they find fulfilment but declining to commit to any kind of religious adherence, then a kind of 'ambient paganism' could well develop into most people's way of dealing with the spiritual side of life; a broad recognition that there exist vaguely defined spiritual powers, and that each person will construe those powers and negotiate their relationship with them in their own way. It will look very different, no doubt, from any paganism that has gone before. But as we have seen, pagan revivals can occur when they are least expected.

# Notes

## Introduction

1. For the fullest discussion of the San Marco Cup see Thornton, Alicia, 'Meaningful Mingling: Classicizing Imagery and Islamicizing Script in a Byzantine Bowl', *The Art Bulletin* 90.1 (March 2008): 32–53.

2. As we shall discuss more fully below, the use of the singular term 'paganism' represents a conceptual shorthand for the totality of pre-Christian religions, and is not intended to reify a single religion of paganism (which never existed).

3. York, Michael, 'Invented Culture/Invented Religion', *Nova Religio* 3 (1999): 135–46, at 141.

4. Gosden, Chris, *The History of Magic: From Alchemy to Witchcraft, from the Ice Age to the Present* (London: Viking, 2020), 237–38.

5. See generally O'Donnell, James J., '*Paganus*', *Classical Folia* 31 (1977): 163–69; Chuvin, Pierre (trans. B. A Archer), *A Chronicle of the Last Pagans* (Cambridge, MA: Harvard University Press, 1990), 7–9; Davies, Owen, *Paganism: A Very Short Introduction* (Oxford: Oxford University Press, 2011), 1–6; Cameron, Alan, *The Last Pagans of Rome* (Oxford: Oxford University Press, 2011), 14–25; and Testa, Rita Lizzi, 'When the Romans became *pagani*' in Rita Lizzi Testa (ed.), *The Strange Death of Pagan Rome* (Turnhout: Brepols, 2013), 31–51. For a discussion of the definition of paganism within the context of medieval northern Europe see Palmer, James T., 'Defining Paganism in the Carolingian World', *Early Medieval Europe* 15 (2007): 402–25.

6. 'Pagan' was not the only term used by the early Christians for followers of pre-Christian religions, and 'gentile' (meaning a worshipper of the 'gods of the nations') was just as common.

7. Marenbon, John, *Pagans and Philosophers: The Problem of Paganism from Augustine to Leibniz* (Princeton, NJ: Princeton University Press, 2015), 5.

8. See Assmann, Jan, 'The Mosaic Distinction: Israel, Egypt, and the Invention of Paganism', *Representations* 56 (1996): 48–67 at 48–52.

9. Flower, Harriet I., *The Dancing Lares and the Serpent in the Garden: Religion at the Roman Street Corner* (Princeton, NJ: Princeton University Press, 2017), ix.

10. Grassigli, Gian Luca, 'Classical Revivals and "Pagan Art"' in Rita Lizzi Testa (ed.), *The Strange Death of Pagan Rome* (Turnhout: Brepols, 2013), 165–69, at 166.

11. Petts, David, *Pagan and Christian: Religious Change in Early Medieval Europe* (London: Bristol Classical Press, 2011), 33–35.

12. On the difficulties of applying the word 'pagan' to Shamanic religious practices see Hutton, Ronald, *Shamans: Siberian Spirituality and the Western Imagination* (London: Continuum, 2001), vii–ix.

13. Pizza, Murphy and Lewis, James R., 'Introduction' in James R. Lewis and Murphy Pizza (eds), *Handbook of Contemporary Paganism* (Leiden: Brill, 2009), 1–12, at 1.

14. Baronas, Darius and Rowell, S. C., *The Conversion of Lithuania: From Pagan Barbarians to Late Medieval Christians* (Vilnius: Institute of Lithuanian Literature and Folklore, 2015), 264.

15. Rountree, Kathryn, 'Introduction: Context is Everything: Plurality and Paradox in Contemporary European Paganisms', in Kathryn Rountree (ed.), *Contemporary Pagan and Native Faith Movements in Europe: Colonialist and Nationalist Impulses* (Oxford: Berghahn, 2015), 1–23, at 8.

16. Yet another terminological debate concerns the use of capital letters for 'Pagan' when referring to contemporary pagans. However, sharply distinguishing contemporary 'Pagans' from ancient 'pagans' also seems to presume a rather simplistic historiography of pagan revivals which this book seeks to avoid, and thus we have chosen to use the lowercase 'pagan' throughout.

17. York, Michael, *Pagan Theology* (New York, NY: New York University Press, 2003), 162.

18. 'Introduction to Paganism', The Pagan Federation, paganfed.org/paganism/, accessed 11 May 2023.

19. Hutton, Ronald, *The Triumph of the Moon: A History of Modern Pagan Witchcraft*, 2nd edn (Oxford: Oxford University Press, 2019), 4–32.

20. Baronas and Rowell, *Conversion of Lithuania*, 261.

21. Young, Francis, *Twilight of the Godlings: The Shadowy Origins of Britain's Supernatural Beings* (Cambridge: Cambridge University Press, 2023), 122–26.

22. Filotas, Bernadette, *Pagans Survivals, Superstitions and Popular Cultures* (Toronto: Pontifical Institute of Medieval Studies, 2005), 72.

23. On nymphs in modern Greece see Purkiss, Diane, *Troublesome Things: A History of Fairies and Fairy Stories* (London: Allen Lane, 2000), 45–46.

24. Bonner, Campbell, 'Some Phases of Religious Feeling in Later Paganism', *Harvard Theological Review* 20.2 (1937): 119–40, at 139–40.

25. Petts, *Pagan and Christian*, 38–40.

26. Baronas, Darius, 'Christians in Late Pagan, and Pagans in Early Christian Lithuania: The Fourteenth and Fifteenth Centuries', *Lithuanian Historical Studies* 19 (2014): 51–81, at 53.

27. Pócs, Éva, 'Small Gods, Small Demons: Remnants of an Archaic Fairy Cult in Central and South-Eastern Europe', in Michael Ostling (ed.), *Fairies, Demons, and Nature Spirits: 'Small Gods' at the Margins of Christendom* (Basingstoke: Palgrave MacMillan, 2018), 255–76, at 263.

28. Chuvin, *Chronicle of the Last Pagans*, 150.

29. Hutton, Ronald, *Pagan Britain* (New Haven, CT: Yale University Press, 2013), viii.

30. Gosden, *History of Magic*, 236–37.

31. Carver, Martin (ed.), *The Cross Goes North: Processes of Conversion in Northern Europe, AD 300–1300* (Woodbridge: Boydell and Brewer, 2006); Petts, *Pagan and Christian.*

32. See, for example, Seznec, Jean, *The Survival of the Pagan Gods* (Princeton, NJ: Princeton University Press, 1981); Wind, Edgar, *Pagan Mysteries in the Renaissance* (London: Penguin, 1967); Allen, Don Cameron, *Mysteriously Meant: The Rediscovery of Pagan Symbolism and Allegorical Interpretation in the Renaissance* (Baltimore, MD: Johns Hopkins University Press, 1970); Godwin, Joscelyn, *The Pagan Dream of the Renaissance* (London: Thames & Hudson, 2002). See also Von Stuckrad, Kocku, 'Visual Gods: From Exorcism to Complexity in Renaissance Studies', *Aries* 6 (2006): 59–85 on the historiography here.

33. Chuvin, *Chronicle of the Last Pagans*; Cameron, *Last Pagans of Rome*; Watts, Edward, *The Final Pagan Generation* (Berkeley, CA: University of California Press, 2020).

34. Gouguenheim, Sylvain, *Les derniers païens: les Baltes face aux chrétiens xiiie–xviiie siècle* (Paris: Passés Composés, 2022).

35. Chuvin, *Chronicle of the Last Pagans*, 2.

36. Hutton, *Pagan Britain*, viii.

37. Adler, Margot, *Drawing Down the Moon* (New York, NY: Viking, 1979).

38. Harvey, Graham, *Listening People, Speaking Earth* (London: Hurst & Company, 1997); Davis, Philip G., *Goddess Unmasked* (Dallas, TX: Spence, 1998); Harvey, Graham and Hardman, Charlotte (eds), *Paganism Today* (London: Thorsons, 1995).

39. Hutton, Ronald, *The Triumph of the Moon: A History of Modern Pagan Witchcraft* (Oxford: Oxford University Press, 1999).

40. Milis, Ludo J. R. (trans. Tanis Guest), *The Pagan Middle Ages* (Woodbridge: Boydell Press, 1998).

41. Jones, Prudence and Pennick, Nigel, *A History of Pagan Europe* (London: Routledge, 1995).

42. Dowden, Ken, *European Paganism: The Realities of Cult from Antiquity to the Middle Ages* (London: Routledge, 2000), 2–3.

43. Clifton, Chas S. and Harvey, Graham (eds), *The Paganism Reader* (New York, NY: Routledge, 2004).

44. Hutton, *Pagan Britain*; Hutton, Ronald, *The Pagan Religions of the Ancient British Isles: Their Nature and Legacy* (Oxford: Blackwell, 1991), 284–341.

45. Siniossoglou, Niketas, *Radical Platonism in Byzantium* (Cambridge: Cambridge University Press, 2016).

46. Williams, Liz, *Miracles of Our Own Making: A History of Paganism* (London: Reaktion, 2021).

47. Gibson, Marion, *Imagining the Pagan Past* (London: Routledge, 2013); Marenbon, *Pagans and Philosophers*; Salih, Sarah, *Imagining the Pagan in Late Medieval England* (Cambridge: D. S. Brewer, 2019); Chatterjee, Paroma, *Between the Pagan Past and Christian Present in Byzantine Culture* (Cambridge: Cambridge University Press, 2021).

48. Clark, Stuart, *Thinking with Demons: The Idea of Witchcraft in Early Modern Europe* (Oxford: Oxford University Press, 1997), viii; Ditchfield, Simon, 'Thinking with Saints: Sanctity and Society in the Early Modern World;' in F. Meltzer and J. Elsner (eds), *Saints: Faith without Borders* (Chicago, IL: University of Chicago Press, 2011), 157–89.

49. Hutton, Ronald, *Queens of the Wild: Pagan Goddesses in Christian Europe: An Investigation* (New Haven, CT: Yale University Press, 2022).

50. For a discussion of reading 'paganism' back on Christianized societies see Hutton, Ronald, 'How Pagan were Medieval English Peasants?' *Folklore* 122 (2011): 235–49.

51. Gimbutas, Marija, *The Balts* (New York: Praeger, 1963), 204.

52. Petts, *Pagan and Christian*, 77–79.

53. Filotas, *Pagan Survivals*, 82–84.

54. See Isidore, *Etym.* 8.11.5.

55. Bode, Georg Heinrich (ed.), *Scriptores rerum mythicarum latini tres Romae nuper reperti* (Celle: E. H. C. Schulze, 1834), vol. 1, 171–72.

56. Hutton, *Queens of the Wild*, 41–74.

57. Young, *Twilight of the Godlings*, 308–309.

## Chapter 1: The First (and Last) Pagans—Ancient Greece and Rome

1. The literature on Graeco-Roman pagan religions is vast, and no attempt is made to summarize it here. The best single studies of Greek and Roman religious life respectively are Burkert, Walter, *Greek Religion* (Malden, MA: Blackwell, 1985), which is somewhat dated but has never really been surpassed; and Beard, Mary, North, John, and Price, Simon, *Religions of Rome* (Cambridge: Cambridge University Press, 1998), which has a rich collection of primary sources. There are also introductory texts available in the Cambridge Companions, Oxford Handbooks and Blackwell Companions series.

2. 'Faites comme les autres, et croyez ce qu'il vous plaira' (Fontenelle, Bernard de, *Histoire des oracles* (Paris: Hachette, 1908 [1687]), 69).

3. Scholars have often taken this line of argument too far, drawing a dichotomy between belief and practice to the point that belief has been treated as irrelevant to ancient religion. For a valuable corrective, see Mackey, Jacob L., *Belief and Cult* (Princeton, NJ: Princeton University Press, 2022).

4.  Mackey, *Belief and Cult*, 290, in reference to the Romans.

5.  *Pluvia defit, causa Christiani sunt*: Augustine, *De civ. Dei*, 2.3. For another example of the same sentiment, see the famous passage at Tertullian, *Apol.*, 40.1–2.

6.  For a contrary perspective, see Festugière, André-Jean, *Personal Religion Among the Greeks* (Berkeley, CA: University of California Press, 1954). But Festugière's work fails to turn up much evidence for this side of Greek religion, at least outside the esoteric-Platonist tradition.

7.  Robertson Smith, W., *Lectures on the Religion of the Semites*, 3rd edn (New York, NY: Macmillan, 1927), 16–17. For a more recent treatment of this point, see Robert Parker, *On Greek Religion* (Ithaca, NY: Cornell University Press, 2011), 31–34.

8.  This is brought out in both the (plural) title and the contents of Lewis Farnell's classic study *The Cults of the Greek States* (Oxford: Clarendon, 1896–1909), 5 vols.

9.  It is often noted that ancient languages did not have a word for 'religion' in the modern Protestantized sense of an individual's belief system. On the evolution of the term, see Smith, Jonathan Z., 'Religion, Religions, Religious', in Mark C. Taylor (ed.), *Critical Terms for Religious Studies* (Chicago, IL: University of Chicago Press, 1998), 269–84.

10. On the esoteric side of Graeco-Roman religious culture, see in general e.g. Luck (ed.), *Arcana Mundi*; Ogden, Daniel, *Magic, Witchcraft and Ghosts in the Greek and Roman Worlds* (Oxford: Oxford University Press, 2009); Bremmer, Jan N., *Initiation into the Mysteries of the Ancient World* (Berlin: De Gruyter, 2014); and Edmonds III, Radcliffe G., *Drawing Down The Moon* (Princeton, NJ: Princeton University Press, 2019).

11. The cult is most famously described in Apuleius, *Metamorph.* 11. See further J. Gwyn Griffiths's commentary in *The Isis-Book (Metamorphoses, Book XI)* (Leiden: Brill, 1975) and Wheeler, Graham John, 'Apuleius and the Esoteric Revival: An Ancient Decadent in Modern Times', *Volupté: Interdisciplinary Journal of Decadence Studies* 2.2 (2019): 260–76.

12. See *Derveni Papyrus*, col. XX; Plato, *Rep.* 364b–c; and Isocrates, *Antid.* 19.5–7.

13. Robert Parker has written in this context: 'It is normal to note that the idea of metempsychosis emerges in India a little before it does in Greece—and then to have trouble in explaining by what channel the one tradition could have affected the other' ('Early Orphism', in Anton Powell (ed.), *The Greek World* (London: Routledge, 1995), 483–510 at 502).

14. For scholarly engagements with the Orphic material, see e.g. Graf, Fritz and Johnston, Sarah Iles (eds), *Ritual Texts for the Afterlife* (New York, NY: Routledge, 2007); Bernabé, Alberto and San Cristóbal, Ana Isabel Jiménez, *Instructions for the Netherworld* (Leiden: Brill, 2008); and Edmonds III, Radcliffe G., *Redefining Ancient Orphism* (Cambridge: Cambridge University Press, 2013).

15. For recent translations published by practising pagans, see e.g. Dunn, Patrick, *The Orphic Hymns* (Woodbury, Ont.: Llewellyn, 2018) and Mastros, Sara Leanne, *Orphic Hymns Grimoire* (Pittsburgh, PA: Mastros Publishing, 2019).

16. *Derveni Papyrus*, col. XVII, line 12. Parallels to these rather clear and striking words can be found in other sources: see Meisner, D. A., '"Zeus the Head, Zeus the Middle": Studies in the History and Interpretation of the Orphic Theogonies', PhD diss., University of Western Ontario, 2015 (online at ir.lib. uwo.ca/etd/3139, accessed 20 September 2023).

17. See generally e.g. Huffman, Carl A., *A History of Pythagoreanism* (Cambridge: Cambridge University Press, 2014).

18. Casaubon, Meric, *A True & Faithful Relation* (London: Garthwait, 1659), 'Preface' (unpaginated).

19. Plato, *Phaedo*, 100e (our translation here and following).

20. Plato, *Symp.* 211d–e.

21. Plato, *Phaedo*, 66b–e.

22. Plato, *Theaet.* 176a–b.

23. See e.g. Plato, *Phaedo*, 106e–115a; *Phaedrus*, 246–254; *Rep.* 614–621.

24. On Hermeticism in general, see e.g. Fowden, Garth, *The Egyptian Hermes* (Princeton, NJ: Princeton University Press, 1993); Ebeling, Florian, *The Secret History of Hermes Trismegistus* (Ithaca, NY: Cornell University Press, 2007); and Slavenburg, Jacob, *The Hermetic Link* (Lake Worth, FL: Ibis, 2012).

25. The standard edition of the *Corpus* in English is Copenhaver, Brian P. (ed.), *Hermetica* (Cambridge: Cambridge University Press, 1992).

26. *Corp. Herm.* 5.10 (translation by Copenhaver, here and subsequently).

27. See *Corp. Herm.*, 12.8, 16.3.

28. See especially Hanegraaff, Wouter J., *Hermetic Spirituality and the Historical Imagination: Altered States of Knowledge in Late Antiquity* (Cambridge: Cambridge University Press, 2022). Hanegraaff is very good on the Hermetic tradition in general, although one might have reservations about some of his positions.

29. This quotation comes not from *Corp. Herm.* but from *The Discourse on the Eighth and Ninth* in Mahé, Jean-Pierre and Meyer, Marvin (ed.), *The Nag Hammadi Scriptures* (New York, NY: HarperCollins, 2007), 57–59.

30. This is no more than the basic skeleton of the Neoplatonic system. Different philosophers could, for example, insert additional levels between the One and Mind; posit an even higher principle above the One ('the Ineffable'); and introduce further entities called 'Henads'. On Neoplatonism generally, see further e.g. Remes, Pauliina, *Neoplatonism* (London: Routledge, 2014); and Dillon, John and Gerson, Lloyd P., *Neoplatonic Philosophy* (Indianapolis, IN: Hackett, 2004).

31. For an example, see Majercik, Ruth, *The Chaldean Oracles* (Leiden: Brill, 1989), 36–39.

32. Edmonds III, Radcliffe G., 'Did the Mithraists Inhale?', *Ancient World* 32.1 (2000): 10–24.

33. Macrobius, *Sat.* 1.23.

34. See Saffrey, H.-D., 'Les Néoplatoniciens et les Oracles Chaldaïques', in *Recherches sur le néoplatonisme après Plotin* (Paris, 1990), 63–79 at 72–74, on the history of

this idea. On the history of the Oracles generally, see Wheeler, Graham John, 'Towards a Reception History of the Chaldaean Oracles', *International Journal of the Classical Tradition* 28 (2021): 261–84.

35.  See Clarke, Emma C., Dillon, John M. and Hershbell, Jackson P. (ed.), *Iamblichus: On the Mysteries* (Atlanta, GA: Society of Biblical Literature, 2003).

36.  See Shaw, Gregory, *Theurgy and the Soul*, 2nd edn (Kettering: Angelico, 2014).

37.  The standard edition of the *PGM* in English is Betz, Hans Dieter, *The Greek Magical Papyri in Translation* (Chicago, IL: University of Chicago Press, 1992). See also now Faraone, Christopher A. and Tovar, Sofía Torallas (eds), *Greek and Egyptian Magical Formularies: Text and Translation, vol. 1* (Berkeley: California Classical Studies, 2022). For a valuable work of scholarship on the *PGM* written by a modern esotericist, see Skinner, Stephen, *Techniques of Graeco-Egyptian Magic* (Singapore: Golden Hoard, 2014).

38.  *PGM* 4.475–834.

39.  On this general subject, Lane Fox, Robin, *Pagans and Christians* (London: Penguin, 1988) is still fundamental. Watts, *Final Pagan Generation* is also interesting. For a readable popular account of the rise of Christianity, see Ehrman, Bart D., *The Triumph of Christianity* (New York, NY: Simon & Schuster, 2018). For a superbly unorthodox exploration of pagans, Christians and Jews in the Roman Empire, see Hopkins, Keith, *A World Full of Gods* (London: Weidenfeld and Nicolson, 1999).

40.  For necessary qualifications to this broad-brush statement, see the Introduction and Chapter 2.

41.  On some relevant texts, see e.g. Assmann, Jan, *Moses the Egyptian* (Cambridge, MA: Harvard University Press, 1997), 47–54; and Liebeschuetz, Wolf, 'The Significance of the Speech of Praetextatus' in Polymnia Athanassiadi and Michael Frede (eds), *Pagan Monotheism in Late Antiquity* (Oxford: Clarendon Press, 1999), 185–205.

42.  Lane Fox, *Pagans and Christians*, 495.

43.  Cf. Ste Croix, G. E. M. de, *Christian Persecution, Martyrdom, and Orthodoxy* (Oxford: Oxford University Press, 2006), 122, 133 37; Clemente, Guido, 'Introduction' in Rita Lizzi Testa (ed.), *The Strange Death of Pagan Rome* (Turnhout: Brepols, 2013), 13–29, at 16–17.

44.  Balagangadhara, S. N., *"The Heathen in His Blindness …": Asia, the West and the Dynamic of Religion* (Leiden: Brill, 1994), 63.

45.  It is interesting to note in this context that a description of a persecutory measure of 257, put by a Christian into the mouth of a Roman, recognizes that those who perform 'Roman rites' (*Romanas caeremonias*) might not be adherents of the 'Roman religion' (*Romanam religionem*): Pontius, *Acta*, 1.

46.  Cf. Ste Croix, *Christian Persecution*, 128–29.

47.  Three works by Platonist philosophers, which survive in fragmentary form, are worthy of particular mention in this connection: Celsus's *True Doctrine* (*c.*170s),

Porphyry's *Contra Christ.* (third century), and the Emperor Julian's *Contra Gal.* (362–63). On Christian apologetics from the other side, see Dulles, Avery, *A History of Apologetics*, rev. edn (San Francisco, CA: Ignatius Press, 2005), ch. 2.

48. Augustine, *De civ. Dei*, 19.23 (our translation).

49. Grassigli, 'Classical Revivals', 167.

50. Petts, *Pagan and Christian*, 27.

51. Gregory, *Ep.* 9.11 (our translation).

52. Gregory, *Ep.* 11.76 (our translation).

53. Hutton, *Pagan Religions*, 284–85.

54. For a fairly recent treatment, which differs somewhat from the classic Christian narrative, see Potter, David, *Constantine the Emperor* (New York, NY: Oxford University Press, 2013).

55. Lucifer, *De reg. apostat.*, 9.

56. Cecconi, Giovanni Alberto 'Alan Cameron's Virius Nicomachus Flavianus', in Lizzi Testa (ed.), *The Strange Death of Pagan Rome* (Turnhout: Brepols, 2013), 151–64, at 157.

57. On Julian generally, Athanassiadi, Polymnia, *Julian: An Intellectual Biography* (London: Routledge, 1992) is a prominent sympathetic treatment and Bowersock, G. W., *Julian the Apostate* (London: Duckworth, 1978) a prominent unsympathetic one. See also e.g. Smith, Rowland, *Julian's Gods* (London: Routledge, 1995) and Murdoch, Adrian, *The Last Pagan* (Stroud: Sutton, 2003).

58. Julian, *Orat.* 5, 179D–180C (our translation).

59. According to the admittedly hostile testimony of his contemporary Gregory Nazianzen (*Orat.* 5.23).

60. *Cod. Theod.* 16.10.6.

61. On this issue, see generally Teitler, H. C., *The Last Pagan Emperor* (New York, NY: Oxford University Press, 2017).

62. On this body of material, see e.g. Baker-Brian, Nicholas and Tougher, Shaun (eds), *Emperor and Author* (Swansea: Classical Press of Wales, 2012). Julian's works are most readily accessible in the Loeb Classical Library series: Julian (ed. Wilmer C. Wright), *Orations 1–5* (Cambridge, MA: Harvard University Press, 1913); Julian (ed. Wilmer C. Wright), *Orations 6–8. Letters to Themistius, To the Senate and People of Athens, To a Priest. The Caesars. Misopogon* (Cambridge, MA: Harvard University Press, 1913); Julian (ed. Wilmer C. Wright), *Letters. Epigrams. Against the Galilaeans. Fragments* (Cambridge, MA: Harvard University Press, 1923).

63. Julian, *Ep.* 19.

64. Julian, *Ep. ad sac.*, 305B–D.

65. See Julian, *Ep. ad sac.*, 300C–304D; *Ep.* 430B. The restrictions on Catholic clerics were ultimately codified in the 1917 *Codex Iuris Canonici*, canons 124–144.

66. Bowersock, *Julian*, 119.

67. See Clifton, Chas, 'An Icon from an Alternate Universe', blog.chasclifton. com/?p=7522 (accessed 6 September 2023) on an Orthodox-style icon of Julian which was created for a modern pagan.

68. For later attitudes to Julian, see Murdoch, *The Last Pagan*, 204–18.

69. Swinburne, Algernon, 'Hymn to Proserpine' in *Poems and Ballads* (London: J. C. Hotten, 1866), 77–84.

70. Cameron, *Last Pagans of Rome*, 12.

71. Cf. Fowden, Garth, 'The Pagan Holy Man in Late Antique Society', *Journal of Hellenic Studies* 102 (1982): 33–59.

72. See generally Cameron, *Last Pagans of Rome*. For alternative perspectives on Cameron's book, see Testa (ed.), *Strange Death of Pagan Rome*.

73. See e.g. Watts, *Final Pagan Generation*, 182, 207.

74. Watts, *Final Pagan Generation*, 192.

75. See e.g. Harl, K. W., 'Sacrifice and Pagan Belief in Fifth- and Sixth-Century Byzantium', *Past and Present* 128 (1990): 7–27.

76. *Cod. Justin.* 1.11.10.

77. Cameron, Alan, 'The Last Days of the Academy at Athens', *Proceedings of the Cambridge Philological Society* 15 (1969): 7–29, at 9.

78. See Siniossoglou, *Radical Platonism*, 58.

79. Constantine VII, *De admin. imp.* 50.

80. Ammianus, *Res gest.* 23.3.1–3; Libanius, *Orat.* 18.214; Sozomen, *Hist. eccles.* 6.1.1.

81. See e.g. Athanassiadi, Polymnia, 'Persecution and Response in Late Paganism: The Evidence of Damascius', *Journal of Hellenic Studies* 113 (1993): 1–29, at 24–27.

82. Green, Tamara M., *The City of the Moon God: Religious Traditions of Harran* (Leiden: Brill, 1992), 112–14.

83. See Hutton, Ronald, *Witches, Druids and King Arthur* (London: Hambledon Continuum, 2006), 138–52. Hämeen-Anttila, Jaakko, *The Last Pagans of Iraq: Ibn Wahshiyya and his* Nabatean Agriculture (Leiden: Brill, 2006), 46 put the consensus dating for the end of paganism in Harran a little earlier, in the ninth or tenth centuries.

84. Steel, Carlos, 'De-Paganizing Philosophy', in Carlos Steel, John Marenbon and Werner Verbeke (eds), *Paganism in the Middle Ages: Threat and Fascination* (Leuven: Leuven University Press, 2012), 19–37, at 25.

## Chapter 2: Dealing with Past and Present Paganism in Medieval Western Christendom

1. Grønlie, Siân (trans.), *Íslendingabók, Kristni Saga: The Book of the Icelanders, The Story of the Conversion* (London: Viking Society for Northern Research, 2006), 9.

2. Bede, *Hist. eccles.* 2.15.

3. Hutton, 'How Pagan were Medieval English Peasants?', 235–49. See also Hutton's chapter 'The Legacy of British Paganism' in Hutton, *Pagan Britain*, 340–96.

4. A notable exception is the writings of the Muslim traveller Ibn Fadlan, who described in detail the religious practices of pagan Rus'. See Frye, Richard N., *Ibn Fadlan's Journey to Russia: A Tenth-Century Traveler from Baghad to the Volga River* (Princeton, NJ: Markus Wiener, 2005).

5. Bede, *Hist. eccles.* 2.13.

6. Young, Francis (ed.), *Pagans in the Early Modern Baltic: Sixteenth-Century Ethnographic Accounts of Baltic Paganism* (Leeds: Arc Humanities Press, 2022), 59–61.

7. On the Polabian revolt see Lübke, Christian, 'The Polabian Alternative: Paganism between Christian Kingdoms' in Przemysław Urbańczyk (ed), *Europe Around the Year 1000* (Warsaw: DiG, 2001), 379–89.

8. Lübke, 'Polabian Alternative', 379–80.

9. Rowell, S. C., *Lithuania Ascending: A Pagan Empire within East-Central Europe, 1295–1345* (Cambridge: Cambridge University Press, 1994), 38–39.

10. Lübke, 'Polabian Alternative', 383–84.

11. On this possibility see Vaitkevičius, Vykintas, 'The Main Features of the State Religion in Thirteenth-Century Lithuania', *Балто-славянские исследования* 16 (2004): 289–356.

12. Álvarez-Pedrosa, Juan Antonio (ed.), *Sources of Slavic Pre-Christian Religion* (Leiden: Brill, 2021), 153.

13. Álvarez-Pedrosa (ed.), *Sources*, 88–91.

14. Orderic Vitalis (ed. Marjorie Chibnall), *The Ecclesiastical History of Orderic Vitalis, Vol. 2, Books III and IV* (Oxford: Clarendon Press, 1969), 226.

15. *Pommersches Urkundbuch: Band I* (Stettin: Königlichen Staats-Archiv zu Stettin, 1868), 13 (no. 32).

16. *Pommersches Urkundbuch*, 15 (no. 34).

17. Reynolds, Burnham W., *The Prehistory of the Crusades: Missionary War and the Baltic Crusades* (London: Bloomsbury, 2016), 19.

18. Nyberg, Tore, *Monasticism in North-Western Europe, 800–1200* (Farnham: Ashgate, 2000), 121–25.

19. Berend, Nora, *At the Gate of Christendom: Jews, Muslims and 'Pagans' in Medieval Hungary, c. 1000–c. 1301* (Cambridge: Cambridge University Press, 2010), 54.

20. Berend, *At the Gate of Christendom*, 68–73.

21. Berend, *At the Gate of Christendom*, 213.

22. Rowell, *Lithuania Ascending*, 10.

23. On Lithuania's early successes see Rowell, *Lithuania Ascending*, 49–81.

24. Rowell, *Lithuania Ascending*, 51–52.

25. Bět'áková, Marta Eva and Blažek, Václav (eds), *Lexicon of Baltic Mythology* (Heidelberg: Winter Verlag, 2021), 153.

26. Mäesalu, Mihkel, 'Taani kuninga asehaldur Konrad Preen ja Jüriöö ülestõus', *Tuna* 2 (2021): 9–24.

27. Rowell, *Lithuania Ascending*, 274–77.

28. Young (ed.), *Pagans in the Early Modern Baltic*, 5.

29. Frost, Robert, *The Oxford History of Poland-Lithuania: The Making of the Polish-Lithuanian Union, 1385–1569* (Oxford: Oxford University Press, 2015), 299.

30. For discussion of this question in relation to post-conversion Lithuania see Rowell, S. C., 'Was Fifteenth-Century Lithuanian Catholicism as Lukewarm as Sixteenth-Century Reformers and Later Commentators Would Have Us Believe?', *Central Europe* 8.2 (2010): 86–106; Baronas, Darius, 'Christians in Late Pagan, and Pagans in Early Christian Lithuania: The Fourteenth and Fifteenth Centuries', *Lithuanian Historical Studies* 19 (2014): 51–81.

31. Young (ed.), *Pagans in the Early Modern Baltic*, 21.

32. Marenbon, *Pagans and Philosophers*, 1–15.

33. On Apuleius in the Middle Ages see Carver, Robert H. F., *The Protean Ass: The Metamorphoses of Apuleius from Antiquity to the Renaissance* (Oxford: Oxford University Press, 2007), 61–107.

34. Marenbon, *Pagans and Philosophers*, 57–66.

35. On the phases of medieval Europe's conversion see Kling, David W., *A History of Christian Conversion* (Oxford: Oxford University Press, 2020), 103–150.

36. Marenbon, *Pagans and Philosophers*, 28–29.

37. Marenbon, *Pagans and Philosophers*, 68–70.

38. Machielsen, Jan, 'Introduction: The Science of Demons' in Jan Machielsen (ed.), *The Science of Demons: Early Modern Authors Facing Witchcraft and the Devil* (London: Routledge, 2020), 1–15, at 3.

39. Kling, *History of Christian Conversion*, 68.

40. On the phenomenon of demonization see Young, *Twilight of the Godlings*, 142–55.

41. Young, *Twilight of the Godlings*, 152–53.

42. Roubeckas, Nickolas, *An Ancient Theory of Religion: Euhemerism from Antiquity to the Present* (London: Routledge, 2017), 165.

43. Roubeckas, *An Ancient Theory of Religion*, 170–73.

44. Williams, Mark, *Ireland's Immortals: A History of the Gods of Irish Myth* (Princeton, NJ: Princeton University Press, 2016), 16.

45. Williams, *Ireland's Immortals*, 20–23.

46. Williams, *Ireland's Immortals*, 25.

47. Freudenberg, Bele and Goetz, Hans-Werner, 'The Christian Perception of Heathens in the Early Middle Ages', *Millennium* 10.1 (2013): 281–91, at 289–90.

48. Freudenberg and Goetz, 'The Christian Perception of Heathens', 290.

49. Young, *Twilight of the Godlings*, 40–41.

50. Green, Richard Firth, 'Refighting Carlo Ginzburg's *Night Battles*' in Craig M. Nakashian and D. P. Franke (eds), *Prowess, Piety, and Public Order in Medieval Society: Essays in Honor of Richard W. Kaeuper* (Leiden: Brill, 2017), 381–402, at 387.

51. Newman, Coree, 'The Good, the Bad, and the Unholy: Ambivalent Angels in the Middle Ages' in Michael Ostling (ed.), *Fairies, Demons, and Nature Spirits* (Basingstoke: Palgrave MacMillan, 2018), 103–122, at 117.

52. Newman, 'The Good, the Bad, and the Unholy', 120.

53. Moitra, Angana, 'From Pagan God to Magical Being: The Changing Face of the Faerie King and Its Cultural Implications' in Désirée Cappa, James E. Christie, Lorenza Gay, Hanna Gentili and Finn Schulze-Feldmann (eds), *Cultural Encounters: Cross-Disciplinary Studies from the Late Middle Ages to the Enlightenment* (Wilmington, DE: Vernon Press, 2018), 23–40, at 27–30.

54. Marenbon, *Pagans and Philosophers*, 201.

55. Marenbon, *Pagans and Philosophers*, 224.

56. Freudenberg and Goetz, 'Christian Perception of Heathens', 283.

57. Marenbon, John, 'Relativism in the Long Middle Ages: Crossing the Ethical Border with Paganism', *Journal of Ethnographic Theory* 5.2 (2015): 345–65, at 346.

58. Marenbon, 'Relativism in the Long Middle Ages', 353–54.

59. Marenbon, 'Relativism in the Long Middle Ages', 356–57.

60. Marenbon, 'Relativism in the Long Middle Ages', 357–58.

61. Marenbon, *Pagans and Philosophers*, 179.

62. Steel, 'De-Paganizing Philosophy', 34.

63. Lievens, Robrecht, 'The "Pagan" Dirc van Delf' in Carlos Steel, John Marenbon and Werner Verbeke (eds), *Paganism in the Middle Ages: Threat and Fascination* (Leuven: Leuven University Press, 2012), 167–94, at 173.

64. Quoted in Lievens, 'The "Pagan" Dirc van Delf', 189.

65. Young, *Twilight of the Godlings*, 275–77.

66. Lievens, 'The "Pagan" Dirc van Delf', 177–78.

67. Slotemaker, John T. and Witt, Jeffrey C., *Robert Holcot* (Oxford: Oxford University Press, 2016), 234.

68. Lievens, 'The "Pagan" Dirc van Delf', 193.

69. Slotemaker and Witt, *Robert Holcot*, 235.

70. Marenbon, *Pagans and Philosophers*, 104–105.

71. Salih, *Imagining the Pagan*, 4.

72. Friedman, Yvonne, 'Christian Hatred of the Other: Theological Rhetoric vs. Political Reality' in Cordelia Hess, and Jonathan Adams (eds), *Fear and Loathing in the North: Jews and Muslims in Medieval Scandinavia and the Baltic Region* (Berlin: De Gruyter, 2015), 187–202, at 198.

73. Cervantes, Fernando, *The Devil in the New World: The Impact of Diabolism in New Spain* (New Haven, CT: Yale University Press, 1994), 12.

74. Young, Francis, *A History of Exorcism in Catholic Christianity* (Basingstoke: Palgrave MacMillan, 2016), 142.

75. Rowell, S. C., 'Unexpected Contacts: Lithuanians at Western Courts, c. 1316–c. 1400', *The English Historical Review* 111 (1996): 557–77.

76. Young (ed.), *Pagans in the Early Modern Baltic*, 20.

77. Freudenberg and Goetz, 'Christian Perception of Heathens', 288–89.

78. Williams, *Ireland's Immortals*, 15.

79. Hutton, *Pagan Britain*, 340.

80. Hutton, *Pagan Britain*, 344–45.

81. Young, *Twilight of the Godlings*, 164–67.

82. Duffy, Eamon, *The Stripping of the Altars: Traditional Religion in England 1400–1580* (New Haven, CT: Yale University Press, 1992), 277–79.

83. Marenbon, 'Relativism in the Long Middle Ages', 348.

84. MacMullen, Ramsay, *Christianity and Paganism in the Fourth to Eighth Centuries* (New Haven, CT: Yale University Press, 1997), 159.

85. MacMullen, *Christianity and Paganism*, 158.

86. Filotas, *Pagans Survivals*, 70–76.

87. Filotas, *Pagan Survivals*, 78–79.

88. Filotas, *Pagan Survivals*, 80–82.

89. Young, *Twilight of the Godlings*, 286.

90. Bozoky, Edina, 'Private Reliquaries and Other Prophylactic Jewels: New Compositions and Devotional Practices in the Fourteenth and Fifteenth Centuries' in Sophie Page (ed.), *The Unorthodox Imagination in Late Medieval Britain* (Manchester: Manchester University Press, 2010), 115–30, at 127.

91. Barlow, Frank, *Thomas Becket* (Berkeley, CA: University of California Press, 1986), 39.

92. Schofield, Phillipp R., *Seals and Their Context in the Middle Ages* (Oxford: Oxbow, 2015), 16.

93. Milis, Ludo, 'The Spooky Heritage of Ancient Paganisms' in Carlos Steel, John Marenbon and Werner Verbeke (eds), *Paganism in the Middle Ages: Threat and Fascination* (Leuven: Leuven University Press, 2012), 1–18, at 10–11.

94. Milis, 'Spooky Heritage', 4.

95. Herzig, Tamar, 'The Bestselling Demonologist: Heinrich Institoris's *Malleus maleficarum*' in Jan Machielsen (ed.), *The Science of Demons: Early Modern Authors Facing Witchcraft and the Devil* (London: Routledge, 2020), 53–67, at 56.

96. Milis, 'Spooky Heritage', 3–4.

97. Marenbon, *Pagans and Philosophers*, 72.

## Chapter 3: Pagan Renaissances

1. [Symonds, John Addington], 'The English Drama during the Reigns of Elizabeth and James: Part 1', *The Cornhill Magazine* 11 (1865): 604–18, at 606. We will come back to Symonds in Chapter 5.

2. Augustine, *De civ. Dei*, 8.5.

3. See Novotný, František, *The Posthumous Life of Plato* (Prague: Academia Pragensis, 1977), 287.

4. See Siniossoglou, *Radical Platonism*, 62–71.

5. Psellus, *Orat. For.* 1.

6. On Psellus and his apparent crypto-paganism, see generally Siniossoglou, *Radical Platonism*, 71–85; also e.g. Burns, Dylan, 'The Chaldean Oracles of Zoroaster, Hekate's Couch, and Platonic Orientalism in Psellos and Plethon', *Aries* 6 (2006): 158–79, at 159–65.

7. For a list of writings by Psellus that relate to the Oracles, see Lewy, Hans, *Chaldaean Oracles and Theurgy*, 3rd edn (Paris: Institut des Etudes Augustiniennes, 2011), Excursus VI. See also Corazzol, Giacomo, 'Le fonti "caldaiche" dell'Oratio: indagine sui presupposti cabbalistici della concezione pichiana dell'uomo', *Accademia* 15 (2013): 9–62, at 19–20 on the works of Psellus and his Byzantine successor Plethon on the *Oracles*.

8. The text can be found in Psellus, Michael (ed. D. J. O'Meara), *Philosophica minora* (Leipzig: Teubner, 1989), vol. 2.

9. See Setton, Kenneth M., 'The Byzantine Background to the Italian Renaissance', *Proceedings of the American Philological Society* 100 (1956): 1–76, at 13.

10. Adapted from the translation of the Russian Orthodox Church, 'Rite of Orthodoxy with Anathemas against Heretics', online at pravoslavie.ru/101610.html, accessed 21 September 2023.

11. See Siniossoglou, *Radical Platonism*, 85–92.

12. Bradshaw, David, *Aristotle East and West: Metaphysics and the Division of Christendom* (Cambridge: Cambridge University Press, 2004), 221–62.

13. See Siniossoglou, *Radical Platonism*, 100–113.

14. On Plethon generally, see the different approaches of e.g. Tambrun, Brigitte, *Pléthon: Le retour de Platon* (Paris: Vrin, 2006); Hladký, Vojtěch, *The Philosophy of Gemistos Plethon* (London: Routledge, 2016); and Siniossoglou, *Radical Platonism*.

15. Opsopaus, John, *The Secret Texts of Hellenic Polytheism* (Woodbury: Llewellyn, 2022).

16. Plethon, *Laws*, preface.

17. Plethon, *Laws* 3.34.

18. Siniossoglou, *Radical Platonism*, 169.

19. See Siniossoglou, *Radical Platonism*, 380; also 391 on the link between pagan cult and Plethon's proto-nationalist ideas.

20. See e.g. Tambrun-Krasker, Brigitte, 'Les Oracles chaldaïques entre idéologie et critique (XVe–XVIIe s.)', in Adrien Lecerf, Saudelli, Lucia and Seng, Helmut (eds), *Oracles Chaldaïques: fragments et philosophie* (Heidelberg: Winter, 2014), 253–77, at 255–60.

21. See Hladký, *Philosophy of Gemistos Plethon*, 35–9.

22. Fragments 6, 8 and 39 in Psellus's collection, which may be found in Psellus (ed. O'Meara), *Philosophica minora*, vol. 2. See also Athanassiadi, Polymnia, 'Byzantine Commentators on the Chaldaean Oracles: Psellos and Plethon', in Katerina Ierodiakonou (ed.), *Byzantine Philosophy and its Ancient Sources* (Oxford: Clarendon, 2002), 237–52 for the contrast between the approaches of Psellus and Plethon.

23. See e.g. Tambrun, Brigitte, 'Marsile Ficin et le commentaire de Pléthon sur les Oracles chaldaïques', *Accademia* 1 (1999): 9–48 at 22–5; Tambrun, *Pléthon*, 80–94, 241–47.

24. George of Trebizond, *Comp.* 3.21.

25. See Vryonis, Speros, 'The "Freedom of Expression" in Fifteenth Century Byzantium', in *La notion de liberté au Moyen Age: Islam, Byzance, Occident* (Paris: Les Belles Lettres, 1985), 261–73; Siniossoglou, *Radical Platonism*, 134–38.

26. See Hladký, *Philosophy of Gemistos Plethon*, 219–20.

27. See Keller, A., 'Two Byzantine Scholars and Their Reception in Italy', *Journal of the Warburg and Courtauld Institutes* 20 (1957): 363–70, at 366–70; Bacchelli, Franco, 'La Considération céleste et les Enseignements de Démétrius Rhaoul Kavàkis', *Noctua* 3.2 (2016): 164–238. Kabakes' ideas about the sun also influenced Copernicus.

28. See Akisik, Aslihan, 'Self and Other in the Renaissance: Laonikos Chalkokondyles and Late Byzantine Intellectuals', PhD diss., Harvard University, 2013, online at core.ac.uk/download/pdf/28943821.pdf, accessed 21 September 2023.

29. See Fantazzi, Charles (ed.), *Michael Marullus: Poems* (Cambridge, MA: Harvard University Press, 2012); Siniossoglou, Niketas, 'Love and Exile in Michael Marullus Tarchaniota', in Natasha Constantinidou and Han Lamers (eds), *Receptions of Hellenism in Early Modern Europe* (Leiden: Brill, 2020), 233–59.

30. Marullus, *Hymns* 2.1.37–60. This passage is influenced by Plato, *Phaedrus*, 246E–247B.

31. Lawson, John Cuthbert, *Modern Greek Folklore and Ancient Greek Religion: A Study in Survivals* (Cambridge: Cambridge University Press, 1910), 41.

32. Larson, Jennifer, *Greek Nymphs: Myth, Cult, Lore* (Oxford: Oxford University Press, 2001), 61.

33. Larson, *Greek Nymphs*, 61–62.

34. Purkiss, *Troublesome Things*, 45–46.

35. Ostling, Michael, 'Introduction: Where've All the Good People Gone?', in Michael Ostling (ed.), *Fairies, Demons, and Nature Spirits: 'Small Gods' at the Margins of Christendom* (Basingstoke: Palgrave MacMillan, 2018), 1–53.

36. Ohnefalsch-Richter, Max, *Ancient Places of Worship in Kypros Catalogued and Described* (Berlin: H. S. Hermann, 1891), 54.

37. Håland, Evy Johanne, *Greek Festivals, Modern and Ancient: A Comparison of Female and Male Values* (Newcastle: Cambridge Scholars Publishing, 2017), vol. 1, 274–75.

38. On the survival of paganism in Christian Greece see Gregory, Timothy E., 'The Survival of Paganism in Christian Greece: A Critical Essay', *The American Journal of Philology* 107.2 (1986): 229–42.

39. Walker, Alicia, 'Magic in Medieval Byzantium', in David J. Collins, *Magic and Witchcraft in the West: From Antiquity to the Present* (Cambridge: Cambridge University Press, 2015), 209–34, at 216–18.

40. Walker, 'Magic in Medieval Byzantium', 227–28.

41. See e.g. Bodnar, Edward W. (ed.), *Cyriac of Ancona: Later Travels* (Cambridge, MA: Harvard University Press, 2003).

42. See further Godwin, *Pagan Dream of the Renaissance*, 21–37. Godwin also published a complete translation of the work as *Hypnerotomachia Poliphili: The Strife of Love in a Dream* (New York, NY: Thames & Hudson, 1999).

43. Joannes Vislicensis, *Bellum Prutenum* in Kruczkiewicz, Bronisław (ed.), *Pauli Crosnensis Rutheni atque Ioannis Vislicensis Carmina* (Kraków: Typis Universitatis Jagellonicae, 1887), 1.90–109; 1.225–56; 2.276–98; 3.1–115.

44. Fracastorius, Hieronymus, *Opera omnia* (Venice: Giunti, 1555), 279v.

45. Archius, Nicolaus, 'In Funerem M. Antonii Turrii, Viri Rarissimi, Epicedion', in *Numerorum libri IV* (Verona: Morone, 1762), 57–63.

46. Disraeli, Isaac, *Curiosities of Literature*, new edn (London: Routledge, 1866), vol. 2, 485.

47. See Machiavelli, Niccolò (ed. Giuseppe Piergili), *Discorsi sopra la prima deca di Tito Livio* (Florence: Successori Le Monnier, 1893), 235–45.

48. See D'Elia, Anthony F., *Pagan Virtue in a Christian World* (Cambridge, MA: Harvard University Press, 2016), 149–83, 274–84.

49. Pius II, *Commentarii* (Frankfurt: Officina Aubriana, 1584), 51: *Aedificavit tamen nobile templum Arimini in honorem divi Francisci, verum ita gentilibus operibus implevit, ut non tam Christianorum quam infidelium daemones adorantium templum esse videretur* (our translation).

50. Perkins, Charles C., *Tuscan Sculptors* (London: Longman, Green, 1864), vol. 1, 169.

51. See further Seznec, *Survival of the Pagan Gods*, 134–37.

52. We may note that Latinizing one's name was in itself unremarkable. The unusual thing about Sanseverino is that he adopted a *new* name—although sometimes authors did this for practical reasons, if their vernacular name could not be elegantly Latinized.

53. See generally D'Elia, Anthony F., *A Sudden Terror* (Cambridge, MA: Harvard University Press, 2009). If there was a conspiracy, Sigismondo Malatesta may have been involved in it.

54. Platina, Bartolomeo (ed. Thomas G. Hendrickson, Alexandra B. Berman, Pascal Croak, Daniel Gridley, Sebastian Herrera, Jin Lee, Graham Rigby. John Robinson, Gabriela C. Sommer, Kent Ueno and James Whittemore), *Lives of the Popes, Paul II* (Oxford, OH: Faenum, 2017), 98–104 (our translation).

55. Piana, Marco, 'Gods in the Garden: Visions of the Pagan Other in the Rome of Julius II', *Journal of Religion in Europe* 12 (2019): 285–309. Gianfrancesco was the nephew of the more famous Giovanni.

56. See e.g. Gentile, Sebastiano, 'Giorgio Gemisto Pletone e la sua influenza sull'umanesimo fiorentino', in Paolo Viti (ed.), *Firenze e il concilio del 1439* (Florence: Olschki, 1994), vol. 2, 813–32.

57. Hankins, James, *Plato in the Italian Renaissance* (Leiden: Brill, 1990), vol. 1, 236.

58. See Monfasani, John, 'A Tale of Two Books: Bessarion's *In Calumniatorem Platonis* and George of Trebizond's *Comparatio Philosophorum Platonis et Aristotelis*', *Renaissance Studies* 22 (2008): 1–15.

59. For a useful introduction to Ficino, see Voss, Angela (ed.), *Marsilio Ficino* (Berkeley, CA: North Atlantic, 2006).

60. See Hankins, James, 'Cosimo de' Medici and the "Platonic Academy"', *Journal of the Warburg and Courtauld Institutes* 53 (1990): 144–62.

61. See Copenhaver (ed.), *Hermetica*, xlvii–l.

62. *Ex pagano Christi miles factus*. See Marcel, Raymond, *Marsile Ficin (1433–1499)* (Paris: Belles Lettres, 1958), 683.

63. See Hutton, *Witches, Druids and King Arthur*, 159–63, 180–81; Hutton, Ronald, 'Astral Magic: The Acceptable Face of Paganism', in Nicholas Campion, Patrick Curry and Michael York (eds), *Astrology and the Academy* (Bristol: Cinnabar, 2004), 10–24, at 11–18. The pagan gods can be found in the form of planetary divinities in the work of members of Ficino's circle—including Giovanni Nesi and Francesco Cattani da Diacceto—and other Renaissance figures, notably the esotericists Heinrich Cornelius Agrippa and Giordano Bruno: see Hutton, *Witches, Druids and King Arthur*, 181–8; Hutton, 'Astral Magic', 19–20.

64. Ficino, Marsilio, *Opera* (Basel: [no publisher], 1561), 933: *ne forte lectores ad priscum deorum daemonumque cultum iamdiu merito reprobatum revocare viderer*.

65. See e.g. Idel, Moshe, '*Prisca Theologia* in Marsilio Ficino and in some Jewish treatments', in Michael J. B. Allen and Valery Rees (eds), *Marsilio Ficino: His Theology, His Philosophy, His Legacy* (Leiden: Brill, 2002), 137–58.

66. Pico della Mirandola, Giovanni (ed. Bertrand Schefer), *Conclusiones DCCCC* (Paris: Editions Allia, 1999), 198.

67. See Hutton, *Witches, Druids and King Arthur*, 180–81. See also Yates, Frances A., *Giordano Bruno and the Hermetic Tradition* (London: Routledge and Kegan Paul, 1964), 78–79, 89–90 on Ficino and Pico's use of the Orphic materials.

68. See Sudduth, Michael, 'Pico della Mirandola's Philosophy of Religion', in M. V. Dougherty (ed.), *Pico della Mirandola: New Essays* (New York, NY: Cambridge University Press, 2008), 61–80, at 76–79.

69. See Hutton, *Witches, Druids and King Arthur*, 188–9; Hutton, 'Astral Magic', 20–21.

70. Knight, Samuel, *The Life of Dr J. Colet*, new edn (Oxford: Clarendon, 1823), 271.

71. Our principal source, Giovio, Paulo, *Historiae sui temporis* (Basel: [no publisher], 1567), vol. 2, 19–20, says vaguely that the bull was 'sacrificed to [the] god/power' (*numini*). For the interpretation of the event as pagan, see Hussovianus, Nicolaus, *In sacrificium nigri tauri Romae* in Hussovianus, Nicolaus (ed. J. Pelczar), *Nicolai Hussoviani Carmina* (Kraków: Sumptibus Academiae Literarum), 100–102.

72. Hutton, *Pagan Britain*, 343–44.

73. See further e.g. Baïf, Jean-Antoine de (ed. Jean Vignes), *Oeuvres complètes I: Euvres en rime, Part 1* (Paris: Honoré Champion, 2002), 778–9, 781–2; Ferguson, Gary, *Queer (Re)Readings in the French Renaissance* (London: Routledge, 2016), 116–17.

74. Meagher, Andrew, *The Popish Mass* (Cork: [no publisher], 1823 [1771]), vi–vii.

75. See Saxl, F., 'Pagan Sacrifice in the Italian Renaissance', *Journal of the Warburg Institute* 2 (1939): 346–67.

76. Bullinger, Heinrich, *De origine erroris* (Zurich: Froschauer, 1539), ch. 35; Calvin, Jean, *Traité des reliques* (Geneva: Labor et Fides, 2000 [1543]).

77. See further Janes, Dominic, *Victorian Reformation* (New York, NY: Oxford University Press, 2009), esp. ch. 4; Kidd, Colin, *The World of Mr Casaubon* (Cambridge: Cambridge University Press, 2016), esp. ch. 3.

78. Voltaire, *Dictionnaire philosophique portatif* (Paris, 1764), 249.

79. Wiseman, Nicholas, *Letters to John Poynder Esq., Upon His Work Entitled 'Popery in Alliance with Heathenism'* (Philadelphia, PA: M. Fithian, 1836), 8–26.

80. See Wheeler, Graham John, 'Discourses of Paganism in the British and Irish Press during the Early Pagan Revival', *The Pomegranate* 19 (2017): 5–24.

## Chapter 4: Paganism in the Enlightenment

1. Bellarmine, Robert, *De controversiis Christianae fidei*, 3.20 in *Opera* (Naples: Giuseppe Giuliano, 1838), vol. 2, 338: *Nulli enim nunc sunt, qui non rideant dogmata Gentilium; nec unquam audimus Christianos depravatos libris Gentilium, deficere ad Gentilismum, ut quotidie deficiunt ad haereticos.*

2. Young (ed.), *Pagans in the Early Modern Baltic*, 17–19.

3. Klein, Andreas, *Early Modern Knowledge about the Sámi: A History of Johannes Schefferus' Lapponia (1673)* (Hanover: Wehrhahn Verlag, 2023), 23–24.

4. Klein, *Early Modern Knowledge about the Sámi*, 31–32.

5. Rasmussen, Siv, 'The Protracted Sámi Reformation—or the Protracted Christianizing Process', in Lars Ivar Hansen, Rognald Heiseldal Bergesen and Ingebjørg Hage (eds), *The Protracted Reformation in Northern Norway: Introductory Studies* (Stamsund: Orkana Akademisk, 2014), 165–84 at 88–89; Willumsen, Liv Helene, 'The Witchcraft Trial against Anders Poulsen, Vadsø 1692: Critical Perspectives', in Håkan Rydving and Konsta Kaikkonen (eds), *Religions around the Arctic: Source Criticism and Comparisons* (Stockholm: Stockholm University Press, 2022), 139–60.

6. Michels, Georg, 'Rescuing the Orthodox: The Church Policies of Archbishop Afanasii of Kholmogory, 1682–1702', in Robert P. Geraci and Michael Khodarkovsky (eds), *Of Religion and Empire: Missions, Conversion, and Tolerance in Tsarist Russia* (Ithaca, NY: Cornell University Press, 2001), 19–37, at 23–24.

7. Pierre, François-Joachim de (Cardinal de Bernis), *Mémoires et Lettres* (Paris: E. Plon et Cie, 1878), vol. 1, 41: 'Les femmes mêmes commencèrent à s'affranchir des préjugés. L'esprit d'incrédulité et le libertinage circulèrent ensemble dans le monde … [L]a corruption devint presque générale, on afficha le matérialisme,

le déisme, le pyrrhonisme; la foi fut réléguée chez le peuple, dans la bourgeoisie et les communautés; il ne fut plus de bon ton de croire à l'Évangile.'

8. See Eilberg-Schwartz, Howard, 'Witches of the West', *Journal of Feminist Studies in Religion* 5 (1989): 77–95.

9. Although it seems that this usage did not entirely come into its own until the latter part of the nineteenth century: see Wheeler, 'Discourses of Paganism', 5–24.

10. Gay, Peter, *The Enlightenment: An Interpretation: The Rise of Modern Paganism* (London: Weidenfeld and Nicolson, 1967), 32, 44.

11. See further Kidd, *World of Mr Casaubon*.

12. [Anon.], *The Connoisseur*, new ed., vol. 2 (London: J. Richardson and Co., 1822 [1756]), 208–13, 209–10.

13. *Ibid.* 212.

14. Jones, William, *The Theological and Miscellaneous Works of the Rev. William Jones* (London: Rivington, 1810), vol. 2, 407.

15. [Hooke, Luke Joseph], *Religionis Naturalis et Revelatae Principia* (Paris: Guérin, 1754 [1752]), vol. 2, appendix 2.

16. It was comparable in this regard to the mythographical works of the twelfth century discussed in Chapter 2, or early modern works like the Polish poet Maciej Sarbiewski's *Dii gentium* (Sarbiewski, Maciej (trans. Krystyna Stawecka), *Dii gentium: Bogowie Pogan* (Warsaw: Ossolineum, 1972)).

17. Hume, David, *The Natural History of Religion* in Hume, David, *Essays and Treatises on Several Subjects* (Basel: J. J. Tourneisen, 1793), vol. 4, 48–50.

18. Along with the broadly equivalent terms 'heathen', 'gentile' and their cognates. Cf. Hutton, *Triumph of the Moon*, 2nd edn, 5–9.

19. See e.g. Pailin, David A., *Attitudes to Other Religions* (Manchester: Manchester University Press, 1984); Hunt, Lynn, Jacob, Margaret C. and Mijnhardt, Wijnand, *The Book That Changed Europe: Picart and Bernard's* Religious Ceremonies of the World (Cambridge, MA: Belknap Press, 2010); and Stroumsa, Guy G., *A New Science* (Cambridge, MA: Harvard University Press, 2010).

20. See e.g. Mulsow, Martin, 'Antiquarianism and Idolatry: The *Historia* of Religions in the Seventeenth Century', in G. Pomata and N. G. Siraisi (eds), *Historia: Empiricism and Erudition in Early Modern Europe* (Cambridge, MA: MIT Press, 2005), 181–210, at 201–203.

21. Rowbotham, Arnold H., 'Voltaire, Sinophile', *PMLA* 47 (1932): 1050–65, at 1056–57.

22. *Caledonian Mercury*, 20 October 1730, 1.

23. See e.g. Ozouf, Mona, *Festivals and the French Revolution* (Cambridge, MA: Harvard University Press, 1988), 97–100.

24. *Saunders's News-Letter*, 25 November 1793, 1.

25. See Ozouf, *Festivals*, 101.

26. See Hornung, Erik, *The Secret Lore of Egypt* (Ithaca, NY: Cornell University Press, 2001), 133–4; Shaw, Matthew, *Time and the French Revolution* (Woodbridge: Boydell, 2011), 67–68.

27. On a more explicitly pagan revival movement among Jacobins in Cephalonia, see Siniossoglou, *Radical Platonism*, 425.

28. One name which does not appear in this paragraph is that of the writer and scholar Fabre d'Olivet (1767–1825). Fabre d'Olivet has been classed as a pagan (see e.g. Faivre, Antoine, *Western Esotericism* (Albany, NY: SUNY Press, 2010), 58; Godwin, *Pagan Dream of the Renaissance*, 249), but he is better seen as a universalizer who sought a single truth behind all religions.

29. Danilewicz, M. L., '"The King of the New Israel": Thaddeus Grabianka (1740–1807)', *Oxford Slavonic Papers* 1 (1968): 49–73, at 58–59.

30. See e.g. the letter preserved in [Anon.], *Biographical Anecdotes of the Founders of the French Republic* (London: Phillips, 1797), 156–57.

31. See Nerval, Gérard de, *Les Illuminés* (Paris: Michel Lévy Frères, 1868), 238–68.

32. See generally Stevenson, David, *The Origins of Freemasonry* (Cambridge: Cambridge University Press, 1988).

33. See, in general, McIntosh, Christopher, *The Rosicrucians*, 3rd edn (York Beach, ME: Weiser, 1998), 42–52; Yates, Frances A., *The Rosicrucian Enlightenment*, new edn (London: Routledge, 2002), 60–62; and the editorial material in Godwin, Joscelyn, McIntosh, Christopher and McIntosh, Donate Pahnke (eds), *Rosicrucian Trilogy: Modern Translations of the Three Founding Documents: Fama Fraternitatis, 1644; Confessio Fraternitatis, 1615; The Chemical Wedding of Christian Rosenkreutz, 1616* (Newburyport, MA: Weiser, 2016).

34. See e.g. Roberts, J. M., *The Mythology of the Secret Societies* (London: Secker and Warburg, 1972).

35. Jacob, Margaret C., 'The Radical Enlightenment and Freemasonry: Where We Are Now', *Philosophica* 88 (2013): 13–29, at 15.

36. British Library MS Add. 23198 ('Matthew Cooke MS'), fols 14b–15. Modern English translation online at albionlodge5.org/uploads/7/8/8/5/7885596/the_matthew_cooke_manuscript_wtranslation.pdf, accessed 22 September 2023.

37. Margaret Jacob wrote that it is 'more akin to ancient paganism than to any modern sect' (*Living the Enlightenment* (New York, NY: Oxford University Press, 1991), 66). Peter Harrison concluded that it is 'rather confused; (*'Religion' and the Religions in the English Enlightenment* (Cambridge: Cambridge University Press, 1990), 90). For further views on the *Pantheisticon*, see e.g. Brown, Michael, *A Political Biography of John Toland* (London: Routledge, 2012), 145–47; Leask, Ian, 'Stoicism unbound: Cicero's *Academica* in Toland's *Pantheisticon*', *British Journal for the History of Philosophy* (2016): 1–21, at 1–2.

38. Jacob, Margaret C., *The Radical Enlightenment*, 2nd edn (Lafayette, LA: Cornerstone, 2006), Appendix.

39. Daniel, Stephen H., *John Toland* (Kingston, Ont.: McGill-Queen's University Press, 1984), 222.

40. See Jacob, *Radical Enlightenment*, 233–36; also 124–28 and Jacob, *Living the Enlightenment*, 91–94.

41. Stevenson, *Origins of Freemasonry*, 233.

42. [Lefranc, Jacques-François], *Le voile levé pour les curieux* ([no place]: [no publisher], 1791), 95: 'adopte, sans répugnance, toutes les rêveries du paganisme'.

43. See Butler, Alison, *Victorian Occultism and the Making of Modern Magic* (Basingstoke: Palgrave Macmillan, 2011), 68–69.

44. Paine, Thomas, *On the Origin of Free-Masonry* (New York, NY: Elliot and Crissy, 1810), 9.

45. See Godwin, Joscelyn, *The Theosophical Enlightenment* (Albany, NY: SUNY Press, 1994), 58 and Gilbert, R. A., 'The Great Chain of Unreason: The Publication and Distribution of "Rejected Knowledge"', in 'England During the Victorian Era', PhD diss., University of London, 2009, 182–84.

46. See Wheeler, 'Apuleius and the Esoteric Revival', 260–76.

47. Leo XIII, *Humanum genus*, 24: *moresque et instituta ethnicorum duodeviginti saeculorum intervallo revocare*. Online at vatican.va/content/leo-xiii/en/encyclicals/documents/hf_l-xiii_enc_18840420_humanum-genus.html, accessed 22 September 2023.

48. On Fransham generally, see Wheeler, Graham John, 'John Fransham, the Norwich Polytheist: An English Pagan in the Eighteenth Century', *Journal of Religious History, Literature and Culture* 6 (2020): 20–49.

49. This is most readily available as [Anon.], 'An Essay on the Oestrum or Enthusiasm of Orpheus', *European Magazine* 18 (1790): 409–13.

50. See Wheeler, 'John Fransham', 48 n.53.

51. Saint, W., *Memoirs of the Life, Character, Opinions, and Writings, of that Learned and Eccentric Man, the Late John Fransham, of Norwich* (Norwich: Berry, 1811), 12.

52. See Wheeler, 'John Fransham', 36.

53. See Wheeler, 'John Fransham', 43–44.

54. There is no definitive modern biography of Taylor, but Critchley, Steven George, 'Pagan Taylor: The Emergence of a Public Character 1785–1804', PhD diss., University of York, 2005, online at etheses.whiterose.ac.uk/14190/1/437615.pdf, accessed 22 September 2023) is a very useful study. See also Raine, Kathleen and Harper, George Mills (eds), *Thomas Taylor the Platonist* (London: Routledge, 1969).

55. Godwin, *Pagan Dream of the Renaissance*, 249.

56. [Anon.], 'The Survival of Paganism', *Fraser's Magazine* 12 (1875): 640–51, at 645.

57. Although his work in this regard also drew on that of the scholar Floyer Sydenham.

58. Taylor has also been credited with a pamphlet advocating polytheism entitled *A New System of Religion* or *The Spirit of all Religions* which was first published in 1790. But this work appears to have been written by the historian and antiquary

John Pinkerton: see O'Flaherty, Patrick, *Scotland's Pariah* (Toronto: University of Toronto Press, 2015), 267–8. See also Addey, Tim, 'Why Thomas Taylor is not the author of *A New System of Religion*', online at prometheustrust.co.uk/Why_Thomas_Taylor_is_not_the_author_of_A_New_System_of_Religion.pdf, accessed 22 September 2023.

59.  See Critchley, 'Pagan Taylor', 190–96.

60.  The translation was reprinted in 1792 and then republished in a second edition in 1824. Taylor made the incorrect claim that the hymns had been used in the Eleusinian Mysteries.

61.  Taylor, Thomas (ed.), *The Hymns of Orpheus* (London: Payne, 1792), 157.

62.  Taylor (ed.), *Hymns of Orpheus*, v–vi.

63.  Bernal, Martin, *Black Athena: The Afroasiatic Roots of Classical Civilisation* (London: Vintage Books, 1991), vol. 1, 322.

64.  See Hutton, *Triumph of the Moon*, 2nd edn, 21–22.

65.  See Hutton, Ronald, *Blood and Mistletoe: The History of the Druids in Britain* (New Haven, CT: Yale University Press, 2009), ch. 11.

66.  See Hutton, *Blood and Mistletoe*, esp. ch. 3.

67.  See Hutton, *Blood and Mistletoe*, ch. 4.

68.  Numa was a legendary king of Rome who was credited with founding the Roman religion.

69.  The full poem can be found in Hall, Augusta (Lady Llanover) (ed.), *The Autobiography and Correspondence of Mary Granville: Second Series* (London: Richard Bentley, 1862), vol. 2, 539–41. See also Cannon, Garland, *The Life and Mind of Oriental Jones* (Cambridge: Cambridge University Press, 1990), 147–48; Hutton, *Blood and Mistletoe*, 131–2.

70.  See Hutton, *Blood and Mistletoe*, ch. 5.

71.  See Ashe, Geoffrey, *Do What You Will* (London: W. H. Allen, 1974), 119–32; Wheeler, Richard, '"Pro Magna Charta" or "Fay ce que Voudras": Political and Moral Precedents for the Gardens of Sir Francis Dashwood at West Wycombe', *New Arcadian Journal* 49/50 (2000): 26–61; Sainsbury, John, *John Wilkes: The Lives of a Libertine* (Aldershot: Ashgate 2006), 109–11, suggesting that the club might not have been as hedonistic as one might assume; Barnett, Suzanne L., *Romantic Paganism: The Politics of Ecstasy in the Shelley Circle* (London: Palgrave Macmillan 2017), 44–53; and Wheeler, Graham John, '"Do What Thou Wilt": The History of a Precept', *Religio* 27 (2019): 17–41.

72.  Walpole, Horace, *Memoirs of the Reign of King George the Third* (London: Bentley, 1845), vol. 1, 174.

73.  See [Anon.], 'Description of the Grand Jubilee at Lord Le Despencer's, at West-Wycombe', *Gentleman's Magazine* 41 (1771): 409. Dashwood's estate also contained other temples, and he rebuilt the local parish church, St Lawrence's, under the inspiration of the Temple of the Sun at Palmyra. It can still be seen today at West Wycombe.

74. See Jones, *Theological and Miscellaneous Works*, 403–404. This text refers to both ceremonies mentioned above.

75. See Hutton, *Triumph of the Moon*, 2nd edn, 161–62.

76. He subsequently repeated his ideas in this area in Knight, Richard Payne, *The Symbolical Language of Ancient Art and Mythology*, new edn (New York, NY: J. W. Bouton, [1818] 1892).

77. In reality, there is a long tradition in Mediterranean Catholic and Orthodox Christianity of offering wax models of body parts at saints' shrines seeking healing, and there is no good reason to connect this practice with survivals of pagan cults.

78. See generally Barnett, *Romantic Paganism*.

79. On this last point, see a well-known letter which he wrote on 22 October 1821 to Thomas Jefferson Hogg, in which he reported that he had 'suspended a garland and raised a small turf altar to the mountain-walking Pan' (Jones, Frederick L. (ed.), *The Letters of Percy Bysshe Shelley* (Oxford: Clarendon Press, 1964), vol. 2, 359–62). It was seemingly not the first time that he had done something like this.

80. See Trelawny, Edward John, *Records of Shelley, Byron and the Author*, new edn (New York, NY: Scribner and Welford, 1887), 138–45, although Trelawny's veracity has been questioned.

81. See Scott, Walter Sidney, *The Athenians* (London: Golden Cockerel, 1943), 43–44.

82. Hutton, *Triumph of the Moon*, 2nd edn, 24. Cf. Luhrmann, T. M., *Persuasions of the Witch's Craft* (Cambridge, MA: Harvard University Press, 1989), 331–32 on play in modern magic.

83. See Wheeler, 'Apuleius and the Esoteric Revival', 271.

## Chapter 5: Poets and Priests—The Victorian Era

1. Symondson, Anthony (ed.), *The Victorian Crisis of Faith* (London: SPCK, 1970).

2. Webb, James, *The Occult Underground* (La Salle: Open Court, 1974), 7 8.

3. Young, G. M., *Portrait of an Age: Victorian England* (London: Oxford University Press, 1977), 116.

4. See Wheeler, 'Discourses of Paganism', 5–24.

5. Lévi, Éliphas, *Transcendental Magic* (London: Redway, 1896), 277–78. 'Patricius' is Francesco Patrizi of Cherso, a Renaissance scholar who produced a collection of the *Chaldaean Oracles*, which had (falsely) come to be ascribed to Zoroaster or Zarathustra.

6. Cf. McIntosh, Christopher, *Eliphas Lévi and the French Occult Revival* (Albany, NY: SUNY Press, 1972), 101–104.

7. See Hallett, Jennifer Rachel, 'Paganism in England 1885–1914', PhD diss., University of Bristol, 2006, online at research-information.bristol.ac.uk/

files/34501523/435432.pdf, ch. 4, accessed 23 September 2023; Wheeler, 'Discourses of Paganism'.

8.   See Shaw, Donald L., 'Darío's Neo-Paganism in Context', *Latin American Literary Review* 38 (2010): 7–22.

9.   Banville, Théodore de, *Les poésies de Théodore de Banville* (Paris: Poulet-Malassis et de Broise, 1857), 164–65 (our translation). In ancient Greece, *thyrsoi* were instruments used in the cult of Dionysus, while Erebos was the realm of darkness.

10.  For the link between Pre-Raphaelitism and the pagan revival, see e.g. Jones and Pennick, *History of Pagan Europe*, 216; Lewis, James R., *Witchcraft Today* (Santa Barbara, CA: ABC-Clio, 1999), xxxiii; Koppen, R. S., *Virginia Woolf, Fashion and Literary Modernity* (Edinburgh: Edinburgh University Press, 2009), 120; Davies, *Paganism*, 100; Delany, Paul, *Fatal Glamour: The Life of Rupert Brooke* (Montreal: McGill-Queen's University Press, 2015), 131.

11.  Gibson, *Imagining the Pagan Past*, 83.

12.  See Étienne, Louis, 'Le paganisme poétique en Angleterre', *Revue des Deux Mondes* 59 (1867), 291–317.

13.  Bartholomew, Michael, 'The Moral Critique of Christian Orthodoxy', in Gerald Parsons (ed.), *Religion in Victorian Britain* (Manchester: Manchester University Press, 1988), vol. 2, 187.

14.  Swinburne, Algernon, *Songs Before Sunrise* (London: Chatto and Windus, 1880), 73–75.

15.  Meredith, George, *Modern Love and Poems of the English Roadside* (London: Chapman and Hall, 1862), 198–99.

16.  As illustrated by the excerpt from Keats quoted in Chapter 4. See further Hutton, *Triumph of the Moon*, 2nd edn, ch. 2. Cf. also Hutton, *Queens of the Wild*, 50–58.

17.  See further the references in Chapter 1, n.11.

18.  See Hallett, 'Paganism in England 1885–1914', 149–74 and Robichaud, Paul, *Pan: The Great God's Modern Return* (London: Reaktion, 2021), ch. 3.

19.  Maugham, Somerset, *Cakes and Ale* (London: Heinemann, 1930), 138–39.

20.  See Hallett, 'Paganism in England 1885–1914', 123–28, 133, 159.

21.  Wilde, Oscar (ed. Bobby Fong and Karl Beckson), *The Complete Works of Oscar Wilde, Vol. 1: Poems and Poems in Prose* (Oxford: Oxford University Press, 2000), 140–43.

22.  On Pan in Machen's works, see further Robichaud, *Pan*, 217–25.

23.  Jenkyns, Richard, *The Victorians and Ancient Greece* (Oxford: Blackwell, 1980), 178.

24.  See Hallett, 'Paganism in England 1885–1914', 137–39, 143, 148, 153–55, 161–70, 178 and Robichaud, *Pan*, 141–49.

25.  Grahame, Kenneth, *Pagan Papers* (London: John Lane, 1904), 189.

26.  See further Hallett, 'Paganism in England 1885–1914', 139–42, 160–64, 177–78; Coste, Bénédicte, 'Late-Victorian Paganism: the case of the *Pagan*

*Review*', *Cahiers Victoriens et Edouardiens* (2015), online at journals.openedition. org/cve/1533, accessed 23 September 2023.

27. See Halloran, William F., *The Life and Letters of William Sharp and 'Fiona Macleod': Volume 1, 1855–1894* (Cambridge: Open Book, 2018), 411–14.

28. Jeffares, A. Norman, *W. B. Yeats: A New Biography* (London: Continuum, 2001), 77–78.

29. *Leamington Spa Courier*, 3 May 1879, 3; 'The Pagan Review', *Saturday Review* 74 (1892), 268–69; Campbell, Lewis, *Religion in Greek Literature* (London: Longmans, Green, and Co., 1898), 376; Chesterton, G. K., *Heretics* (London: John Lane, 1905), ch. 12.

30. See Hutton, *Blood and Mistletoe*, 271–74.

31. See Hutton, *Blood and Mistletoe*, ch. 8.

32. See further *Western Mail*, 15 January 1884, 3, which contains a contemporary report of the whole affair.

33. See Lillie, Arthur, *Madame Blavatsky and Her 'Theosophy'* (London: Swan Sonnenschein and Co, 1895), 54–56.

34. Hallett, 'Paganism in England 1885–1914', 75; and see generally Chapter 3.

35. Carpenter, Edward, *Civilisation: Its Cause and Cure* (London: George Allen and Unwin, 1921), 73.

36. Knight, William (ed.), *Memorials of Thomas Davidson* (Boston, MA: Ginn and Company, 1907), 7.

37. See Hallett, 'Paganism in England 1885–1914', 132–33, 149, 158, 161; Reid, Kelly Anne, 'The Love Which Dare Not Speak Its Name: An Examination of Pagan Symbolism and Morality in *Fin de siecle* Decadent Fiction', *The Pomegranate* 10 (2008): 130–41.

38. See e.g. Hilliard, David, 'UnEnglish and Unmanly: Anglo-Catholicism and Homosexuality', *Victorian Studies* 25 (1982): 181–210.

39. Blain, Virginia, '"Michael Field, the Two-headed Nightingale": lesbian text as palimpsest', *Women's History Review* 5 (1996): 239–57, at 249.

40. Spiritualism is generally dated to the Fox sisters in New York State in 1848, but it can be traced back to the work of the Swedish mystic Emanuel Swedenborg (1688–1772).

41. See e.g. Howe, Ellic, *Magicians of the Golden Dawn* (London: Routledge and Kegan Paul, 1972), 1–25; Regardie, Israel, *The Golden Dawn*, 7th edn (St Paul, MN: Llewellyn, 2016), 3–6; Godwin, *The Theosophical Enlightenment*, 223–24; Küntz, Darcy, *The Complete Golden Dawn Cipher Manuscript* (Sequim WA: Holmes, 1996), 11–15; McIntosh, Christopher, '"Fräulein Sprengel" and the Origins of the Golden Dawn: A Surprising Discovery', *Aries* 11 (2011): 249–57.

42. See Gilbert, R. A., 'Provenance Unknown: A Tentative Solution to the Riddle of the Cipher Manuscript of the Golden Dawn', in Götz von Olenhusen, Albrecht (eds), *Wege und Abwege* (Freiburg: Hochschul, 1990), 79–89; Gilbert, R. A., 'Supplement to "Provenance Unknown": The Origins of the Golden Dawn', in

Darcy Küntz (ed.), *The Golden Dawn Source Book* (Edmonds, WA: Holmes, 1996), 11–13; and also Gilbert, R. A., 'From Cipher to Enigma: The Role of William Wynn Westcott in the creation of the Hermetic Order of the Golden Dawn', in Carroll Runyon (ed.), *Secrets of the Golden Dawn Cypher Manuscript* (Silverado, CA: CHS, 1997), 204–22, at 214–15.

43. See e.g. Wheeler, Graham John, 'A Microcosm of the Esoteric Revival: The Histories of the Lesser Banishing Ritual of the Pentagram', *Correspondences* 8.2 (2020): 1–40.

44. Machen, Arthur, *Things Near and Far* (London: Martin Secker, 1923), 153–54. The significance of 1809 is that it was the date of a watermark on some sheets of the cipher MS on which the rituals were based. Cf. Aleister Crowley's complaint, in his publication of the rituals, of 'the "mixed-biscuit" type of symbol which is … chosen so as to "show off" superficial knowledge' (Crowley, Aleister, 'The Temple of Solomon the King (Book II)', *The Equinox* 1.2 (1909): 217–334, at 266). For a more favourable assessment, see Bogdan, Henrik, *Western Esotericism and Rituals of Initiation* (Albany, NY: SUNY Press, 2007), 121–22 (quoting in turn Gerald Yorke to the same effect).

45. Müller is a particularly interesting character: see further e.g. Dorson, Richard M., 'The Eclipse of Solar Mythology', in Thomas A. Sebeok (ed.), *Myth: A Symposium* (Philadelphia, PA: American Folklore Society, 1955), 15–38; Nicholls, Angus, 'Max Müller and the Comparative Method', *Comparative Critical Studies* 12 (2015): 213–34. Egil Asprem makes the comparison with Frazer's *Golden Bough* explicit in '*Kabbalah Recreata*: Reception and Adaptation of Kabbalah in Modern Occultism', *The Pomegranate* 9.2 (2007): 132–53, at 133–34.

46. Gilbert, R. A., *The Golden Dawn Scrapbook* (York Beach, ME: Weiser, 1997), 23.

47. The standard edition of the texts of the order is Regardie, *The Golden Dawn*.

48. See Wheeler, 'Apuleius and the Esoteric Revival', 271–72.

49. See Roukema, Aren, *Esotericism and Narrative* (Leiden: Brill, 2018), 77–78.

50. Cf. Roukema, *Esotericism and Narrative*, 97.

51. Asprem, '*Kabbalah Recreata*', 136.

52. See Hallett, 'Paganism in England 1885–1914', 214–18; Tully, Caroline, 'Samuel Liddell MacGregor Mathers and Isis', in Dave Evans and Dave Green (eds), *Ten Years of Triumph of the Moon* (Harpenden: Hidden Publishing, 2009), 62–74.

53. Hallett, 'Paganism in England 1885–1914', 217.

54. Rimbaud, Arthur, *Poésies* (Paris: Gallimard, 1999), 66–67 (our translation).

55. See Bois, Jules, *Les petites religions de Paris* (Paris: Chailley, 1894), esp. 3–19, 185–90.

56. Hutton, *Triumph of the Moon*, 2nd edn, 31.

57. Leland, Charles G., *Aradia or the Gospel of the Witches* (London: David Nutt, 1899).

58. Jarcke, Karl Ernst, 'Ein Hexenprozess', in *Annalen der Deutschen und Auslandischen Criminal-Rechts-Pflege* 1 (1828): 431–56, at 450: 'zunächst eine Tradition aus der heidnisch-germanischen Zeit, eine im Volke lebende heidnisch Naturkunde und

Natur-Religion gewesen sey, die auch ihre … Ceremonien und Sakramente hatte.'

59. See generally Hutton, *Triumph of the Moon*, 2nd edn, 141–8, and the essays in Pazzaglini, Mario and Pazzaglini, Dina (eds), *Aradia or the Gospel of the Witches* (Blaine, MN: Phoenix, 1998). For the evidence that Maddalena existed (her legal name was Margherita Taluti), see Jacobs, Joseph and Nutt, Alfred (eds), *The International Folk-Lore Conference 1891: Papers and Transactions* (London: David Nutt, 1892), 454 (Raven Grimassi first drew attention to this reference in an unpublished paper delivered at the 2008 Pantheacon conference).

60. See Hutton, *Queens of the Wild*, ch. 4.

61. Hutton, *Queens of the Wild*, 22.

62. Gouguenheim, *Les derniers païens*, 247.

63. Tamm, Marek, 'History as Cultural Memory: Mnemohistory and the Construction of the Estonian Nation', *Journal of Baltic Studies* 39.4 (2008): 499–516; Prusinowska, Justyna, 'They are Still Coming Back. Heroes for Time of Crisis: Vidvuds and Lāčplēsis' in Ieva Kalniņa (ed.), *Literatūra un Reliģija: Svētie un Grēcinieki* (Riga: Latvijas Universitātes Akadēmiskais apgāds, 2018), 66–84.

## Chapter 6: The Emergence of Modern Paganism

1. The term may have come from her sister Vanessa. Cf. Bell, Quentin, *Virginia Woolf* (London: Vintage, 2017), 172–74 (with notes).

2. This was Frances Cornford's description of him as a student in her poem 'Youth' (1910).

3. See Delany, Paul, *The Neo-Pagans* (New York, NY: Free Press, 1987), 101.

4. Jones, Nigel *Rupert Brooke* (London: Head of Zeus, 2014), 164.

5. See e.g. *Cambridge Magazine* 2 (1912), 53.

6. Keynes, Geoffrey (ed.), *The Letters of Rupert Brooke* (London: Faber and Faber, 1968), 282–83.

7. Keynes (ed.), *Letters of Rupert Brooke*, 287–88.

8. See Hallett, 'Paganism in England', 92–96.

9. Haggard, H. Rider, *The Days of My Life* (London: Longmans, Green and Company, 1926), vol. 1, ch. 11. The work was written in 1910–12.

10. Farjeon, Eleanor, *Edward Thomas* (London: Faber and Faber, 2010), 34–35.

11. See generally Hutton, *Triumph of the Moon*, 2nd edn, 168–76.

12. See Hutton, *Triumph of the Moon*, 2nd edn, 171–72.

13. Hutton, *Triumph of the Moon*, 2nd edn, 173–75.

14. On the Kibbo Kift, see generally Pollen, Annebella, *The Kindred of the Kibbo Kift* (London: Donlon, 2015).

15. Hutton, *Triumph of the Moon*, 2nd edn, 175.

16. There are a number of biographies of Crowley on the market, of which the most detailed and sympathetic is Kaczynski, Richard, *Perdurabo: The Life of Aleister Crowley*, rev. edn (Berkeley, CA: North Atlantic, 2010). The best general introduction to Crowley's life is Lachman, Gary, *Aleister Crowley* (New York, NY: Penguin, 2014).

17. Symonds, John and Grant, Kenneth (eds), *The Confessions of Aleister Crowley* (New York, NY: Farrar Straus and Giroux, 1970), ch. 86.

18. He also borrowed from the later Graeco-Egyptian period: notably, his *Liber Samekh* contains a rite adapted from *PGM* 5.96–172.

19. Hart, George, *The Routledge Dictionary of Egyptian Gods and Goddesses*, 2nd edn (Routledge: London, 2005), 10.

20. See Tully, Caroline, 'Walk Like an Egyptian: Egypt as Authority in Aleister Crowley's Reception of *The Book of the Law*', *The Pomegranate* 12 (2010): 20–47.

21. See e.g. 'Black magic funeral at Brighton', *Daily Herald*, 6 December 1947, 3.

22. For a biography of Fortune, see Knight, Gareth, *Dion Fortune and the Inner Light* (Loughborough: Thoth, 2000).

23. Hutton, Ronald, 'The Roots of Modern Paganism', in Graham Harvey and Charlotte Hardman (eds), *Paganism Today* (London: Thorsons, 1995), 3–15, at 5.

24. See Hutton, *Triumph of the Moon*, 2nd edn, 187–94; Robichaud, *Pan*, 235–34.

25. See generally Knight, Gareth, *Dion Fortune's Rites of Isis and of Pan* (Cheltenham: Skylight, 2013).

26. Murray, Margaret Alice, *The Witch-Cult in Western Europe* (Oxford: Clarendon Press, 1921).

27. See e.g. Hutton, *Triumph of the Moon*, 2nd edn, 199–200; Sheppard, Kathleen L., *The Life of Margaret Alice Murray* (Lanham, MD: Lexington, 2013), 168–69.

28. See Hutton, *Triumph of the Moon*, 2nd edn, 155–56.

29. Murray, Margaret Alice, *The God of the Witches* (London: Oxford University Press, 1970 [1931]).

30. See e.g. 'Midland "Black Magic" Murders?', *Birmingham Gazette*, 2 September 1950, 1.

31. Murray, Margaret Alice, *The Divine King in England* (London: Faber and Faber, 1954).

32. See e.g. Truzzi, Marcello, 'Towards a Sociology of the Occult: Notes on Modern Witchcraft', in Irving I. Zaretsky and Mark P. Leone (eds), *Religious Movements in Contemporary America* (Princeton, NJ: Princeton University Press, 1974), 628–45, at 640–41; Cohn, Norman, *Europe's Inner Demons: The Demonisation of Christians in Medieval Christendom*, new edn (London: Pimlico, 2005), 153.

33. Wheeler, Graham John, 'An Esbat among the Quads: An Episode of Witchcraft at Oxford University in the 1920s', *The Pomegranate* 20.2 (2018): 157–78.

34. See Heselton, Philip, *In Search of the New Forest Coven* ([no place of publication]: Fenix Flames, 2020). Others would doubt the existence of the coven: see

e.g. Chas S. Clifton's review, 'Philip Heselton, *Gerald Gardner and the Cauldron of Inspiration*', *The Pomegranate* 6.2 (2004): 267–70.

35. Murray, Linda J., *A Zest for Life: The Story of Alexander Keiller* (Swindon: Morven, 1999), 23. See also Trubshaw, Bob, 'Keiller's occult connections' (2015), online at indigogroup.co.uk/avebury/keiller01.htm, accessed 24 September 2023; Worthington, Andy, 'Mystics and Mavericks: The Pagan Reinvention of Avebury', in Joanne Parker (ed.), *Written on Stone: The Cultural Reception of British Prehistoric Monuments* (Newcastle: Cambridge Scholars, 2009), 100–10, at 101–102.

36. See e.g. Lewis, *Witchcraft Today*, 54; Lewis, James R., *Odd Gods* (Amherst, MA: Prometheus, 2001), 313, 315; Kelly, Aidan A., *Inventing Witchcraft* (Loughborough: Thoth, 2008), 20; Clarke, Peter B. (ed.), *Encyclopaedia of New Religious Movements* (London: Routledge, 2009), 682.

37. See Hutton, *Triumph of the Moon*, 2nd edn, 298.

38. O'Donnell, Elliott, *Strange Cults and Secret Societies of Modern London* (London: Philip Allen, 1934), 129; see generally 125–46.

39. O'Donnell, *Strange Cults*, 233, 235; see generally 233–39.

40. See Clifton, Chas S., *Her Hidden Children: The Rise of Wicca and Paganism in America* (Lanham, MD: AltaMira, 2006), 139–42; Galtsin, Dmitry, 'Gleb Botkin and the Church of Aphrodite', *The Pomegranate* 14 (2012): 91–107.

41. Dmitry Galtsin, 'Gleb Botkin', 103.

42. Waldron, David, *The Sign of the Witch* (Durham, NC: Carolina Academic Press, 2008), 136.

43. This is apparent from comments made by public figures at the time. See e.g. *Western Mail*, 3 September 1936, 8 (William John MP); *Daily Mirror*, 8 February 1937, 12 (the poet Patience Strong); *Lancashire Evening Post*, 19 July 1937, 3 (Bishop Herbert of Blackburn).

44. *Tewkesbury Register*, 16 December 1939, 4 (typographical errors corrected).

45. Pius XI, *Non abbiamo bisogno* (1931), 44, online at vatican.va/content/pius-xi/en/encyclicals/documents/hf_p-xi_enc_29061931_non-abbiamo-bisogno.html, accessed 24 September 2023; Pius XI, *Mit brennender Sorge* (1937), 17, online at vatican.va/content/pius-xi/en/encyclicals/documents/hf_p-xi_enc_14031937_mit-brennender-sorge.html, accessed 24 September 2023.

46. See Badger, William and Purkiss, Diane, 'English Witches and SS Academics', *Preternature* 6 (2017): 125–53.

47. Noakes, J. and Pridham, G. (eds), *Nazism 1919–1945 Volume 2: State, Economy and Society 1933–1939* (Exeter: Exeter University Press, 1984), 497–98.

48. See Poewe, Karla and Hexham, Irving, 'Jakob Wilhelm Hauer's New Religion and National Socialism', *Journal of Contemporary Religion* 20:2 (2005): 195–215.

49. See in general Goodrick-Clarke, Nicholas, *The Occult Roots of Nazism: The Ariosophists of Austria and Germany, 1890–1935* (Wellingborough: Aquarian Press, 1985); Schnurbein, Stefanie von, *Norse Revival: Transformations of Germanic*

*Paganism* (Leiden: Brill, 2016), ch. 1. Cf. also Goodrick-Clarke, Nicholas, *Black Sun: Aryan Cults, Esoteric Nazism, and the Politics of Identity* (New York, NY: New York University Press, 2003).

50. Dühring, Eugen, *Die Judenfrage*, 5th edn (Nowawes-Neuendorf bei Berlin: Ulrich Dühring, 1901 [1880]), 32–33.

51. 'Das Einschleichen mystisch veranlagter, okkulter Jenseitsforscher darf daher in der Bewegung nicht geduldet werden'. The quote is from Hitler's speech on the second day of the 1938 Nuremberg rally (6 September 1938).

52. Winter, Barbara, *The Australia-First Movement and the 'Publicist', 1936–1942* (Brisbane: Glass House, 2005), 39–47.

53. [Mills, Alexander Rud], *The First Guide Book to the Anglecyn Church of Odin* (Sydney: A. R. Mills, 1936). The saints venerated in the text ranged from John Locke to Florence Nightingale.

54. Werth, Paul W., 'Big Candles and "Internal Conversion": The Mari Animist Reformation and Its Russian Appropriations', in Robert P. Geraci and Michael Khodarkovsky (eds), *Of Religion and Empire: Missions, Conversion, and Tolerance in Tsarist Russia* (Ithaca, NY: Cornell University Press, 2001), 144–72, at 152–56.

55. On contemporary traditional religion in the Mari El Republic see Knorre, Boris, 'Neopaganism in the Mari El Republic' in Kaarina Aitamurto and Scott Simpson (eds), *Modern Pagan and Native Faith Movements in Central and Eastern Europe* (London: Routledge, 2014), 249–65.

56. Čuplinskas, Indrė and Motiejūnaitė, Jūratė, 'The *vaidilutė*: how Lithuanian Catholic youth made a pagan priestess Christian', *Journal of Baltic Studies* 53.2 (2022): 169–85.

57. *Pranskevičiūtė, Rasa*, 'Contemporary Paganism in Lithuanian Context: Principal Beliefs and Practices of Romuva' in Kaarina Aitamurto and Scott Simpson (eds), *Modern Pagan and Native Faith Movements in Central and Eastern Europe* (London: Routledge, 2014), 77–93.

58. Stasulane, Anita and Ozoliņš, Gatis, 'Transformations of Neopaganism in Latvia: From Survival to Revival', *Open Theology* 3 (2017): 235–48, at 237–38.

59. Misāne, Agita, 'Inter-war Right-wing Movements in the Baltic States and their Religious Affiliations', *Acta Ethnographica Hungarica* 46.1–2 (2001): 75–87, at 79.

60. Misāne, 'Inter-war Right-wing Movements', 80–83.

61. Misāne, 'Inter-war Right-wing Movements', 83–86.

62. Strmiska, Michael P., 'Pagan Politics in the 21st Century: "Peace and Love" or "Blood and Soil"?', *The Pomegranate* 20.1 (2018): 5–44, at 20.

63. Nastevics, Ugis, 'Latvian Religion—Dievturība?', *Religiski-Filozofiski Raksti* 24 (2018): 82–104.

64. On Rodnoverie see Shnirelman, Victor A., 'Russian Neopaganism: from Ethnic Religion to Racial Violence', in Kaarina Aitamurto and Scott Simpson (eds), *Modern Pagan and Native Faith Movements in Central and Eastern Europe* (London:

Routledge, 2014), 62–75; Aitamurto, Kaarina, *Paganism, Traditionalism, Nationalism: Narratives of Russian Rodnoverie* (London: Routledge, 2016).

65. On Sámi religious revival see Kraft, Siv Ellen, 'Sami Neo-shamanism in Norway: Colonial Grounds, Ethnic Revival and Pagan Pathways', in Kaarina Aitamurto and Scott Simpson (eds), *Modern Pagan and Native Faith Movements in Central and Eastern Europe* (London: Routledge, 2014), 25–42.

66. For an imperfect list of his books, see 'Gerald Gardner's Library', web.archive. org/web/20010607172853/http://www.newwiccanchurch.com/gbglibidx. htm, accessed 24 September 2023.

67. The standard treatments of Gardner's life and the genesis of Wicca include Hutton, *Triumph of the Moon*, 2nd edn; Heselton, Philip, *Witchfather: A Life of Gerald Gardner* (Loughborough: Thoth, 2012), 2 vols; and, more controversially, Kelly, *Inventing Witchcraft*.

68. It bears emphasizing that the neo-Druids had not gone away by this point; nor had their Christianizing tendencies. Hutton describes one 1948 ceremony at Stonehenge: 'The liturgy neatly blended Christian and pagan themes, speaking at one moment of a single supreme being, and at another of the material world as being in the custody of a sun god and an earth goddess' (Hutton, *Blood and Mistletoe*, 376).

69. Graves, Robert, *The White Goddess* (London: Faber and Faber, 2010 [1948]).

70. Graves, Robert, *The Greek Myths* (Harmondsworth: Penguin, 2017 [1955]), 13. It is also worth noting that Graves published a translation of Apuleius' *Golden Ass* with Penguin in 1950.

71. Gardner, Gerald B., *High Magic's Aid* (Clevedon: Aurinia, 2010 [1949]); Gardner, Gerald B., *Witchcraft Today* (New York, NY: Citadel, 2004 [1954]); Gardner, Gerald B., *The Meaning of Witchcraft* (Boston, MA: Weiser, 2004 [1959]).

72. Gardner, *Witchcraft Today*, 140.

73. Gardner, *The Meaning of Witchcraft*, 237. At least some of this book is believed to have been ghostwritten by Gardner's pupil Doreen Valiente.

74. Rose, Elliot, *A Razor for a Goat* (Toronto: University of Toronto Press, 1989 [1962]), ch. 10.

75. See Wheeler, 'Apuleius and the Esoteric Revival', 260–76.

76. See Gardner, *The Meaning of Witchcraft*, 171–74. 'Seems to have' because, again, this material may have come from Doreen Valiente.

77. A middle-aged businessman in a suburban Masonic hall may be initiated into 'the craft', undergo being blindfolded and stabbed with a sharp object, swear an oath, encounter 'working tools' and hear a 'charge', all while his teenage daughter goes through the same experiences in the coven meeting next door.

78. Murray had also linked the god of the witches with Pan: see Murray, *The God of the Witches*, 28.

79. Gardner, *Witchcraft Today*, 42.

## Epilogue: Pagan Pasts, Pagan Futures?

1.  Milis, 'Spooky Heritage', 2.
2.  MacMullen, *Christianity and Paganism*, 158.
3.  Hutton, *Triumph of the Moon*, 2nd edn, 425.
4.  Hutton, *Queens of the Wild*, 159–92.

# Select Bibliography

Adler, Margot, *Drawing Down the Moon* (New York: Viking, 1979)

Aitamurto, Kaarina, *Paganism, Traditionalism, Nationalism: Narratives of Russian Rodnoverie* (London: Routledge, 2016). https://doi.org/10.4324/9781315599304

Aitamurto, Kaarina and Simpson, Scott (eds), *Modern Pagan and Native Faith Movements in Central and Eastern Europe* (London: Routledge, 2014). https://doi.org/10.4324/9781315729008

Allen, Don Cameron, *Mysteriously Meant: The Rediscovery of Pagan Symbolism and Allegorical Interpretation in the Renaissance* (Baltimore, MD: Johns Hopkins University Press, 1970)

Allen, Michael J. B. and Rees, Valery (eds), *Marsilio Ficino: His Theology, His Philosophy, His Legacy* (Leiden: Brill, 2002)

Álvarez-Pedrosa, Juan Antonio (ed.), *Sources of Slavic Pre-Christian Religion* (Leiden: Brill, 2021). https://doi.org/10.1163/9789004441385

[Anon.], *Biographical Anecdotes of the Founders of the French Republic* (London: Phillips, 1797)

[Anon.], *The Connoisseur*, new ed., vol. 2 (London: J. Richardson and Co., 1822 [1756])

Archius, Nicolaus, 'In Funerem M. Antonii Turrii, Viri Rarissimi, Epicedion', in *Numerorum libri IV* (Verona: Morone, 1762), 57–63

Ashe, Geoffrey, *Do What You Will* (London: W. H. Allen, 1974)

Asprem, Egil, '*Kabbalah Recreata*: Reception and Adaptation of Kabbalah in Modern Occultism', *The Pomegranate* 9.2 (2007): 132–53. https://doi.org/10.1558/pome.v9i2.132

Assmann, Jan, 'The Mosaic Distinction: Israel, Egypt, and the Invention of Paganism', *Representations* 56 (1996): 48–67. https://doi.org/10.2307/2928707

Assmann, Jan, *Moses the Egyptian* (Cambridge, MA: Harvard University Press, 1997). https://doi.org/10.4159/9780674020306

Athanassiadi, Polymnia, *Julian: An Intellectual Biography* (London: Routledge, 1992)

Athanassiadi, Polymnia, 'Persecution and Response in Late Paganism: The Evidence of Damascius', *Journal of Hellenic Studies* 113 (1993): 1–29. https://doi.org/10.2307/632395

Athanassiadi, Polymnia and Frede, Michael (eds), *Pagan Monotheism in Late Antiquity* (Oxford: Clarendon Press, 1999). https://doi.org/10.1093/oso/9780198152521.001.0001

Bacchelli, Franco, 'La Considération céleste et les Enseignements de Démétrius Rhaoul Kavàkis', *Noctua* 3.2 (2016): 164–238

Badger, William and Purkiss, Diane, 'English Witches and SS Academics', *Preternature* 6 (2017): 125–53. https://doi.org/10.5325/preternature.6.1.0125

Baïf, Jean-Antoine de (ed. Jean Vignes), *Oeuvres complètes I: Euvres en rime, Part 1* (Paris: Honoré Champion, 2002)

Baker-Brian, Nicholas and Tougher, Shaun (eds), *Emperor and Author* (Swansea: Classical Press of Wales, 2012). https://doi.org/10.2307/j.ctvvn9n9

Balagangadhara, S. N., *"The Heathen in His Blindness …": Asia, the West and the Dynamic of Religion* (Leiden: Brill, 1994). https://doi.org/10.1163/9789004378865

Banville, Théodore de, *Les poésies de Théodore de Banville* (Paris: Poulet-Malassis et de Broise, 1857)

Barlow, Frank, *Thomas Becket* (Berkeley, CA: University of California Press, 1986)

Baronas, Darius, 'Christians in Late Pagan, and Pagans in Early Christian Lithuania: The Fourteenth and Fifteenth Centuries', *Lithuanian Historical Studies* 19 (2014): 51–81. https://doi.org/10.30965/25386565-01901003

Baronas, Darius and Rowell, S. C., *The Conversion of Lithuania: From Pagan Barbarians to Late Medieval Christians* (Vilnius: Institute of Lithuanian Literature and Folklore, 2015)

Barnett, Suzanne L., *Romantic Paganism: The Politics of Ecstasy in the Shelley Circle* (London: Palgrave Macmillan 2017)

Beard, Mary, North, John, and Price, Simon, *Religions of Rome* (Cambridge: Cambridge University Press, 1998)

Bell, Quentin, *Virginia Woolf* (London: Vintage, 2017), 172–4

Bellarmine, Robert, *Opera* (Naples: Giuseppe Giuliano, 1838), 12 vols

Berend, Nora, *At the Gate of Christendom: Jews, Muslims and 'Pagans' in Medieval Hungary, c. 1000–c. 1301* (Cambridge: Cambridge University Press, 2010)

Bernabé, Alberto and San Cristóbal, Ana Isabel Jiménez, *Instructions for the Netherworld* (Leiden: Brill, 2008)

Bernal, Martin, *Black Athena: The Afroasiatic Roots of Classical Civilisation* (London: Vintage Books, 1987–2006), 3 vols

Bět'áková, Marta Eva and Blažek, Václav (eds), *Lexicon of Baltic Mythology* (Heidelberg: Winter Verlag, 2021)

Betz, Hans Dieter, *The Greek Magical Papyri in Translation* (Chicago, IL: University of Chicago Press, 1992). https://doi.org/10.1093/oso/9780195044508.003.0009

Blain, Virginia, '"Michael Field, the Two-headed Nightingale": lesbian text as palimpsest', *Women's History Review* 5 (1996): 239–57. https://doi.org/10.1080/09612029600200117

Bode, Georg Heinrich (ed.), *Scriptores rerum mythicarum latini tres Romae nuper reperti* (Celle: E. H. C. Schulze, 1834), 2 vols

Bodnar, Edward W. (ed.), *Cyriac of Ancona: Later Travels* (Cambridge, MA: Harvard University Press, 2003)

Bogdan, Henrik, *Western Esotericism and Rituals of Initiation* (Albany, NY: SUNY Press, 2007). https://doi.org/10.1353/book5196

Bois, Jules, *Les petites religions de Paris* (Paris: Chailley, 1894)

Bonner, Campbell, 'Some Phases of Religious Feeling in Later Paganism', *Harvard Theological Review* 20.2 (1937): 119–40. https://doi.org/10.1017/S0017816000022197

Bowersock, G. W., *Julian the Apostate* (London: Duckworth, 1978)

Bradshaw, David, *Aristotle East and West: Metaphysics and the Division of Christendom* (Cambridge: Cambridge University Press, 2004). https://doi.org/10.1017/CBO9780511482489

Bremmer, Jan N., *Initiation into the Mysteries of the Ancient World* (Berlin: De Gruyter, 2014). https://doi.org/10.1515/9783110299557

Brown, Michael, *A Political Biography of John Toland* (London: Routledge, 2012). https://doi.org/10.3318/dib.008584.v2

Bullinger, Heinrich, *De origine erroris* (Zurich: Froschauer, 1539)

Burkert, Walter, *Greek Religion* (Malden, MA: Blackwell, 1985)

Burns, Dylan, 'The Chaldean Oracles of Zoroaster, Hekate's Couch, and Platonic Orientalism in Psellos and Plethon', *Aries* 6 (2006): 158–79. https://doi.org/10.1163/157005906777811925

Butler, Alison, *Victorian Occultism and the Making of Modern Magic* (Basingstoke: Palgrave Macmillan, 2011). https://doi.org/10.1057/9780230294707

Calvin, Jean, *Traité des reliques* (Geneva: Labor et Fides, 2000 [1543])

Cameron, Alan, 'The Last Days of the Academy at Athens', *Proceedings of the Cambridge Philological Society* 15 (1969): 7–29. https://doi.org/10.1017/S1750270500030207

Cameron, Alan, *The Last Pagans of Rome* (Oxford: Oxford University Press, 2011). https://doi.org/10.1093/acprof:oso/9780199747276.001.0001

Campbell, Lewis, *Religion in Greek Literature* (London: Longmans, Green, and Co., 1898)

Campion, Nicholas, Curry, Patrick and York, Michael (eds), *Astrology and the Academy* (Bristol: Cinnabar, 2004)

Cannon, Garland, *The Life and Mind of Oriental Jones* (Cambridge: Cambridge University Press, 1990). https://doi.org/10.1017/CBO9780511527142

Cappa, Désirée, Christie, James E., Gay, Lorenza, Gentili, Hanna and Schulze-Feldmann, Finn (eds), *Cultural Encounters: Cross-Disciplinary Studies from the Late Middle Ages to the Enlightenment* (Wilmington, DE: Vernon Press, 2018)

Carpenter, Edward, *Civilisation: Its Cause and Cure* (London: George Allen and Unwin, 1921). https://doi.org/10.5962/bhl.title.17382

Carver, Martin (ed.), *The Cross Goes North: Processes of Conversion in Northern Europe, AD 300–1300* (Woodbridge: Boydell and Brewer, 2006)

Carver, Robert H. F., *The Protean Ass: The Metamophoses of Apuleius from Antiquity to the Renaissance* (Oxford: Oxford University Press, 2007). https://doi.org/10.1093/acprof:oso/9780199217861.001.0001

Casaubon, Meric, *A True & Faithful Relation* (London: Garthwait, 1659)

Cervantes, Fernando, *The Devil in the New World: The Impact of Diabolism in New Spain* (New Haven, CT: Yale University Press, 1994)

Chatterjee, Paroma, *Between the Pagan Past and Christian Present in Byzantine Culture* (Cambridge: Cambridge University Press, 2021). https://doi.org/10.1017/9781108985628

Chesterton, G. K., *Heretics* (London: John Lane, 1905)

Clark, Stuart, *Thinking with Demons: The Idea of Witchcraft in Early Modern Europe* (Oxford: Oxford University Press, 1997)

Clifton, Chas S., 'Philip Heselton, *Gerald Gardner and the Cauldron of Inspiration*', *The Pomegranate* 6.2 (2004): 267–70. https://doi.org/10.1558/pome.6.2.267.53122

Clifton, Chas S. and Harvey, Graham (eds), *The Paganism Reader* (New York: Routledge, 2004)

Chuvin, Pierre (trans. B. A Archer), *A Chronicle of the Last Pagans* (Cambridge, MA: Harvard University Press, 1990)

Clarke, Emma C., Dillon, John M. and Hershbell, Jackson P. (ed.), *Iamblichus: On the Mysteries* (Atlanta, GA: Society of Biblical Literature, 2003)

Clarke, Peter B. (ed.), *Encyclopaedia of New Religious Movements* (London: Routledge, 2009)

Clifton, Chas S., *Her Hidden Children: The Rise of Wicca and Paganism in America* (Lanham, MD: AltaMira, 2006), 139–42

Cohn, Norman, *Europe's Inner Demons: The Demonisation of Christians in Medieval Christendom*, new edn (London: Pimlico, 2005)

Collins, David J., *Magic and Witchcraft in the West: From Antiquity to the Present* (Cambridge: Cambridge University Press, 2015)

Colonna, Francesco (trans. Joscelyn Godwin), *Hypnerotomachia Poliphili: The Strife of Love in a Dream* (New York, NY: Thames & Hudson, 1999)

Constantinidou, Natasha and Lamers, Han (eds), *Receptions of Hellenism in Early Modern Europe* (Leiden: Brill, 2020). https://doi.org/10.1163/9789004402461

Copenhaver, Brian P. (ed.), *Hermetica* (Cambridge: Cambridge University Press, 1992)

Corazzol, Giacomo, 'Le fonti "caldaiche" dell'Oratio: indagine sui presupposti cabbalistici della concezione pichiana dell'uomo', *Accademia* 15 (2013): 9–62

Crowley, Aleister, 'The Temple of Solomon the King (Book II)', *The Equinox* 1.2 (1909): 217–334

Čuplinskas, Indrė and Motiejūnaitė, Jūratė, 'The *vaidilutė*: how Lithuanian Catholic youth made a pagan priestess Christian', *Journal of Baltic Studies* 53.2 (2022): 169–85. https://doi.org/10.1080/01629778.2021.1990973

D'Elia, Anthony F., *A Sudden Terror* (Cambridge, MA: Harvard University Press, 2009)

D'Elia, Anthony F., *Pagan Virtue in a Christian World* (Cambridge, MA: Harvard University Press, 2016)

Daniel, Stephen H., *John Toland* (Kingston, Ont.: McGill-Queen's University Press, 1984). https://doi.org/10.1515/9780773564022

Danilewicz, M. L., '"The King of the New Israel": Thaddeus Grabianka (1740–1807)', *Oxford Slavonic Papers* 1 (1968): 49–73

Davies, Owen, *Paganism: A Very Short Introduction* (Oxford: Oxford University Press, 2011). https://doi.org/10.1093/actrade/9780199235162.001.0001

Davis, Philip G., *Goddess Unmasked* (Dallas, TX: Spence, 1998)

Delany, Paul, *The Neo-Pagans* (New York, NY: Free Press, 1987). https://doi.org/10.1515/9780773582774

Delany, Paul, *Fatal Glamour: The Life of Rupert Brooke* (Montreal: McGill-Queen's University Press, 2015)

Dillon, John and Gerson, Lloyd P., *Neoplatonic Philosophy* (Indianapolis, IN: Hackett, 2004)

Disraeli, Isaac, *Curiosities of Literature*, new edn (London: Routledge, 1866), 3 vols

Dowden, Ken, *European Paganism: The Realities of Cult from Antiquity to the Middle Ages* (London: Routledge, 2000)

Duffy, Eamon, *The Stripping of the Altars: Traditional Religion in England 1400–1580* (New Haven, CT: Yale University Press, 1992)

Dühring, Eugen, *Die Judenfrage*, 5th edn (Nowawes-Neuendorf bei Berlin: Ulrich Dühring, 1901 [1880])

Dulles, Avery, *A History of Apologetics*, rev. edn (San Francisco, CA: Ignatius Press, 2005)

Dunn, Patrick, *The Orphic Hymns* (Woodbury, Ont.: Llewellyn, 2018)

Ebeling, Florian, *The Secret History of Hermes Trismegistus* (Ithaca, NY: Cornell University Press, 2007)

Edmonds III, Radcliffe G., 'Did the Mithraists Inhale?', *Ancient World* 32.1 (2000): 10–24

Edmonds III, Radcliffe G., *Redefining Ancient Orphism* (Cambridge: Cambridge University Press, 2013). https://doi.org/10.1017/CBO9781139814669

Edmonds III, Radcliffe G., *Drawing Down The Moon* (Princeton, NJ: Princeton University Press, 2019). https://doi.org/10.23943/princeton/9780691156934.001.0001

Ehrman, Bart D., *The Triumph of Christianity* (New York, NY: Simon & Schuster, 2018)

Eilberg-Schwartz, Howard, 'Witches of the West', *Journal of Feminist Studies in Religion* 5 (1989): 77–95

Étienne, Louis, 'Le paganisme poétique en Angleterre', *Revue des Deux Mondes* 59 (1867), 291–317

Evans, Dave and Green, Dave (eds), *Ten Years of Triumph of the Moon* (Harpenden: Hidden Publishing, 2009)

Faivre, Antoine, *Western Esotericism* (Albany, NY: SUNY Press, 2010)

Fantazzi, Charles (ed.), *Michael Marullus: Poems* (Cambridge, MA: Harvard University Press, 2012)

Faraone, Christopher A. and Tovar, Sofía Torallas (eds), *Greek and Egyptian Magical Formularies: Text and Translation, vol. 1* (Berkeley: California Classical Studies, 2022). https://doi.org/10.3998/mpub.12227202

Farjeon, Eleanor, *Edward Thomas* (London: Faber and Faber, 2010)

Farnell, Lewis, *The Cults of the Greek States* (Oxford: Clarendon, 1896–1909), 5 vols

Ferguson, Gary, *Queer (Re)Readings in the French Renaissance* (London: Routledge, 2016). https://doi.org/10.4324/9781315245485

Festugière, André-Jean, *Personal Religion Among the Greeks* (Berkeley, CA: University of California Press, 1954). https://doi.org/10.1525/9780520317079

Ficino, Marsilio, *Opera* (Basel: [no publisher], 1561)

Filotas, Bernadette, *Pagans Survivals, Superstitions and Popular Cultures* (Toronto: Pontifical Institute of Medieval Studies, 2005)

Flower, Harriet I., *The Dancing Lares and the Serpent in the Garden: Religion at the Roman Street Corner* (Princeton, NJ: Princeton University Press, 2017)

Fontenelle, Bernard de, *Histoire des oracles* (Paris: Hachette, 1908 [1687])

Fowden, Garth, 'The Pagan Holy Man in Late Antique Society', *Journal of Hellenic Studies* 102 (1982): 33–59. https://doi.org/10.2307/631125

Fowden, Garth, *The Egyptian Hermes* (Princeton, NJ: Princeton University Press, 1993)

Fracastorius, Hieronymus, *Opera omnia* (Venice: Giunti, 1555)

Freudenberg, Bele and Goetz, Hans-Werner, 'The Christian Perception of Heathens in the Early Middle Ages', *Millennium* 10.1 (2013): 281–91. https://doi.org/10.1515/mjb.2013.10.1.281

Frost, Robert, *The Oxford History of Poland-Lithuania: The Making of the Polish-Lithuanian Union, 1385–1569* (Oxford: Oxford University Press, 2015). https://doi.org/10.1093/acprof:oso/9780198208693.001.0001

Frye, Richard N., *Ibn Fadlan's Journey to Russia: A Tenth-Century Traveler from Baghad to the Volga River* (Princeton, NJ: Markus Wiener, 2005)

Galtsin, Dmitry, 'Gleb Botkin and the Church of Aphrodite', *The Pomegranate* 14 (2012): 91–107. https://doi.org/10.1558/pome.v14i1.91

Gardner, Gerald B., *High Magic's Aid* (Clevedon: Aurinia, 2010 [1949])

Gardner, Gerald B., *Witchcraft Today* (New York, NY: Citadel, 2004 [1954])

Gardner, Gerald B., *The Meaning of Witchcraft* (Boston, MA: Weiser, 2004 [1959])

Gay, Peter, *The Enlightenment: An Interpretation: The Rise of Modern Paganism* (London: Weidenfeld and Nicolson, 1967)

Geraci, Robert P. and Khodarkovsky, Michael (eds), *Of Religion and Empire: Missions, Conversion, and Tolerance in Tsarist Russia* (Ithaca, NY: Cornell University Press, 2001)

Gibson, Marion, *Imagining the Pagan Past* (London: Routledge, 2013). https://doi.org/10.4324/9780203068304

Gilbert, R. A., *The Golden Dawn Scrapbook* (York Beach, ME: Weiser, 1997)

Gimbutas, Marija, *The Balts* (New York: Praeger, 1963)

Giovio, Paulo, *Historiae sui temporis* (Basel: [no publisher], 1567), 2 vols

Godwin, Joscelyn, *The Theosophical Enlightenment* (Albany, NY: SUNY Press, 1994)

Godwin, Joscelyn, *The Pagan Dream of the Renaissance* (London: Thames & Hudson, 2002)

Godwin, Joscelyn, McIntosh, Christopher and McIntosh, Donate Pahnke (eds), *Rosicrucian Trilogy: Modern Translations of the Three Founding Documents: Fama Fraternitatis, 1644; Confessio Fraternitatis, 1615; The Chemical Wedding of Christian Rosenkreutz, 1616* (Newburyport, MA: Weiser, 2016)

Götz von Olenhusen, Albrecht (ed.), *Wege und Abwege* (Freiburg: Hochschul, 1990)

Goodrick-Clarke, Nicholas, *The Occult Roots of Nazism: The Ariosophists of Austria and Germany, 1890–1935* (Wellingborough: Aquarian Press, 1985)

Goodrick-Clarke, Nicholas, *Black Sun: Aryan Cults, Esoteric Nazism, and the Politics of Identity* (New York, NY: New York University Press, 2003)

Gosden, Chris, *The History of Magic: From Alchemy to Witchcraft, from the Ice Age to the Present* (London: Viking, 2020)

Gouguenheim, Sylvain, *Les derniers païens: les Baltes face aux chrétiens xiiie–xviiie siècle* (Paris: Passés Composés, 2022)

Graf, Fritz and Johnston, Sarah Iles (eds), *Ritual Texts for the Afterlife* (New York, NY: Routledge, 2007). https://doi.org/10.4324/9780203961346

Grahame, Kenneth, *Pagan Papers* (London: John Lane, 1904)

Graves, Robert, *The White Goddess* (London: Faber and Faber, 2010 [1948])

Graves, Robert, *The Greek Myths* (Harmondsworth: Penguin, 2017 [1955])

Green, Tamara M., *The City of the Moon God: Religious Traditions of Harran* (Leiden: Brill, 1992). https://doi.org/10.1163/9789004301429

Gregory, Timothy E., 'The Survival of Paganism in Christian Greece: A Critical Essay', *The American Journal of Philology* 107.2 (1986): 229–42. https://doi.org/10.2307/294605

Griffiths, J. Gwyn (ed.), *The Isis-Book (Metamorphoses, Book XI)* (Leiden: Brill, 1975)

Grønlie, Siân (trans.), *Íslendingabók, Kristni Saga: The Book of the Icelanders, The Story of the Conversion* (London: Viking Society for Northern Research, 2006)

Haggard, H. Rider, *The Days of My Life* (London: Longmans, Green and Company, 1926), 2 vols

Håland, Evy Johanne, *Greek Festivals, Modern and Ancient: A Comparison of Female and Male Values* (Newcastle: Cambridge Scholars Publishing, 2017), 2 vols

Hall, Augusta (Lady Llanover) (ed.), *The Autobiography and Correspondence of Mary Granville: Second Series* (London: Richard Bentley, 1861–62), 6 vols

Halloran, William F., *The Life and Letters of William Sharp and 'Fiona Macleod': Volume 1, 1855–1894* (Cambridge: Open Book, 2018). https://doi.org/10.11647/OBP.0142.12

Hämeen-Anttila, Jaakko, *The Last Pagans of Iraq: Ibn Wahshiyya and his Nabatean Agriculture* (Leiden: Brill, 2006). https://doi.org/10.1163/9789047409083

Hanegraaff, Wouter J., *Hermetic Spirituality and the Historical Imagination: Altered States of Knowledge in Late Antiquity* (Cambridge: Cambridge University Press, 2022). https://doi.org/10.1017/9781009127936

Hankins, James, 'Cosimo de' Medici and the "Platonic Academy"', *Journal of the Warburg and Courtauld Institutes* 53 (1990): 144–62. https://doi.org/10.2307/751344

Hankins, James, *Plato in the Italian Renaissance* (Leiden: Brill, 1990), 2 vols. https://doi.org/10.1163/9789004452367

Hansen, Lars Ivar, Bergesen, Rognald Heiseldal and Hage, Ingebjørg (eds), *The Protracted Reformation in Northern Norway: Introductory Studies* (Stamsund: Orkana Akademisk, 2014)

Harl, K. W., 'Sacrifice and Pagan Belief in Fifth- and Sixth-Century Byzantium', *Past and Present* 128 (1990): 7–27. https://doi.org/10.1093/past/128.1.7

Harrison, Peter, *'Religion' and the Religions in the English Enlightenment* (Cambridge: Cambridge University Press, 1990). https://doi.org/10.1017/CBO9780511627972

Hart, George, *The Routledge Dictionary of Egyptian Gods and Goddesses*, 2nd edn (Routledge: London, 2005). https://doi.org/10.4324/9780203023624

Harvey, Graham, *Listening People, Speaking Earth* (London: Hurst & Company, 1997)

Harvey, Graham and Hardman, Charlotte (eds), *Paganism Today* (London: Thorsons, 1995)

Heselton, Philip, *Witchfather: A Life of Gerald Gardner* (Loughborough: Thoth, 2012), 2 vols

Heselton, Philip, *In Search of the New Forest Coven* ([no place of publication]: Fenix Flames, 2020)

Hess, Cordelia and Adams, Jonathan (eds), *Fear and Loathing in the North: Jews and Muslims in Medieval Scandinavia and the Baltic Region* (Berlin: De Gruyter, 2015). https://doi.org/10.1515/9783110346473

Hilliard, David, 'UnEnglish and Unmanly: Anglo-Catholicism and Homosexuality', *Victorian Studies* 25 (1982): 181–210

Hladký, Vojtěch, *The Philosophy of Gemistos Plethon* (London: Routledge, 2016). https://doi.org/10.4324/9781315554723

[Hooke, Luke Joseph], *Religionis Naturalis et Revelatae Principia* (Paris: Guérin, 1752–54), 3 vols

Hopkins, Keith, *A World Full of Gods* (London: Weidenfeld and Nicolson, 1999)

Hornung, Erik, *The Secret Lore of Egypt* (Ithaca, NY: Cornell University Press, 2001)

Howe, Ellic, *Magicians of the Golden Dawn* (London: Routledge and Kegan Paul, 1972)

Huffman, Carl A., *A History of Pythagoreanism* (Cambridge: Cambridge University Press, 2014). https://doi.org/10.1017/CBO9781139028172

Hume, David, *Essays and Treatises on Several Subjects* (Basel: J. J. Tourneisen, 1793), 4 vols

Hunt, Lynn, Jacob, Margaret C. and Mijnhardt, Wijnand, *The Book That Changed Europe: Picart and Bernard's Religious Ceremonies of the World* (Cambridge, MA: Belknap Press, 2010). https://doi.org/10.2307/j.ctv134vmq4

Hussovianus, Nicolaus (ed. J. Pelczar), *Nicolai Hussoviani Carmina* (Kraków: Sumptibus Academiae Literarum)

Hutton, Ronald, *The Pagan Religions of the Ancient British Isles: Their Nature and Legacy* (Oxford: Blackwell, 1991)

Hutton, Ronald, *The Triumph of the Moon: A History of Modern Pagan Witchcraft* (Oxford: Oxford University Press, 1999)

Hutton, Ronald, *Shamans: Siberian Spirituality and the Western Imagination* (London: Continuum, 2001)

Hutton, Ronald, *Witches, Druids and King Arthur* (London: Hambledon Continuum, 2006)

Hutton, Ronald, *Blood and Mistletoe: The History of the Druids in Britain* (New Haven, CT: Yale University Press, 2009)

Hutton, Ronald, 'How Pagan were Medieval English Peasants?', *Folklore* 122 (2011): 235–49. https://doi.org/10.1080/0015587X.2011.608262

Hutton, Ronald, *Pagan Britain* (New Haven, CT: Yale University Press, 2013)

Hutton, Ronald, *The Triumph of the Moon: A History of Modern Pagan Witchcraft*, 2nd edn (Oxford: Oxford University Press, 2019)

Hutton, Ronald, *Queens of the Wild: Pagan Goddesses in Christian Europe: An Investigation* (New Haven, CT: Yale University Press, 2022). https://doi.org/10.12987/9780300265279

Ierodiakonou, Katerina (ed.), *Byzantine Philosophy and its Ancient Sources* (Oxford: Clarendon, 2002). https://doi.org/10.1093/oso/9780199246137.001.0001

Jacob, Margaret C., *Living the Enlightenment* (New York, NY: Oxford University Press, 1991)

Jacob, Margaret C., *The Radical Enlightenment*, 2nd edn (Lafayette, LA: Cornerstone, 2006)

Jacob, Margaret C., 'The Radical Enlightenment and Freemasonry: Where We Are Now', *Philosophica* 88 (2013): 13–29. https://doi.org/10.21825/philosophica.82132

Jacobs, Joseph and Nutt, Alfred (eds), *The International Folk-Lore Conference 1891: Papers and Transactions* (London: David Nutt, 1892)

Janes, Dominic, *Victorian Reformation* (New York, NY: Oxford University Press, 2009). https://doi.org/10.1093/acprof:oso/9780195378511.001.0001

Janko, Richard (ed.), 'The Derveni Papyrus ("Diagoras of Melos, *Apopyrgizontes Logoi?*"): A New Translation', *Classical Philology* 96.1 (2001): 1–32. https://doi.org/10.1086/449521

Jarcke, Karl Ernst, 'Ein Hexenprozess', *Annalen der Deutschen und Auslandischen Criminal-Rechts-Pflege* 1 (1828): 431–56

Jeffares, A. Norman, *W. B. Yeats: A New Biography* (London: Continuum, 2001)

Jenkyns, Richard, *The Victorians and Ancient Greece* (Oxford: Blackwell, 1980)

Jones, Frederick L. (ed.), *The Letters of Percy Bysshe Shelley* (Oxford: Clarendon Press, 1964), 2 vols

Jones, Nigel, *Rupert Brooke* (London: Head of Zeus, 2014)

Jones, Prudence and Pennick, Nigel, *A History of Pagan Europe* (London: Routledge, 1995)

Jones, William, *The Theological and Miscellaneous Works of the Rev. William Jones* (London: Rivington, 1810), 6 vols

Julian (ed. Wilmer C. Wright), *Orations 1–5* (Cambridge, MA: Harvard University Press, 1913)

Julian (ed. Wilmer C. Wright), *Orations 6–8. Letters to Themistius, To the Senate and People of Athens, To a Priest. The Caesars. Misopogon* (Cambridge, MA: Harvard University Press, 1913). https://doi.org/10.4159/DLCL. emperor_julian-letter_senate_people_athens.1913

Julian (ed. Wilmer C. Wright), *Letters. Epigrams. Against the Galilaeans. Fragments* (Cambridge, MA: Harvard University Press, 1923). https://doi.org/10.4159/ DLCL.emperor_julian-fragments.1923

Kaczynski, Richard, *Perdurabo: The Life of Aleister Crowley*, rev. edn (Berkeley, CA: North Atlantic, 2010)

Kalniņa, Ieva (ed.), *Literatūra un Reliģija: Svētie un Grēcinieki* (Riga: Latvijas Universitātes Akadēmiskais apgāds, 2018). https://doi.org/10.22364/lursug

Keller, A., 'Two Byzantine Scholars and Their Reception in Italy', *Journal of the Warburg and Courtauld Institutes* 20 (1957): 363–70. https://doi.org/10.2307/750788

Kelly, Aidan A., *Inventing Witchcraft* (Loughborough: Thoth, 2008)

Keynes, Geoffrey (ed.), *The Letters of Rupert Brooke* (London: Faber and Faber, 1968)

Kidd, Colin, *The World of Mr Casaubon* (Cambridge: Cambridge University Press, 2016). https://doi.org/10.1017/9781139226646

Klein, Andreas, *Early Modern Knowledge about the Sámi: A History of Johannes Schefferus' Lapponia (1673)* (Hanover: Wehrhahn Verlag, 2023)

Kling, David W., *A History of Christian Conversion* (Oxford: Oxford University Press, 2020). https://doi.org/10.1093/oso/9780195320923.001.0001

Knight, Gareth, *Dion Fortune and the Inner Light* (Loughborough: Thoth, 2000)

Knight, Gareth, *Dion Fortune's Rites of Isis and of Pan* (Cheltenham: Skylight, 2013)

Knight, Richard Payne, *The Symbolical Language of Ancient Art and Mythology*, new edn (New York, NY: J. W. Bouton, [1818] 1892)

Knight, Samuel, *The Life of Dr J. Colet*, new edn (Oxford: Clarendon, 1823)

Knight, William (ed.), *Memorials of Thomas Davidson* (Boston, MA: Ginn and Company, 1907)

Koppen, R. S., *Virginia Woolf, Fashion and Literary Modernity* (Edinburgh: Edinburgh University Press, 2009). https://doi.org/10.3366/edinburgh/9780748638727. 001.0001

Kruczkiewicz, Bronisław (ed.), *Pauli Crosnensis Rutheni atque Ioannis Vislicensis Carmina* (Kraków: Typis Universitatis Jagellonicae, 1887)

Küntz, Darcy, *The Complete Golden Dawn Cipher Manuscript* (Sequim WA: Holmes, 1996)

Küntz, Darcy (ed.), *The Golden Dawn Source Book* (Edmonds, WA: Holmes, 1996)

Lachman, Gary, *Aleister Crowley* (New York, NY: Penguin, 2014)

Lane Fox, Robin, *Pagans and Christians* (London: Penguin, 1988)

Larson, Jennifer, *Greek Nymphs: Myth, Cult, Lore* (Oxford: Oxford University Press, 2001). https://doi.org/10.1093/oso/9780195144659.001.0001

Lawson, John Cuthbert, *Modern Greek Folklore and Ancient Greek Religion: A Study in Survivals* (Cambridge: Cambridge University Press, 1910)

Leask, Ian, 'Stoicism unbound: Cicero's *Academica* in Toland's *Pantheisticon*', *British Journal for the History of Philosophy* (2016): 1–21. https://doi.org/10.1080/09608788.2016.1230090

Lecerf, Adrien, Lucia, Saudelli, and Seng, Helmut (eds), *Oracles Chaldaïques: fragments et philosophie* (Heidelberg: Winter, 2014)

[Lefranc, Jacques-François], *Le voile levé pour les curieux* ([no place]: [no publisher], 1791)

Leland, Charles G., *Aradia or the Gospel of the Witches* (London: David Nutt, 1899)

Lévi, Éliphas, *Transcendental Magic* (London: Redway, 1896)

Lewis, James R., *Witchcraft Today* (Santa Barbara, CA: ABC-Clio, 1999)

Lewis, James R., *Odd Gods* (Amherst, MA: Prometheus, 2001)

Lewis, James R. and Pizza, Murphy (eds), *Handbook of Contemporary Paganism* (Leiden: Brill, 2009)

Lewy, Hans, *Chaldaean Oracles and Theurgy*, 3rd edn (Paris: Institut des Etudes Augustiniennes, 2011)

Lillie, Arthur, *Madame Blavatsky and Her 'Theosophy'* (London: Swan Sonnenschein and Co, 1895)

Luck, Georg (ed.), *Arcana Mundi: Magic and the Occult in the Greek and Roman Worlds*, 2nd edn (Baltimore, MD: Johns Hopkins University Press, 2006). https://doi.org/10.1353/mrw.0.0014

Luhrmann, T. M., *Persuasions of the Witch's Craft* (Cambridge, MA: Harvard University Press, 1989)

McIntosh, Christopher, *Eliphas Lévi and the French Occult Revival* (Albany, NY: SUNY Press, 1972)

McIntosh, Christopher, *The Rosicrucians*, 3rd edn (York Beach, ME: Weiser, 1998)

McIntosh, Christopher, '"Fräulein Sprengel" and the Origins of the Golden Dawn: A Surprising Discovery', *Aries* 11 (2011): 249–57. https://doi.org/10.1163/156798911X581261

MacMullen, Ramsay, *Christianity and Paganism in the Fourth to Eighth Centuries* (New Haven, CT: Yale University Press, 1997)

Machiavelli, Niccolò (ed. Giuseppe Piergili), *Discorsi sopra la prima deca di Tito Livio* (Florence: Successori Le Monnier, 1893)

Machielsen, Jan (ed.), *The Science of Demons: Early Modern Authors Facing Witchcraft and the Devil* (London: Routledge, 2020). https://doi.org/10.4324/9780203702512

Mackey, Jacob L., *Belief and Cult* (Princeton, NJ: Princeton University Press, 2022)

Mäesalu, Mihkel, 'Taani kuninga asehaldur Konrad Preen ja Jüriöö ülestõus', *Tuna* 2 (2021): 9–24

Mahé, Jean-Pierre and Meyer, Marvin (ed.), *The Nag Hammadi Scriptures* (New York, NY: HarperCollins, 2007)

Majercik, Ruth, *The Chaldean Oracles* (Leiden: Brill, 1989). https://doi.org/10.1163/9789004296718

Makdisi, George, Sourdel, Dominique and Sourdel-Thomine, Janine (eds), *La notion de liberté au Moyen Age: Islam, Byzance, Occident* (Paris: Les Belles Lettres, 1985)

Marcel, Raymond, *Marsile Ficin (1433–1499)* (Paris: Belles Lettres, 1958)

Marenbon, John, *Pagans and Philosophers: The Problem of Paganism from Augustine to Leibniz* (Princeton, NJ: Princeton University Press, 2015). https://doi.org/10.23943/princeton/9780691142555.001.0001

Marenbon, John, 'Relativism in the Long Middle Ages: Crossing the Ethical Border with Paganism', *Journal of Ethnographic Theory* 5.2 (2015): 345–65. https://doi.org/10.14318/hau5.2.019

Mastros, Sara Leanne, *Orphic Hymns Grimoire* (Pittsburg, PA: Mastros Publishing, 2019)

Maugham, Somerset, *Cakes and Ale* (London: Heinemann, 1930)

Meagher, Andrew, *The Popish Mass* (Cork: [no publisher], 1823 [1771])

Meltzer, F. and Elsner, J. (eds), *Saints: Faith without Borders* (Chicago, IL: University of Chicago Press, 2011). https://doi.org/10.7208/chicago/9780226519937.001.0001

Meredith, George, *Modern Love and Poems of the English Roadside* (London: Chapman and Hall, 1862)

Milis, Ludo J. R. (trans. Tanis Guest), *The Pagan Middle Ages* (Woodbridge: Boydell Press, 1998)

[Mills, Alexander Rud], *The First Guide Book to the Anglecyn Church of Odin* (Sydney: A. R. Mills, 1936)

Misāne, Agita, 'Inter-war Right-wing Movements in the Baltic States and their Religious Affiliations', *Acta Ethnographica Hungarica* 46.1–2 (2001): 75–87. https://doi.org/10.1556/AEthn.46.2001.1-2.9

Monfasani, John, 'A Tale of Two Books: Bessarion's *In Calumniatorem Platonis* and George of Trebizond's *Comparatio Philosophorum Platonis et Aristotelis*', *Renaissance Studies* 22 (2008): 1–15. https://doi.org/10.1111/j.1477-4658.2007.00469.x

Murdoch, Adrian, *The Last Pagan* (Stroud: Sutton, 2003)

Murray, Linda J., *A Zest for Life: The Story of Alexander Keiller* (Swindon: Morven, 1999)

Murray, Margaret Alice, *The Witch-Cult in Western Europe* (Oxford: Clarendon Press, 1921)

Murray, Margaret Alice, *The God of the Witches* (London: Oxford University Press, 1970 [1931])

Murray, Margaret Alice, *The Divine King in England* (London: Faber and Faber, 1954)

Nakashian, Craig M. and Franke, D. P. (eds), *Prowess, Piety, and Public Order in Medieval Society: Essays in Honor of Richard W. Kaeuper* (Leiden: Brill, 2017). https://doi.org/10.1163/9789004341098

Nastevics, Ugis, 'Latvian Religion – Dievturība?', *Religiski-Filozofiski Raksti* 24 (2018): 82–104

Nerval, Gérard de, *Les Illuminés* (Paris: Michel Lévy Frères, 1868)

Nicholls, Angus, 'Max Müller and the Comparative Method', *Comparative Critical Studies* 12 (2015): 213–34. https://doi.org/10.3366/ccs.2015.0168

Noakes, J. and Pridham, G. (eds), *Nazism 1919–1945 Volume 2: State, Economy and Society 1933–1939* (Exeter: Exeter University Press, 1984)

Novotný, František, *The Posthumous Life of Plato* (Prague: Academia Pragensis, 1977)

Nyberg, Tore, *Monasticism in North-Western Europe, 800–1200* (Farnham: Ashgate, 2000)

O'Donnell, Elliott, *Strange Cults and Secret Societies of Modern London* (London: Philip Allen, 1934)

O'Donnell, James J., '*Paganus*', *Classical Folia* 31 (1977): 163–9

O'Flaherty, Patrick, *Scotland's Pariah* (Toronto: University of Toronto Press, 2015)

Ogden, Daniel, *Magic, Witchcraft and Ghosts in the Greek and Roman Worlds* (Oxford: Oxford University Press, 2009)

Ohnefalsch-Richter, Max, *Ancient Places of Worship in Kypros Catalogued and Described* (Berlin: H. S. Hermann, 1891)

Opsopaus, John, *The Secret Texts of Hellenic Polytheism* (Woodbury: Llewellyn, 2022)

Orderic Vitalis (ed. Marjorie Chibnall), *The Ecclesiastical History of Orderic Vitalis, Vol. 2, Books III and IV* (Oxford: Clarendon Press, 1969). https://doi.org/10.1093/actrade/9780198222040.book.1

Ostling, Michael (ed.), *Fairies, Demons, and Nature Spirits* (Basingstoke: Palgrave MacMillan, 2018). https://doi.org/10.1057/978-1-137-58520-2

Ozouf, Mona, *Festivals and the French Revolution* (Cambridge, MA: Harvard University Press, 1988)

Page, Sophie (ed.), *The Unorthodox Imagination in Late Medieval Britain* (Manchester: Manchester University Press, 2010)

Pailin, David A., *Attitudes to Other Religions* (Manchester: Manchester University Press, 1984)

Paine, Thomas, *On the Origin of Free-Masonry* (New York, NY: Elliot and Crissy, 1810)

Palmer, James T., 'Defining Paganism in the Carolingian World', *Early Medieval Europe* 15 (2007): 402–25. https://doi.org/10.1111/j.1468-0254.2007.00214.x

Parker, Joanne (ed.), *Written on Stone: The Cultural Reception of British Prehistoric Monuments* (Newcastle: Cambridge Scholars, 2009)

Parsons, Gerald (ed.), *Religion in Victorian Britain* (Manchester: Manchester University Press, 1988), 5 vols

Pazzaglini, Mario and Pazzaglini, Dina (eds), *Aradia or the Gospel of the Witches* (Blaine, MN: Phoenix, 1998)

Perkins, Charles C., *Tuscan Sculptors* (London: Longman, Green, 1864), 2 vols

Petts, David, *Pagan and Christian: Religious Change in Early Medieval Europe* (London: Bristol Classical Press, 2011). https://doi.org/10.5040/9781849668439

Piana, Marco, 'Gods in the Garden: Visions of the Pagan Other in the Rome of Julius II', *Journal of Religion in Europe* 12 (2019): 285–309. https://doi.org/10.1163/18748929-01203003

Pico della Mirandola, Giovanni (ed. Bertrand Schefer), *Conclusiones DCCCC* (Paris: Editions Allia, 1999)

Pierre, François-Joachim de (Cardinal de Bernis), *Mémoires et Lettres* (Paris: E. Plon et Cie, 1878), 2 vols

Pius II, *Commentarii* (Frankfurt: Officina Aubriana, 1584)

Platina, Bartolomeo (ed. Thomas G. Hendrickson, Alexandra B. Berman, Pascal Croak, Daniel Gridley, Sebastian Herrera, Jin Lee, Graham Rigby. John Robinson, Gabriela C. Sommer, Kent Ueno and James Whittemore), *Lives of the Popes, Paul II* (Oxford, OH: Faenum, 2017)

Poewe, Karla and Hexham, Irving, 'Jakob Wilhelm Hauer's New Religion and National Socialism', *Journal of Contemporary Religion* 20:2 (2005): 195–215. https://doi.org/10.1080/13537900500067752

Pollen, Annebella, *The Kindred of the Kibbo Kift* (London: Donlon, 2015)

Pomata, G. and Siraisi, N. G. (eds), *Historia: Empiricism and Erudition in Early Modern Europe* (Cambridge, MA: MIT Press, 2005). https://doi.org/10.7551/mitpress/3521.001.0001

*Pommersches Urkundbuch: Band I* (Stettin: Königlichen Staats-Archiv zu Stettin, 1868)

Potter, David, *Constantine the Emperor* (New York, NY: Oxford University Press, 2013)

Powell, Anton (ed.), *The Greek World* (London: Routledge, 1995). https://doi.org/10.4324/9780203269206

Psellus, Michael (ed. D. J. O'Meara), *Philosophica minora* (Leipzig: Teubner, 1989) 2 vols

Purkiss, Diane, *Troublesome Things: A History of Fairies and Fairy Stories* (London: Allen Lane, 2000)

Raine, Kathleen and Harper, George Mills (eds), *Thomas Taylor the Platonist* (London: Routledge, 1969)

Regardie, Israel, *The Golden Dawn*, 7th edn (St Paul, MN: Llewellyn, 2016)

Reid, Kelly Anne, 'The Love Which Dare Not Speak Its Name: An Examination of Pagan Symbolism and Morality in *Fin de siecle* Decadent Fiction', *The Pomegranate* 10 (2008): 130–41. https://doi.org/10.1558/pome.v10i2.130

Remes, Pauliina, *Neoplatonism* (London: Routledge, 2014). https://doi.org/10.4324/9781315711751

Reynolds, Burnham W., *The Prehistory of the Crusades: Missionary War and the Baltic Crusades* (London: Bloomsbury, 2016). https://doi.org/10.5040/9781474211123

Rimbaud, Arthur, *Poésies* (Paris: Gallimard, 1999)

Roberts, J. M., *The Mythology of the Secret Societies* (London: Secker and Warburg, 1972)

Robertson Smith, W., *Lectures on the Religion of the Semites*, 3rd edn (New York, NY: Macmillan, 1927)

Robichaud, Paul, *Pan: The Great God's Modern Return* (London: Reaktion, 2021)

Rose, Elliot, *A Razor for a Goat* (Toronto: University of Toronto Press, 1989 [1962])

Roubeckas, Nickolas, *An Ancient Theory of Religion: Euhemerism from Antiquity to the Present* (London: Routledge, 2017)

Roukema, Aren, *Esotericism and Narrative* (Leiden: Brill, 2018)

Rountree, Kathryn (ed.), *Contemporary Pagan and Native Faith Movements in Europe: Colonialist and Nationalist Impulses* (Oxford: Berghahn, 2015). https://doi.org/10.2307/j.ctt9qctm0

Rowbotham, Arnold H., 'Voltaire, Sinophile', *PMLA* 47 (1932): 1050–65. https://doi.org/10.2307/457929

Rowell, S. C., *Lithuania Ascending: A Pagan Empire within East-Central Europe, 1295–1345* (Cambridge: Cambridge University Press, 1994)

Rowell, S. C., 'Unexpected Contacts: Lithuanians at Western Courts, c. 1316–c. 1400', *The English Historical Review* 111 (1996): 557–77. https://doi.org/10.1093/ehr/CXI.442.557

Rowell, S. C., 'Was Fifteenth-Century Lithuanian Catholicism as Lukewarm as Sixteenth-Century Reformers and Later Commentators Would Have Us Believe?', *Central Europe* 8.2 (2010): 86–106. https://doi.org/10.1179/174582110X12871342860045

Runyon, Carroll (ed.), *Secrets of the Golden Dawn Cypher Manuscript* (Silverado, CA: CHS, 1997)

Rydving, Håkan and Kaikkonen, Konsta (eds), *Religions around the Arctic: Source Criticism and Comparisons* (Stockholm: Stockholm University Press, 2022). https://doi.org/10.16993/bbu

Saffrey, H.-D., *Recherches sur le néoplatonisme après Plotin* (Paris: Vrin, 1990)

Sainsbury, John, *John Wilkes: The Lives of a Libertine* (Aldershot: Ashgate 2006)

Saint, W., *Memoirs of the Life, Character, Opinions, and Writings, of that Learned and Eccentric Man, the Late John Fransham, of Norwich* (Norwich: Berry, 1811)

Ste Croix, G. E. M. de, *Christian Persecution, Martyrdom, and Orthodoxy* (Oxford: Oxford University Press, 2006)

Salih, Sarah, *Imagining the Pagan in Late Medieval England* (Cambridge: D. S. Brewer, 2019). https://doi.org/10.1515/9781787445819

Sarbiewski, Maciej (trans. Krystyna Stawecka), *Dii gentium: Bogowie Pogan* (Warsaw: Ossolineum, 1972)

Saxl, F., 'Pagan Sacrifice in the Italian Renaissance', *Journal of the Warburg Institute* 2 (1939): 346–67. https://doi.org/10.2307/750043

Schnurbein, Stefanie von, *Norse Revival* (Leiden: Brill, 2016)

Schofield, Phillipp R., *Seals and Their Context in the Middle Ages* (Oxford: Oxbow, 2015). https://doi.org/10.2307/j.ctvh1dsk8

Scott, Walter Sidney, *The Athenians* (London: Golden Cockerel, 1943)

Sebeok, Thomas A. (ed.), *Myth: A Symposium* (Philadelphia, PA: American Folklore Society, 1955)

Setton, Kenneth M., 'The Byzantine Background to the Italian Renaissance', *Proceedings of the American Philological Society* 100 (1956): 1–76

Seznec, Jean, *The Survival of the Pagan Gods* (Princeton, NJ: Princeton University Press, 1981)

Shaw, Donald L., 'Darío's Neo-Paganism in Context', *Latin American Literary Review* 38 (2010): 7–22

Shaw, Gregory, *Theurgy and the Soul*, 2nd edn (Kettering: Angelico, 2014)

Shaw, Matthew, *Time and the French Revolution* (Woodbridge: Boydell, 2011). https://doi.org/10.1515/9781846158476

Sheppard, Kathleen L., *The Life of Margaret Alice Murray* (Lanham, MD: Lexington, 2013)

Siniossoglou, Niketas, *Radical Platonism in Byzantium* (Cambridge: Cambridge University Press, 2016)

Skinner, Stephen, *Techniques of Graeco-Egyptian Magic* (Singapore: Golden Hoard, 2014)

Slavenburg, Jacob, *The Hermetic Link* (Lake Worth, FL: Ibis, 2012)

Slotemaker, John T. and Witt, Jeffrey C., *Robert Holcot* (Oxford: Oxford University Press, 2016). https://doi.org/10.1093/acprof:oso/9780199391240.001.0001

Smith, Rowland, *Julian's Gods* (London: Routledge, 1995)

Stasulane, Anita and Ozoliņš, Gatis, 'Transformations of Neopaganism in Latvia: From Survival to Revival', *Open Theology* 3 (2017): 235–48. https://doi.org/10.1515/opth-2017-0019

Steel, Carlos, Marenbon, John and Verbeke, Werner (eds), *Paganism in the Middle Ages: Threat and Fascination* (Leuven: Leuven University Press, 2012). https://doi.org/10.2307/j.ctt9qf0hm

Stevenson, David, *The Origins of Freemasonry* (Cambridge: Cambridge University Press, 1988). https://doi.org/10.1017/CBO9780511560828

Strmiska, Michael P., 'Pagan Politics in the 21st Century: "Peace and Love" or "Blood and Soil"?', *The Pomegranate* 20.1 (2018): 5–44. https://doi.org/10.1558/pome.35632

Stroumsa, Guy G., *A New Science* (Cambridge, MA: Harvard University Press, 2010)

Sudduth, Michael, 'Pico della Mirandola's Philosophy of Religion', in M. V. Dougherty (ed.), *Pico della Mirandola: New Essays* (New York, NY: Cambridge University Press, 2008), 61–80. https://doi.org/10.1017/CBO9780511619274.005

Swinburne, Algernon, *Poems and Ballads* (London: J. C. Hotten, 1866)

Swinburne, Algernon, *Songs Before Sunrise* (London: Chatto and Windus, 1880)

[Symonds, John Addington], 'The English Drama during the Reigns of Elizabeth and James: Part 1', *The Cornhill Magazine* 11 (1865): 604–18

Symonds, John and Grant, Kenneth (eds), *The Confessions of Aleister Crowley* (New York, NY: Farrar Straus and Giroux, 1970)

Symondson, Anthony (ed.), *The Victorian Crisis of Faith* (London: SPCK, 1970)

Tambrun, Brigitte, 'Marsile Ficin et le commentaire de Pléthon sur les Oracles chaldaïques', *Accademia* 1 (1999): 9–48

Tambrun, Brigitte, *Pléthon: Le retour de Platon* (Paris: Vrin, 2006)

Tamm, Marek, 'History as Cultural Memory: Mnemohistory and the Construction of the Estonian Nation', *Journal of Baltic Studies* 39.4 (2008): 499–516. https://doi.org/10.1080/01629770802468865

Taylor, Mark C. (ed.), *Critical Terms for Religious Studies* (Chicago, IL: University of Chicago Press, 1998)

Taylor, Thomas (ed.), *The Hymns of Orpheus* (London: Payne, 1792)

Teitler, H. C., *The Last Pagan Emperor* (New York, NY: Oxford University Press, 2017)

Testa, Lizzi (ed.), *The Strange Death of Pagan Rome* (Turnhout: Brepols, 2013)

Thornton, Alicia, 'Meaningful Mingling: Classicizing Imagery and Islamicizing Script in a Byzantine Bowl', *The Art Bulletin* 90.1 (March 2008): 32–53. https://doi.org/10.1080/00043079.2008.10786381

Trelawny, Edward John, *Records of Shelley, Byron and the Author*, new edn (New York, NY: Scribner and Welford, 1887)

Tully, Caroline, 'Walk Like an Egyptian: Egypt as Authority in Aleister Crowley's Reception of *The Book of the Law*', *The Pomegranate* 12 (2010): 20–47. https://doi.org/10.1558/pome.v12i1.20

Urbańczyk, Przemysław (ed.), *Europe Around the Year 1000* (Warsaw: DiG, 2001)

Vaitkevičius, Vykintas, 'The Main Features of the State Religion in Thirteenth-Century Lithuania', *Балто-славянские исследования* 16 (2004): 289–356

Viti, Paolo (ed.), *Firenze e il concilio del 1439* (Florence: Olschki, 1994), 2 vols

Voltaire, *Dictionnaire philosophique portatif* (Paris, 1764)

Von Stuckrad, Kocku, 'Visual Gods: From Exorcism to Complexity in Renaissance Studies', *Aries* 6 (2006): 59–85. https://doi.org/10.1163/157005906775248743

Voss, Angela (ed.), *Marsilio Ficino* (Berkeley, CA: North Atlantic, 2006)

Waldron, David, *The Sign of the Witch* (Durham, NC: Carolina Academic Press, 2008)

Walpole, Horace, *Memoirs of the Reign of King George the Third* (London: Bentley, 1845), 4 vols

Watts, Edward, *The Final Pagan Generation* (Berkeley, CA: University of California Press, 2020). https://doi.org/10.1525/9780520959491

Webb, James, *The Occult Underground* (La Salle: Open Court, 1974)

Wheeler, Graham John, 'Discourses of Paganism in the British and Irish Press during the Early Pagan Revival', *The Pomegranate* 19 (2017): 5–24. https://doi.org/10.1558/pome.27926

Wheeler, Graham John, 'An Esbat among the Quads: An Episode of Witchcraft at Oxford University in the 1920s', *The Pomegranate* 20.2 (2018): 157–78. https://doi.org/10.1558/pom.34209

Wheeler, Graham John, 'Apuleius and the Esoteric Revival: An Ancient Decadent in Modern Times', *Volupté: Interdisciplinary Journal of Decadence Studies* 2.2 (2019): 260–76

Wheeler, Graham John, '"Do What Thou Wilt": The History of a Precept', *Religio* 27 (2019): 17–41

Wheeler, Graham John, 'A Microcosm of the Esoteric Revival: The Histories of the Lesser Banishing Ritual of the Pentagram', *Correspondences* 8.2 (2020): 1–40

Wheeler, Graham John, 'John Fransham, the Norwich Polytheist: An English Pagan in the Eighteenth Century', *Journal of Religious History, Literature and Culture* 6 (2020): 20–49. https://doi.org/10.16922/jrhlc.6.1.2

Wheeler, Graham John, 'Towards a Reception History of the Chaldaean Oracles', *International Journal of the Classical Tradition* 28 (2021): 261–84. https://doi.org/10.1007/s12138-020-00562-3

Wheeler, Richard, '"Pro Magna Charta" or "Fay ce que Voudras": Political and Moral Precedents for the Gardens of Sir Francis Dashwood at West Wycombe', *New Arcadian Journal* 49/50 (2000): 26–61

Wilde, Oscar (ed. Bobby Fong and Karl Beckson), *The Complete Works of Oscar Wilde, Vol. 1: Poems and Poems in Prose* (Oxford: Oxford University Press, 2000), https://doi.org/10.1093/actrade/9780198119609.book.1

Williams, Liz, *Miracles of Our Own Making: A History of Paganism* (London: Reaktion, 2021)

Williams, Mark, *Ireland's Immortals: A History of the Gods of Irish Myth* (Princeton, NJ: Princeton University Press, 2016). https://doi.org/10.2307/j.ctvc775gk

Winter, Barbara, *The Australia-First Movement and the 'Publicist', 1936–1942* (Brisbane: Glass House, 2005)

Wiseman, Nicholas, *Letters to John Poynder Esq., Upon His Work Entitled 'Popery in Alliance with Heathenism'* (Philadelphia, PA: M. Fithian, 1836)

Yates, Frances A., *Giordano Bruno and the Hermetic Tradition* (London: Routledge and Kegan Paul, 1964)

Yates, Frances A., *The Rosicrucian Enlightenment*, new edn (London: Routledge, 2002). https://doi.org/10.4324/9780203166017

York, Michael, 'Invented Culture/Invented Religion', *Nova Religio* 3 (1999): 135–46. https://doi.org/10.1525/nr.1999.3.1.135

York, Michael, *Pagan Theology* (New York, NY: New York University Press, 2003)

Young, Francis, *A History of Exorcism in Catholic Christianity* (Basingstoke: Palgrave MacMillan, 2016). https://doi.org/10.1007/978-3-319-29112-3

Young, Francis (ed.), *Pagans in the Early Modern Baltic: Sixteenth-Century Ethnographic Accounts of Baltic Paganism* (Leeds: Arc Humanities Press, 2022). https://doi.org/10.1017/9781802700213

Young, Francis, *Twilight of the Godlings: The Shadowy Origins of Britain's Supernatural Beings* (Cambridge: Cambridge University Press, 2023). https://doi.org/10.1017/9781009330343

Young, G. M., *Portrait of an Age: Victorian England* (London: Oxford University Press, 1977)

Zaretsky, Irving I. and Leone, Mark P. (eds), *Religious Movements in Contemporary America* (Princeton, NJ: Princeton University Press, 1974)

## Unpublished PhD dissertations

Akisik, Aslihan, 'Self and Other in the Renaissance: Laonikos Chalkokondyles and Late Byzantine Intellectuals', PhD diss., Harvard University, 2013, online at core.ac.uk/download/pdf/28943821.pdf

Critchley, Steven George, 'Pagan Taylor: The Emergence of a Public Character 1785–1804', PhD diss., University of York, 2005, online at etheses.whiterose.ac.uk/14190/1/437615.pdf

Gilbert, R. A., 'England During the Victorian Era', PhD diss., University of London, 2009

Hallett, Jennifer Rachel, 'Paganism in England 1885–1914', PhD diss., University of Bristol, 2006, online at research-information.bristol.ac.uk/files/34501523/435432.pdf

Meisner, D. A., '"Zeus the Head, Zeus the Middle": Studies in the History and Interpretation of the Orphic Theogonies', PhD diss., University of Western Ontario, 2015


## Web sources

*Cahiers Victoriens et Edouardiens*, journals.openedition.org/cve/

Gerald Gardner's Library, web.archive.org/web/20010607172853/http://www.newwiccanchurch.com/gbglibidx.htm

Indigo Group, indigogroup.co.uk

Letter from Hardscrabble Creek, blog.chasclifton.com

Matthew Cooke Manuscript: Translation, albionlodge5.org/uploads/7/8/8/5/7885596/the_matthew_cooke_manuscript_wtranslation.pdf

Rite of Orthodoxy with Anathemas against Heretics, pravoslavie.ru/101610.html

The Pagan Federation, paganfed.org/paganism/

The Prometheus Trust, prometheustrust.co.uk

The Vatican, vatican.va

# Index

Milton Keynes UK
Ingram Content Group UK Ltd.
UKHW032313161024
449556UK00001B/3